BAPTISTS
and
CHRISTIAN UNITY

BAPTISTS
and
CHRISTIAN UNITY

William R. Estep

BROADMAN PRESS
Nashville, Tennessee

To the memory of
H. D. Schultz
one-time faculty member
of Berea College

422-318

DEWEY DECIMAL CLASSIFICATION NUMBER: 262
Library of Congress catalog card number: 67-12169
Printed in the United States of America
4.JUL6613

Acknowledgments

This work has been in the making so long that it is impossible to acknowledge my indebtedness to everyone who has made it possible. In a very real sense it is an ecumenical production, drawing upon the labors of writers and theologians across the centuries and from widely separated theological positions. However, without specific and direct help on the part of particular individuals, this contribution to the current ecumenical dialogue would not have materialized. To these friends, I wish to express my appreciation.

Albert Outler of Perkins School of Theology, Southern Methodist University, read the first three chapters and offered many suggestions for their improvement. Leo Garrett of Southern Baptist Theological Seminary, Louisville, Kentucky, made a careful, critical evaluation of the fourth chapter. My colleagues of the School of Theology, Southwestern Baptist Theological Seminary: Robert A. Baker, chairman, Department of Church History; Leon McBeth, associate professor of church history, and T. B. Maston, professor emeritus of Christian ethics, read the manuscript in its entirety. From their numerous comments I have greatly profited. J. P. Allen, pastor of the Broadway Baptist Church, also read the manuscript and shared with the author insights regarding the subject from yet another dimension of the Christian ministry.

Three young women have typed and retyped portions of the manuscript—my daughter, Rhoda; Mrs. Russell Wilson; and Miss Billy Green. To each of them, I wish to say thank you. Doubtless, this is not a perfect production. But for whatever errors in judgment and fact it may embody, I assume full responsibility.

Contents

BAPTISTS AND THE COUNCILS

CONCLUSION

1

Ecumenicity in Perspective

"Ecumenical" is not exactly a new term in Christian history; but to many Baptists, as well as others in the mid-twentieth century, it is. The term rarely appeared in Baptist literature the three centuries prior to 1938, nor in Anabaptist writings of the sixteenth century.

From Luther's cry for an ecumenical council at Leipzig, in 1519, until the International Missionary Conference at Edinburgh, in 1910, a period of four hundred years, Protestants practically abandoned the word. The Roman Catholic Church continued to conduct its own councils, which it termed ecumenical. But even Rome did not bother with such councils for almost a hundred years prior to 1961.

Today the situation is greatly altered. The term "ecumenical" is a part of every alert churchman's vocabulary. Indeed, the word is so freely bandied about in some circles that any precise connotation it might have once possessed has been quite obscured. This may mean that far too many possess only the most superficial knowledge of things ecumenical. Confusion is frequently the result. However, it also indicates that ecumenicity is very much in the air. It has caught the popular fancy. Particularly since New Delhi and Vatican Council II, many Baptists are asking more and more questions requiring factual answers.

Use of the Term

The word in its original meaning refers to the whole inhabited earth. In its adjectival form, as applied to church councils from Nicaea (A.D. 325) on, it means "of the whole church." In this way Rome has continued to claim exclusive rights to the term, considering herself the whole church, even after the schism between the East and the West in 1054, the Reformation in 1517, and subsequent secessions.

1

Since 1910, the term has been used by Protestants to describe the movement toward the reunion of Christendom which crystallized at the Edinburgh International Missionary Conference.

Thus, the World Council of Churches and its related organizations fell heir to a term to which they have given new substance. Most frequently, from 1910 to 1961, the term has been applied to this historical development. But Vatican Council II and Pope John's references to Vatican Council II as an ecumenical council changed all of this. Many Protestants wholly misunderstood the pontiff's use of the term. They automatically applied a New Delhi connotation to the phraseology of John XXIII. It was not entirely their fault. The term lent itself to ambiguity in this context.

"Ecumenical" and its cognates will be used in this work with reference to all movements and organizations which look toward a greater degree of unity in Christendom than exists at present. It is not an evaluative term. The immediate context alone can determine the exact meaning. Consequently, the World Council and the various national affiliates, the Roman Catholic Church's Vatican Council II, and the fundamentalist organizations are placed in the same category. Actual mergers of denominations or merger proposals, and the spirit of oneness in Christ manifested in numerous individuals and movements not commonly recognized as ecumenical, are so designated.

Purpose of Study

This work is not a book *for* or *against* the ecumenical movement or any of its structures. It does not attempt to tell any Baptist body what its relationship to the various councils ought to be. Rather, it does make an attempt to describe, inform, and explain the ecumenical movement for a Baptist audience. Consequently, the non-Baptist reader is likely to come to a more perfect understanding of Baptists and their peculiarities.

The book is written from the assumption that Baptists must increasingly face the challenge of ecumenical Christianity. There is no escaping it. This challenge, at present, most Baptists are either unprepared or unwilling to accept. The decisions for or against alignment with various ecumenical structures have often been arrived at without sufficient information and under extenuating pressures. It is fairly obvious that a responsible decision can only be made on the basis of reliable information and proper theological understanding.

One of the major aims of this study is to provide Baptists with a more complete picture of ecumenicity in all of its varied hues. For many Baptists, ecumenicity wears but one face. However, historically and theologically, this is not true. At the same time, ecumenical claims of success and actual performance sometimes vary. This work attempts to present most of the facets of the modern ecumenical movement accurately.

If the movement has suffered from caricature, it is completely unintentional and unconscious. Some ecumenical experiments and dreams have hardly been mentioned. For example, COCU is not discussed.[1] The Church of South India is only mentioned in passing. The enormous and commendable relief programs of the World Council and the various national councils receive no attention. These omissions are intentional since, obviously, such a work makes no claim to comprehensiveness beyond the rather narrow, self-imposed limits.

The Historical Perspective

Perhaps to a well-versed student of the ecumenical movement, a discussion of ecumenicity prior to specific treatment of the Baptists may seem unnecessary. But for the neophyte or the busy pastor, the historical survey of the concept of unity in its various manifestations is as necessary as those which deal specifically with the Baptists. For one to determine what the Baptist relationship to the various councils should be without the benefit of the historical approach assumed here is to attempt a premature decision based on partial information.

The chapter on Catholic ecumenism may seem entirely out of place. Actually, the only excuse for its insertion is that Vatican Council II has raised many questions in the minds of Protestants that cannot long go unanswered. Rome can no longer be ignored in her claim for a share of ecumenical limelight. Baptists, as other evangelicals, can ill afford misinformation or no information on Catholic ecumenicity in the light of the stakes involved.

Most works on the ecumenical movement never concern them-

---

[1]In 1960, Eugene Carson Blake delivered a sermon in Grace Cathedral in San Francisco in which he called for the reorganization of the Protestant denominations in the United States into one church structure. The resultant movement is known as the Consultation on Church Union. Eight major denominations are now involved in discussing the possibilities of merger in line with the Blake proposal. The movement is more commonly known as COCU.

selves with fundamentalist ecumenical structures. In a sense their omission has ample justification. These structures have not developed out of the movement which first became articulate at Edinburgh in 1910. They are, rather, reactionary developments. However, a discussion of their ecumenical views is certainly as justified as that of Rome. In fact, as far as true ecumenical insight and commitment are concerned, they demand consideration. From the standpoint of Baptist involvement they can hardly be overlooked.

Organization

The sequence of chapters can be seen at a glance from the table of contents. However, the relationship of the parts to the whole may not be quite so clear.

Chapters 2, 3, and 4 are devoted to a historical survey—from the emergence of the concept of Christian unity among the ante-Nicene fathers to New Delhi. Chronology and event have determined the dividing lines. Chapters 5 and 6 present ecumenicity within the Roman Catholic context on the one hand and that of the competitive fundamentalists on the other. A volume or volumes could be and have been devoted to each of these subjects. They are treated here in just enough detail to fill in information necessary for an ecumenical understanding otherwise impossible.

Chapters 7, 8, and 9 are devoted to a discussion of various Baptist bodies and their relationship to the world, national, and local councils. Baptists can possibly learn something about themselves in these pages. It is probable too that some who have been rather quick to level blanket indictments at the Baptists, when nothing more constructive appeared, may realize that their opinions have been arrived at from inadequate information rather than thorough knowledge. On the other hand, it may be that the characteristics which they detest most about Baptists find much support in these chapters. Possibly it is too much to hope that contemporary stereotypes of Baptists will disappear and all misunderstandings will be erased. At least there is an attempt to understand the ecumenical movement and to be understood by responsible ecumenists.

Chapter 10, as inadequate as it may appear to many zealous champions of the ecumenical movement, is the conclusion. In a sense, no conclusion can be the final word for Baptists on the ecumenical movement. Both the ecumenical movement and Baptists are very much alive and quite capable of change which may produce new avenues of approach and new relationships. Christian unity is, indeed, as Robert Handy has suggested, a never-ending quest and an ever-present reality.

2

Schism and the Ecumenical Ideal (A.D. 95-1648)

There has rarely, if ever, been a time in the history of Christianity when the church has not been faced with the problem of schism. From the days of the New Testament to the present hour, Christians have been divided in their allegiance. Party loyalty has at times taken precedence over Christ and denominational convictions over the ecumenical ideal. Apparently sectarian divisiveness has become an abiding characteristic of the Christian religion. Never considered the ideal, the schismatic condition of Christendom has been tackled with varying degrees of success through the centuries. Thus, some understanding of the problem of schism and attempted solutions is necessary in order to put this discussion of the ecumenical movement within its historical context.

From Clement to Nicaea

Doubtless the seeds of division were already present during the lifetime of the apostles (Acts 15; 1 Cor. 1:10-17; Gal. 2:11-21; Titus 1:5-16). And by the close of the New Testament era they threatened to disrupt the tranquility of more than one congregation. The church at Corinth became the focal point of anxiety that prompted a letter of admonition from the church at Rome. This letter, *The First Epistle of Clement to the Corinthians,* provides the modern reader with an excellent source for study of the problem of schism and the early church.

For some reason which cannot now be ascertained with certainty, the church at Corinth, or some members of that church, had sought advice from the church at Rome concerning a problem of sedition against the presbyters of the church. Perhaps Clement was personally acquainted with certain members of the church from a previous visit to Corinth.[1] The letter is addressed to "the Church of God sojourning at Corinth" and written in the name of "the Church of God which sojourns at Rome." The impression of equality of the congregations within the Christian fraternity given by the salutation is further enhanced with the reference to the members of the church as my "dear brethren."

Clement betrays no paternal attitude in his rather sharp admonitions to the "dear brethren." To the contrary, he takes special pains to couch his advice in a most fraternal and self-effacing manner. "These things, beloved," he asserts, "we write unto you, not merely to admonish you of your duty, but also to remind ourselves. For we are struggling on the same arena, and the same conflict is assigned to both of us."[2]

Clement finds it impossible to conceal his revulsion at the treatment which the presbyters had received at the hands of some of the members of the church when he declares: "Why do we divide and tear in pieces the members of Christ, and raise up strife against our own body, and have reached such a height of madness as to forget that 'we are members one of another?' "[3] Having registered his feelings, Clement then proceeds to enumerate the evil effects of schism. "Your schism has subverted [the faith of] many, has discouraged many, has given rise to doubt in many, and has caused grief to us all. And still your sedition continueth."[4]

The way out of this deplorable situation, according to Clement, is found in the guidelines set forth in the Holy Scriptures (Old Testament), the life and teachings of Christ, and the example of the apostles, Peter and Paul.[5]

Upon the basis of these citations and numerous other arguments and illustrations, Clement calls the factions at Corinth to repentance

---

[1]Roberts and Crombie, *The Writings of the Apostolic Fathers*, p. 7.
[2]*Ibid.*, p. 12.
[3]*Ibid.*, p. 40.
[4]*Ibid.*, p. 41.
[5]Peter is mentioned and his sufferings for the cause of Christ, but the manner and place of his death are passed over in silence. Much more attention is given to Paul, of whom Clement writes: "Owing to envy, Paul also obtained the reward of patient endurance, after being seven times thrown into captivity, compelled to flee, and stoned. After preaching in the east and west, he gained the illustrious reputation due to his faith, having taught righteousness to the whole world, and come to the extreme limit of the west, and suffered martyrdom under the prefects." *Ibid.*, p. 11.

and reconciliation with God and the brethren. Finally, in a Pauline vein, love is acclaimed as the sure balm of healing. "The height to which love exalts is unspeakable," opines Clement. "Love beareth all things, is long-suffering in all things. There is nothing base, nothing arrogant in love. Love admits of no schisms: love gives rise to no seditions: love does all things in harmony."[6] Such love, Clement suggests, may demand the sacrifice of one's self for the good of the church—the will of the individual out of love will be subject to the will of the majority.[7]

The proffered solution to the problem of schism in the Corinthian church is simply an appeal to the Christian conscience of the offending brethren. Schism, in this instance, is viewed as a problem which can be solved by spiritual means alone.

Ignatius of Antioch

By the time of the Ignatian epistles (107-130), the problem of schism had become much more formidable. Not only were there problems of discipline with which to deal but also doctrine. For Ignatius the solution to these problems lay in submission to the authority of the bishop.

Doubtless some of these epistles are heavily interpolated and others may not be the work of Ignatius, bishop of Antioch, at all. However, it seems a justifiable inference to hold that by the middle of the second century there had emerged, as far as some churches are concerned, a threefold ministry—bishops, presbyters, and deacons. Of the three, the bishop is viewed as the seat of authority, the preserver of unity and orthodoxy. However, in the Ignatian epistles, the concept is that of a pastor who has emerged as the center of authority and ruler over the presbyters in the local church. His authority does not extend to other churches or presbyters in other churches.

A few excerpts will illustrate the Ignatian approach to the problem of schism in the churches of the second century. In the *Epistle to the Ephesians,* chapter 4, the writer exhorts:

So then it becometh you to run in harmony with the mind of the bishop; which things also ye do. For your honourable presbytery, which is worthy of God, is attuned to the bishop, even as its strings to a lyre.

---

[6] *Ibid.,* p. 42.
[7] *Ibid.,* p. 45.

. . . It is therefore profitable for you to be in blameless unity, that ye may also be partakers of God always.[8]

It is clear from this passage, according to the writer, that the presbyters were given a supporting and subordinate role to the bishop.

In the *Epistle to the Smyrnaeans,* an analogy is drawn between the heavenly hierarchy and the earthly.

[But] shun divisions, as the beginning of evils. Do ye all follow your bishop, as Jesus Christ followed the Father, and the presbytery as the Apostles; and to the deacons pay respect, as God's commandment. Let no man do aught of things pertaining to the Church apart from the bishop.[9]

The analogy is a familiar one in the writings ascribed to Ignatius. It finds similar expression in many other places but particularly in the *Epistle to the Magnesians,* chapters 2 and 6.[10]

A further departure from the approach of Clement to the problem of schism in the local church appears in the quasi-sacramental significance which Ignatius attaches to a proper relationship to one's bishop. To oppose the bishop or to participate in a schism is in Ignatian thought disastrous. The force of this concept in the *Epistle to the Philadelphians* is unavoidable.

For as many as are of God and of Jesus Christ are also with the bishop. And as many as shall, in the exercise of repentance, return into the unity of the church, these, too, shall belong to God, that they may live according to Jesus Christ. Do not err, my brethren. If any man follows him that makes a schism in the church, he shall not inherit the kingdom of God.[11]

It is clear in the writings of Ignatius that schism, regardless of the reason, is viewed as a grievous sin that can only be forgiven by an unqualified submission to the authority of the bishop. Ignatius never dealt with the problem of schism between the churches.

Irenaeus and Heresy

Half a century or more later, the Gnostic heresy in a variety of forms introduced a perverted gospel which wrought dissension and

---

[8]Lightfoot, *The Apostolic Fathers,* p. 64.
[9]*Ibid.,* p. 84.
[10]Roberts and Crombie, pp. 172-78.
[11]*Ibid.,* pp. 223-24.

schism from Nag Hamadi to Rome. In the ensuing controversy, Irenaeus arose as the great champion of orthodoxy. His five books entitled *Against Heresies* are extant in a rather poorly rendered Latin version. His other works exist, if at all, only in fragments. However, from them it is possible to gain many insights relative to the problem of schism and Christianity of the second century.

Irenaeus, probably a native of Asia Minor, was pastor of the church at Lyons (185) when he penned his monumental work against the Gnostics. The development of gnosticism as a heretical Christian movement was only one of a number of significant changes which had taken place since the Ignatian epistles were written. Schism takes on a broader connotation in the writings of Irenaeus. The emphasis is no longer upon the churches but rather upon *the church*.

In addition to refuting the absurd pretensions of the Gnostic systems, Irenaeus points out the way to preserve the unity of the Catholic Church and save it from the inroads of heresy. This unity can be preserved, according to Irenaeus, in three ways: by adherence to Scripture, the apostolic tradition, and the historic episcopate. The use of the term "Scripture" includes the New Testament as well as the Old. Irenaeus refers to every book of the New Testament except Philemon and 3 John. Of course the Scriptures are subject to interpretation and the Gnostics made the most of this, as Irenaeus indicated when he wrote:

> When they are refuted from Scripture, they turn to accuse the Scriptures themselves—the text is not good, they are not authentic, they contradict each other, one cannot discover the truth from Scripture if one does not know the tradition. For the truth, they say, has not been handed down in writing but orally, and that is why Paul said, "Howbeit we speak wisdom among the perfect: yet a wisdom not of this world."[12]

The correct interpretation of Scripture may be found, declared Irenaeus, in the tradition of the apostles. This tradition finds its most succinct expression in the Rule of Faith. The Rule of Faith is a creedal formulation which later becomes, in greatly altered form, the Apostles' Creed.

> The Church, though dispersed throughout the whole world to the ends of the earth, received from the apostles and their disciples the

---

[12]Greenslade, *Early Latin Theology*, V, 67.

faith in one God, the Father almighty, "who made heaven and earth, the sea, and all that in them is," and in one Christ Jesus, the Son of God, incarnate for our salvation, and in the Holy Ghost, who preached through the prophets the dispensations of God and the comings and the birth of the Virgin and the passion and the resurrection from the dead, and the reception into heaven of the beloved, Christ Jesus our Lord, in the flesh, and his coming from heaven in the glory of the Father to sum up all things and to raise up all flesh of all mankind, that unto Christ Jesus our Lord and God and Saviour and King, according to the good pleasure of the invisible Father, "every knee should bow, of things in heaven, and things on earth, and things under the earth, and that every tongue should confess" him, and to execute just judgment upon all; to send "spiritual wickedness" and the angels who transgressed and became apostate, and the impious and unrighteous and unjust and blasphemous among men, into eternal fire, but upon the righteous and the holy and those who keep his commandments and persevere in his love—some from the beginning, some from repentance—to bestow the gift of life and incorruption, surrounding them with eternal glory.[13]

Irenaeus claimed that the "Church, though dispersed throughout the whole world, keeps the faith carefully, as dwelling in one house; and she believes these doctrines as though she had one soul and one heart."[14] However, he admits that this argument has little weight with the heretics. "But again," he writes, "when we challenge them by the tradition which comes from the apostles and is guarded in the churches through the successions of the presbyters, they oppose tradition, saying that they, being wiser not only than the presbyters but even than the apostles, have discovered the unadulterated truth."[15] His final argument, then, is not an appeal to Scripture or to tradition but to an unbroken succession from the apostles themselves. Irenaeus is convinced that the succession from the apostles through the presbyters guarantees the purity of the faith and is the only sure means by which the unity of the church can be preserved. He affirms:

By the same order and the same succession the tradition in the Church from the apostles and the preaching of the truth have reached us. And this is complete proof that there is one and the same life-giving faith which has been preserved in the Church from the apostles up till now and has been handed on in truth.[16]

---

[13]*Ibid.*, pp. 65-66.
[14]*Ibid.*, p. 66.
[15]*Ibid.*, p. 68.
[16]*Ibid.*, p. 68.

Since Irenaeus feels that it is impossible to present a list for all the churches, the increasingly influential church at Rome is selected to illustrate his theory of apostolic succession. He begins by referring to that "very ancient and universally known church founded and established at Rome by the two apostles Peter and Paul." [17]

Agreement with the doctrinal position of the church of Rome becomes for Irenaeus the sole criterion of orthodoxy. "For with this church, on account of its more weighty origin, every church, that is, the faithful from all quarters, must necessarily agree, since in it the tradition from the apostles has always been preserved by those who come to it from all quarters.[18] Unfortunately for Irenaeus' theory, his argument rests upon the most dubious evidence. It is obviously a pious fable, devoid of historical fact, that the church of Rome was founded by Peter and Paul.[19] But his argument was at least an insistence that the Christian revelation was historically mediated and produced a living, tangible movement and an apostolic witness to the revelation of God in Christ that could not be discounted by the Gnostic vagaries.

All advocates of apostolic succession can find in Irenaeus, in embryonic form at least, the basic guidelines of their position. He writes:

Wherefore it is incumbent to obey the presbyters who are in the church—those who, as I have shown, possess the succession from the apostles; those who, together with the succession of the episcopate, have received the certain gift of truth, according to the good pleasure of the Father. But [it is also incumbent] to hold in suspicion others who depart from the primitive succession, and assemble themselves together in any place whatsoever, [looking upon them] either as heretics of perverse minds, or as schismatics puffed up and self-pleasing, or again as hypocrites, acting thus for the sake of lucre and vainglory.[20]

Irenaeus applies the basic assumptions of Ignatius to the catholic or universal church. Thus, the succession of the church at Rome becomes for him the means of the transmission of the apostolic tradi-

---

[17]*Ibid.*, p. 69.

[18]*Ibid.*

[19]See Elliott-Binns, *The Beginnings of Western Christendom,* pp. 93-95, for an objective and brief discussion of Peter in Rome. The most extensive recent discussion of the Petrine tradition is that of Oscar Cullmann, *Peter,* trans. Floyd Filson (Philadelphia: The Westminster Press, 1953).

[20]Roberts and Rambaut, *The Writings of Irenaeus,* I, 462.

tion by which the Scriptures must be interpreted and the unity of Christendom preserved.

Tertullian

Tertullian is an enigma. A champion of unity and orthodoxy, he became a Montanist, spending twenty of his thirty-year ministry as a schismatic. It is he who made known the teachings of Irenaeus on the Scriptures, the Rule of Faith, and apostolic succession. The Latin did what the Greek of Irenaeus could never do—it popularized the concepts which Cyprian was to use in systematizing his views of the church.

However, Tertullian was no slavish imitator of Irenaeus. He had a profound distrust of philosophy. "What has Jerusalem to do with Athens, the Church with the Academy, the Christian with the heretic?" he asked. "Our principles come from the Porch of Solomon, who had himself taught that the Lord is to be sought in simplicity of heart. I have no use for a Stoic or a Platonic or dialectic Christianity."[21]

He felt that the sum total of what one was to believe was contained in the Rule of Faith, which, he assumed, was the apostolic legacy. The test then of apostolicity is, for Tertullian, conformity to the Rule of Faith. To this he was later to add discipline and the presence of the Holy Spirit. Callistus, the bishop of Rome (218-22), had taken a rather lax position in regard to discipline in the church, much to Tertullian's displeasure.

I hear that an edict has been issued, and that a peremptory one. The Sovereign Pontiff, indeed, the bishop of bishops, puts forth his edict: "To those who have done penance, remit the sins of adultery and fornication." What an edict! Who is going to endorse that with a "Well done"? And where will this bounteous gift be posted up? Then Tertullian sarcastically answers, "On the spot, I suppose, on the very doors of the brothels, just by the advertisements of lust."[22]

Tertullian the Montanist further departs from Tertullian the Catholic when the primacy of the Holy Spirit over the bishops is asserted in his treatise entitled *De Pudicitia.*

It is the Spirit who gathers together the Church which the Lord made

---

[21]Greenslade, 36.
[22]*Ibid.*, p. 74.

to consist in three. From that beginning, the whole number of those who agree in this faith takes its being as the Church from its founder and consecrator. Therefore the Church will indeed pardon sins, but the Church which is spirit, through a spiritual man, not the Church which is a collection of bishops. Law and judgment belong to the Lord, not the servant; to God, not the priest.[23]

The voice of dissent had been effectively raised by one who had the ear of the church, only to be silenced and reinterpreted by Cyprian.

Cyprian and the Episcopacy

The culmination of two centuries of thought on the nature and function of the church is found in Cyprian's masterpiece *De Unitate*. Evaluations of this work differ, due to factors other than merit.

The work is thus important as a landmark in the development of the episcopal conception of the Church by divine right. Otherwise, it is but a mediocre performance, which is vitiated by the tendency to mistake dogmatism for history, to ignore the fact of historical development, and to identify the Church with Old Testament institutions.[24]

Cyprian was greatly influenced by Tertullian. Both had practiced law before their conversion to Christianity. Both were of Latin extraction and natives of North Africa. Both brought creative minds and facile pens into the service of the church. It was Cyprian who "saved" Tertullian for the Catholic Church. While ignoring much of Tertullian's Montanist and more biblical emphases, he systematized his earlier views regarding the church.

By the middle of the third century the monarchial bishopric had given way to the metropolitan bishopric. Cyprian was the bishop of Carthage and quite naturally saw in his conflict with the presbyters who had objected to his election that the episcopacy was ordained of God to preserve the unity of the one visible church. It apparently never occurred to him to question his presuppositions relative to the office of bishop in the third century in the light of the Scriptures of the first. Where the bishop is, for Cyprian, there is the church. And "he who will not have the church for his mother cannot have God for his father."

The aggregate of the bishops thus became for Cyprian the concrete

<hr>

[23]*Ibid.*, pp. 76-77.
[24]MacKinnon, *From Christ to Constantine*, p. 308.

realization in time and space of the universal visible church. Green-slade has summarized Cyprian's views:

The Church is a single, visible body, using the apostolic Scriptures in addition to the Old Testament, maintaining the traditional apostolic faith, living under the institutions which have been handed down from apostolic times; and it is further linked with the apostles by the succession of bishops in each see.[25]

If the bishopric is the structure around which the church exists in history, the sign of unity which binds laity to the bishops in an indissoluble union is the sacraments. In this manner church, ministry, and sacrament become the means of salvation as well as the integral elements of the universal church.

Tertullian taught, in his Montanist days, that where the Holy Spirit's presence and power are felt there is the church.

Cyprian reversed the order in insisting that where the church is there is the Holy Spirit, and outside the church there is no salvation. "Further, outside this one visible communion there is no spiritual vitality and no salvation, for the Holy Spirit and the gifts of the Spirit were and are bestowed by Christ upon the Church alone."[26]

If you abandon the Church and join yourself to an adulteress, you are cut off from the promises of the Church. If you leave the Church of Christ you will not come to Christ's rewards, you will be an alien, an outcast, an enemy. You cannot have God for your father unless you have the Church for your mother. . . . He who does not keep this unity does not keep the law of God, nor the faith of the Father and the Son—nor life and salvation.[27]

Since, in Cyprian's scheme of things, the bishop is the key to it all, he found it necessary to spell out the requirements of the office. In Cyprian's opinion, a true bishop must be ordained in the church by those in apostolic succession and to a vacant see. Cyprian's final position was forged upon the anvil of controversy: first, his own with the dissenting North African presbyters; second, that of Cornelius with Novatian; and finally the baptismal controversy with Stephen.

Cyprian enjoins the bishops of the church gathered at the Council of Carthage (251) to unity. "It is particularly incumbent upon those

---

[25]*Op cit.*, 120.
[26]*Ibid.*, 121.
[27]*Ibid.*, 127-28.

of us who preside over the Church as bishops to uphold this unity firmly and to be its champions, so that we may prove the episcopate also to be itself one and undivided." [28]

It is in this context that the controversial primacy clause occurs in chapter 4 of *De Unitate*. Two versions of this work exist. One is termed the *Primacy Text* and the other the *Received Text*. The *Primacy Text* has been extensively used to bolster papal claims of Petrine authority. Defenders of the *Received Text* on the other hand believe this version to have stronger manuscript support.[29] This interesting and controversial section of *De Unitate* reads, after quoting Matthew 16:18-19 and a reference to the resurrection encounter of Peter with Christ:

> Certainly the rest of the apostles were exactly what Peter was, but primacy is given to Peter (*primatus Petro datur*) and one Church and one chair is demonstrated. And they are all shepherds but the flock is shown to be one, which is to be fed by all the apostles in unanimous agreement. He who does not hold this unity of Peter, does he believe he holds the faith? He who deserts the chair of Peter on whom the Church was founded, does he trust that he is in the Church?[30]

It is conceivable that Cyprian wrote such a passage as he attempted to champion the cause of Cornelius, the newly elected bishop of Rome, against the claims of Novatian. Cyprian had little regard for Novatian, holding that he was a schismatic "who usurped for himself the name of a bishop though no one had given him a bishopric." It was of little import to Cyprian that the Novatianists claimed to hold an identical creed, the Trinitarian concept of God, and the sacraments. They were outside the church and this alone was sufficient to declare them apostate.[31] Cyprian's theology suffered at the hands of his ecclesiology. For Cyprian a mechanical union structured around the episcopacy was the pearl of great price.

If, indeed, Cyprian ever championed the primacy of Peter, he did not believe that primacy to be a hereditary possession of the bishop of Rome, or else he found it expedient to abandon such a position when he found himself in conflict with Stephen (254-57), the successor of Cornelius. It was Stephen's position that baptism outside the

---

[28]*Ibid.*, 126.
[29]See *ibid.*, 122.
[30]Cited in *ibid.*, 142.
[31]*Ibid.*, 154.

church, with water, and in the name of the Holy Trinity constituted a valid baptism. Therefore, he refused to baptize anew Novatianists who wished to return to the church. For Cyprian this was an impossible position.

Threatened with excommunication by Stephen, Cyprian called a second council at Carthage on September 1, 256, with eighty-six bishops present. The council unanimously declared that baptism outside the church was invalid. This was a personal affront and a formal challenge to the authority of the bishop of Rome. Nevertheless, Cyprian's emphasis upon the episcopacy, the value of corporeal union, his concept of the church, and exaltation of the bishop of Rome went a long way in making such future dissent from the dictates of Rome a precarious act at best. In Cyprian's works, modern advocates of the episcopacy, the ecumenical movement, and Roman Catholicism find much support.

Constantine and Nicaea

In Cyprian's teachings were present most of the basic concepts which were to convert Christianity into a persecuting religion. It is not surprising then that, when circumstances arose which put the power of the state on the side of the bishops, pagans, heretics, and schismatics began to feel the sting of the lash. The sword became not only an accepted method of preserving the unity of the church but a tool of evangelism as well. With the rise to power of Constantine, a series of events was set in motion which would do exactly this.[32]

The Edict of Milan, 313, marked a turning point in the history of Christianity. Constantine, who now favored Christianity even though not baptized until the eve of his death, and Licinius, a pagan, agreed in issuing the proclamation that put Christianity on equal footing with all other religions of the Roman Empire.[33]

---

[32]See Philip Schaff's discussion of the Edict of Milan in *The Progress of Religious Freedom* (New York: Charles Scribner's Sons, 1889), pp. 4-7. Of it he writes: "This famous Edict changed the current of history," p. 5. For the text of this edict see Henry Bettenson, *Documents of the Christian Church* (London: Oxford University Press, 1963), pp. 22-23. One form of the edict or rescript (since it was sent to an individual) was translated by Eusebius, *The Ecclesiastical History, II,* 444-46. Also see Baker, *A Summary of Christian History,* pp. 65 ff., for a brief but factual discussion of Constantine in the changing relationship of Christianity to the Roman Empire.

[33]See MacKinnon, pp. 535-36.

However, Licinius did not abide by the provisions of the edict and began a fresh persecution of the Christians in the eastern section of the Empire.

Constantine, thus armed with a pretext for conflict, waged war with his coemperor and, defeating him in the battles of Adrianople and Chrysopolis, became sole emperor in 323. Now he was free to do openly what he had begun to do cautiously as early as 313. It was clearly his policy to advance the cause of Christianity at the expense of paganism.[34]

The church became the beneficiary of large gifts of money. Laws were enacted that forced recognition of the rights and privileges of Christians in every province of the Empire. Bishops Hosius of Cordova and Eusebius of Caesarea were made the emperor's most trusted advisers. It is not difficult to see why Eusebius pictures such state of affairs as idyllic.

Yea, and Emperors, the most exalted, by successive enactments on behalf of the Christians, confirmed still further and more widely God's bounty towards us; and bishops constantly received even personal letters from the Emperor, and honours and gifts of money.

He continues in chapter 3 to describe the unity of the church.

After this there was brought about that spectacle for which we all prayed and longed: festivals of dedication in the cities and consecrations of the newly built houses of prayer, assemblages of bishops, comings together of those from far off foreign lands, kindly acts on the part of laity towards laity, union between the members of Christ's body as they met together in complete harmony.[35]

Christianity, under Constantine's patronage, was actually, if not legally, rapidly becoming the official religion of the Empire. To this fact numerous acts testify.[36]

Constantine obviously saw in the religion that persecution could not stamp out great possibilities for holding together his vast and heterogeneous empire. Schism within the church would destroy much of the value of the Christian religion as a cohesive force and therefore it could not be tolerated. It must be dealt with and healed by

---

[34]*Ibid.*, p. 538.
[35]*Op cit.*, 395, 397.
[36]MacKinnon, pp. 538 ff.

peaceable means if possible and if not, then by coercion and the application of physical penalties. The Donatists were apparently the first Christians to feel the heavy hand of persecution by Christians. Unfortunately, they were by no means the last.

During the latter period of Constantine's reign, the Novatians, Valentinians, Marcionites, Paulicians, Montanists or Kataphrygians, and Arians were numbered among those listed as pestilent criminals and enemies of the truth who are forbidden to assemble in public or private and whose property is to be confiscated and turned over to the Catholic Church.[37]

Shortly after his victory over Maxentius, Constantine was evidently informed of the Donatist schism. He felt it his responsibility to seek to resolve the difficulty, according to an extant letter to Miltiades, bishop of Rome.[38] From the beginning of his involvement in the controversy, it was obvious that Constantine had no intention of giving in to the Donatists. His sympathies were with the majority. After the various hearings (Synod of Arles, 314, and Milan, 316), Constantine grew weary of the long, drawn-out proceedings and the recalcitrance of the schismatics. He then pursued a policy of persecution for four years which was abandoned in 321 as fruitless. The Donatists, who had first invited the imperial judgment of their cause, eventually challenged the right of Caesar to dictate the affairs of the church.

The Arian controversy posed a greater threat in the eyes of Constantine than the African schism ever could. For one thing, it had the potential of splitting the Empire into two warring camps. Constantine correctly recognized that whereas the Donatist controversy involved personalities and pestiferous problems of ecclesiology, it did not contain the explosive potential of a full-fledged theological controversy over the nature of the Christian deity. After Arius and his party had been defeated and Nicene orthodoxy left in command of the field, Constantine editorialized:

Now that the impious hostility of the tyrants has been for ever removed by the power of God, our Saviour, . . . I pray that that spirit which delights in evil may devise no other means for exposing the divine law

---

[37]*Ibid.*, p. 546. For a recent study of the Donatists see W. H. C. Freud, *The Donatist Church: A Movement of Protest in Roman North Africa* (Oxford: Clarendon press, 1952).
[38]Eusebius, 455.

to blasphemous calumny; for in my opinion intestine strife within the
Church of God is far more evil and dangerous than any kind of war
and conflict; and these our differences appear more grievous than any
outward trouble.[39]

The Arians were banished, but no protest was heard from either
Eusebius or Athanasius. Athanasius was to protest vigorously when,
with the change of emperors, his lot became that of the exile. Apparently the church was fast reaching the place of willingness to
pay the price of submission for the benefits of state patronage.
Subsequently, the voices of Donatus, Athanasius, and Hosius of Cordova on behalf of religious freedom were forgotten with dreadful
consequences.

From Theodosius to Charlemagne

Ambrose, bishop of Milan, contributed much to the emerging
medieval pattern of *corpus christianum*. In the mind of Ambrose,
it was the responsibility of the state to enforce the edicts of the
church with police power, if necessary. The emperor must also "pro-
tect the true religion and the true Church against its rivals; that is,
he should prohibit heretical worship and the pagan cults."[40]

Once the Catholic Church had felt the power it could invoke at
will, it began to rely increasingly upon the arm of the flesh to fight
the battles of the Lord. The secular power of worldly princes became particularly useful against schism. Thus, Ambrose in address-
ing the Emperor Gratian concerning the Photinian schism reveals
the implementation of these concepts.

There is also the matter of the Photinians. By an earlier law you
decree that they should not assemble together, and by the law governing the episcopal Council, you forbade them to join us. We now learn
that they are still attempting to meet inside the city of Sirmium, and
ask your Grace once more to forbid their meetings and to order due
respect to be shown first to the catholic Church and secondly to your
own laws, so that, under God's protection, by your care for the peace
and quiet of the Church, you may reign in triumph.[41]

Under the influence of Ambrose, the church also began to flex

---

[39]MacKinnon, p. 551.
[40]Greenslade, 180.
[41]*Ibid.*, 189.

its political muscles. Ambrose virtually excommunicated Eugenius, throwing the weight of the church on the side of Theodosius. After his victory at the river Frigidus, Theodosius I (378-95) became the sole emperor and repaid the support of the church by making Christianity the official religion of the Empire.

But it was Theodosius II who was responsible for the codification of the laws regarding religion which the church was to use against heretics and schismatics through the centuries. The state and the church had embraced a unitive concept of society, but from different motives. However, it eventuated in the union of church and state.

With the fall of the Roman Empire, the church emerged as the one stabilizing force in a convulsive age. Thus it preserved practically all that remained of the once proud Empire. Amid the decay and ruin, the grand edifice of medieval Catholicism began to emerge.

In the West, Leo I and Gregory I and their successors became the heirs of both the Petrine legacy of fabled lore and the *Pontifex Maximus* tradition of pagan Rome. Greatly augmented by forged documents, the *Donation of Constantine,* and the *Pseudo-Isidorian Decretals,* the church by the end of the ninth century had become a temporal as well as a spiritual power. In reality, the papal states comprised a significant political entity within themselves. With the crowning of Charlemagne (800) and the creation of the Holy Roman Empire, Leo III made explicit that which had been firmly believed by the faithful for generations. He expressed the concept a few days before the coronation when, under fire by his enemies and faced with an investigating council called by Charlemagne, he declared: "the Apostolic See has the right to judge everyone but can itself be judged by no one."[42]

Charlemagne, taken by surprise as he knelt before the altar at St. Peter's in Rome, was crowned by Leo and acclaimed by the forewarned congregation as "Charles Augustus, crowned by God, great and peaceful emperor of the Romans, long life and victory."[43] By this act, Leo declared quite eloquently that church was over state and pope over emperor. The unitive concept of church and society thus survived the barbarian invasions and provided the ideal

---

[42]Cited by Cannon, *History of Christianity in the Middle Ages,* p. 81.
[43]*Ibid.*

toward which both popes and emperors were to strive for a millenium, but not always harmoniously.

Medieval Schism and Unity

The Great Schism (1054) rudely shattered the ecumenical ideal as no other division had previously. The causes of separation between Eastern and Western Christianity were deep and varied. Subsequent attempts at reunion, although often promising, ended in frustration. Both councils and crusades not only failed to unite the two "Catholic churches" but added to the misunderstanding and ill will already apparent. By the close of the fifteenth century the division between East and West took on the aspects of permanency.

From the ninth century on, heresy grew and the heretics vastly multiplied. The Cyprianic dream of the one universal, undivided, visible church had begun to disintegrate even in the West. Crusades were launched against the Waldenses; John Huss was burned at the stake; and the Inquisition, with varying degrees of success, attempted to enforce outward conformity wherever it could compel the secular power to do its bidding. The Jew, Moor, and pagan became increasingly subject to the overbearing demands of a power-hungry hierarchy.

As the political prowess of the church increased, it suffered from a corresponding decline in spiritual perception. The papacy was unable to extricate itself from the immoral web in which it had become entangled. Simply to mention the pornocracy, the Babylonian captivity, and the papal schism is reminder enough of the depths of degradation to which the Roman Church had sunk. The Reformation was the inevitable reaction to this sordid state of affairs. As the Middle Ages came to a close, many were beginning to feel that the church must be reformed at any cost, even at the loss of unity.

The Reformers and Ecumenicity

Few Reformers were willing to face the consequences of any radical reform. Erasmus determined to stay within the Roman Church, believing that the only reform justifiable was that which left intact the structure, doctrines, and laws of medieval Catholicism. It was an Erasmian position that the Roman Catholic Church had within canon law all the resources necessary for a genuine reformation. The influence of Erasmus in sixteenth-century Europe was great. Both Luther and Calvin felt called upon to defend their positions as advocates of reform who had no intention of rending the seamless robe of Christ.

Luther, Calvin, and Zwingli viewed the Roman Catholic Church as a fallen church. "Luther dated the fall with Sabianus and Boniface III, but Zwingli pinpointed it with Hildebrand and the 'assertion of hierarchial power.' "[44] Calvin was inclined to date the fall with Gregory the Great. But neither Luther, Calvin, nor Zwingli agreed with the Anabaptists in holding that the fall was total and the Roman Church completely apostate.

All three felt that they were simply remodeling a structure upon the same time-honored foundation, and that they were in vital communion with the one true church of Christ. Infant baptism became the outward symbol of this basic assumption. It was, in addition to other things, the historic mark of the continued witness of the undivided apostolic church in history.

The concept enters into Luther's definition of the church: "For where the Gospel is being preached and the Sacraments are rightly used, there is the holy Christian Church."[45]

Again, in discussing the invisible nature of the church, Luther wrote: "It is a high, deeply hidden thing, the Church, so that no one may either know or see it, except as it is known from Baptism, Sacrament and the Word."[46]

Calvin also included the sacraments as marks of the true church. However, for both Reformers, doctrinal purity was of far greater importance than a mere mechanical union. The Reformers, therefore, represent a return to a pre-Cyprianic view of the unity of the church and could be classified as both anti-Cyprian and anti-Erasmus. They were unwilling, though, to go as far as either the Anabaptists or the Inspirationists (*Spiritualisten*) in the restoration of the true church.

The Radical Reformers

The fall of the church in Anabaptist thought was absolute. The Anabaptists dated the fall with the union of church and state which, according to them, was first implemented by Constantine the Great.

---

[44]Estep, *The Anabaptist Story*, p. 177.
[45]Cited by Mueller, *Church and State in Luther and Calvin*, p. 6.
[46]*Ibid.*, p. 10.

All sorts of dire consequences accompanied the fall. They believed that when infant baptism became the prevailing practice (407), the character of the church as a fellowship of the regenerate was seriously altered. With the formal union of state and church under Theodosius I, the fall was complete. In no sense then could the Anabaptists accept the Church of Rome as the true church. To them, therefore, Luther, Zwingli, and Calvin by the introduction of the *Landeskirchen* and the maintenance of infant baptism, remained to some extent within the fallen church.

Anabaptists did feel a kinship, however, with every regenerate man who, because of his relationship to Christ, is a part of that universal invisible church. The Anabaptists had no interest in making such a concept of unity visible. They were primarily concerned with building visible churches upon the foundation of Christ and the apostles. Apostolic succession, corporate unity, and political power had absolutely no attraction for them. It was their conviction that they stood in relation to Christ and the apostles where first-century Christians stood. And in the light of the New Testament revelation they could build anew the true church (*rechte Kirche*) upon an apostolic foundation. They can be classified as exponents of a theory of radical discontinuity.

In some ways the Inspirationist Caspar Schwenckfeld was the most ecumenically minded Reformer of the sixteenth century. He rejected all sacraments and refused to institute a church. It was his conviction that the sacraments should not be reinstituted until authorized by a direct revelation from God. The true church in Schwenckfeld's mind was made up of believers of every nation.

> We believe, know and confess that there is a holy Christian Church on earth today; namely, the company of all chosen believers and saints of God, who have the spirit of Christ, which is called the Catholic Church, correctly speaking; whose head is Christ, as she is his body and the congregation of God; whose members are scattered hither and yon throughout the whole world and known only to Christ her head, her Lord and King. The firm foundation of God standeth, having this seal: The Lord knoweth them that are his, 2 Tim. 2:19.[47]

Schwenckfeld never organized his followers into local churches. His ecumenicity was hardly that of Cyprian or the *corpus christianum* of his day.

---

[47]Cited by Schultz, *Caspar Schwenckfeld von Ossig*, p. 326.

Even though the advocates of the Magisterial Reform held tenaciously to a doctrine of ecclesiological continuity, often the effects of their teachings belied their stand. The continuity which they proclaimed so loudly with Rome and Israel was apparently obvious, at times, only to them. The end result was often much the same as that achieved by the advocates of radical discontinuity—the disintegration of the medieval *corpus christianum* and the birth of numerous variegated sects. The Holy Roman Empire's days were numbered. Its heart, the Roman Catholic Church, had failed and it only awaited the coup de grace by a Bonaparte to fall to its knees. Whatever else the Reformation achieved, it shattered the embodiment of an ecumenical ideal which had endured for a millenium.[48]

---

[48]See McNeill, *Unitive Protestantism,* p. 144, for an ecumenical interpretation of the Reformation. In this work the author calls Martin Bucer of Strassburg "the most zealous exponent of the ideal of church unity of his age."

3

The Ecumenical Movement
(A.D. 1648-1938)

That the Reformation shattered the *corpus christianum* of the Middle Ages was fairly obvious. What was not so obvious was the fact that some Reformers did not consider the new state of affairs the ideal. Among the Catholic exponents of the conciliation, Desiderius Erasmus was easily the most irenical. He never felt that Luther's extreme measures were necessary in reforming the church. And when Luther's efforts resulted in divisions that rocked the whole of Christendom, Erasmus clung to the bosom of the Roman Church.

In his attempt to mediate between the Utraquists (1519-21) and Rome, Erasmus was torn between two loyalties. His evangelical sympathies were clearly on the side of these disciples of Huss. But his innate desire for order and security compelled him to champion the cause of Rome. Consequently, he advised the Bohemian evangelicals to "follow Christ and seek reunion with Rome." Three years before his death, increasingly weary over the poor prospects of peace in Christendom, he wrote: "We have had enough of quarrels: perhaps sheer weariness may bring us together to concord."[1]

Unfortunately, Erasmus never lived to witness any substantial improvement over the situation which he deplored so eloquently. The forces of Roman Catholic reaction were too strong. If Erasmus had been chosen to represent the Catholic party at Augsburg in 1530, the course of Christian history might have taken a different turn.

It was the Lutheran faction personified in Philip Melanchthon which more nearly appropriated the spirit of Erasmus in the Augs-

---

[1]Cited by McNeill in "The Ecumenical Idea and Efforts to Realize It, 1517-18," in Rouse and Neill, *A History of the Ecumenical Movement, 1517-1948*, p. 36.

burg negotiations. But the concessions of Melanchthon could not change the basic theological stance of the Reformers and the adamant Catholic theologians were not prepared to accept anything less than complete capitulation. Thus, the irenic spirit of Luther's chief theologian came to naught.

Other attempts to arrive at a consensus between various factions of the Reformation were only partially successful.[2] By the time of the Peace of Westphalia (1648) the Protestant picture was still one of divided loyalties in which political and national considerations, at times, weighed quite as heavily as the strictly theological.

On the other hand, with the advent of the Council of Trent (1545-64), Rome's position had begun to harden. As papal influence gained the ascendancy, the Catholic position became increasingly intolerant. From Trent to the first session of Vatican Council II, called by John XXIII (1962), with few exceptions Rome thought of ecumenicity in terms of Protestant surrender and Protestants talked of ecumenicity in terms of self-preservation. Yet the ecumenical vision, although often eclipsed, did not fall from the sky.

Ecumenical Antecedents

From 1648 to 1910 many were the voices raised on behalf of Christian unity. The closer one comes to Edinburgh, 1910, the more insistent and unified the voices become, until like a swelling chorus the ecumenical movement becomes an irrepressible reality.

Pietism.—The first of these antecedents was Pietism. The Pietist emphasis upon the life of the spirit minimized the externals of confessional Lutheranism and produced a new era of interchurch fellowship and cooperation.

Count Nikolaus Ludwig von Zinzendorf (1700-60) became the best known exponent of this type of ecumenicity. Nominally a Lutheran and educated at the Pietist center of learning, the University of Halle, Zinzendorf became a bishop of the Unitas Fratrum (Moravians).

It was as a Moravian that he achieved fame both as a missionary and as an ecumenical pioneer. His efforts were not confined to Protestantism alone. For some time he carried on a rather extensive correspondence with the French Catholic Cardinal de Noailles. In

---

[2]*Ibid.*, p. 67. See McNeill, *Unitive Protestantism*, for a detailed discussion of the Wittenberg Concord., pp. 152-62.

1725, in order to acquaint French Catholics with a popular Protestant devotional work, he had Arndt's four books on *True Christianity* translated into French and published. Two years later Zinzendorf edited and published a hymnbook containing Protestant and Catholic hymns.[3] The cautious cardinal was greatly relieved when Zinzendorf turned his attention elsewhere.

Somewhat less ambitious were Zinzendorf's efforts to unite all German-speaking religious groups in Penn's colony into one harmonious body designated as "one congregation of God in the Spirit." Zinzendorf himself directed the first seven "Pennsylvania Synods." The experiment (1742) gave him an opportunity to introduce his Tropus concept of Christian unity. However, upon the occasion of the third synod, dissension set in which finally disrupted the movement, leaving it in the hands of the Moravians.[4]

The immediate results of Zinzendorf's efforts were frustrating indeed. The Lutherans were stimulated to draw anew the lines of demarcation between themselves and the Moravians. This was soon accomplished under the able leadership of Henry Melchior Muhlenberg. The Reformed, Mennonites, and Dunkards also strengthened their denominational structures. Pietism, however, continued its leavening process during the First Great Awakening (1726-55).

Through the evangelistic efforts of George Whitefield and his fellow evangelists, who ignored denominational lines, the foundation of a common evangelical heritage was formed for all Protestant denominations in the colonies. Even though some divisive side effects developed from the Great Awakening, the overall thrust gave American Christianity a common Pietistic understanding which led to many interdenominational ventures in the century which followed.

Nineteenth-century societies.—The first quarter of the nineteenth century saw a rash of organizations. Among them were the American Bible Society (1816), the American Sunday School Union (1824), and the American Tract Society (1825). It was a pietistic purpose which called into existence these interdenominational societies. The founders of the American Tract Society declared that it was their goal "to diffuse a knowledge of our Lord Jesus as redeemer of sinners, and to promote the interest of vital godliness,

---

[3]Elisabeth H. Zorb, "Count Zinzendorf, an 18th-Century Ecumenist," *The Ecumenical Review*, IX, No. 4 (July, 1957), 422.
[4]*Ibid.*, 426-27.

sound morality and good citizenship by the distribution of Christian literature in many languages throughout the world."[5]

By mid-century, the World's Evangelical Alliance had come into existence. The organizational meeting was held at London in August, 1846. All Protestant denominations were invited to send representatives. Some eight hundred persons responded. Zinzendorf would have been gratified when the delegates in this initial meeting declared it their purpose to:

> Confess the reality of the one Church, not to create it; while recognizing the essential unity of the Church, they deplore the divisions, confess their sinfulness, and do now take steps toward attaining a state of mind and feeling more in accord with the spirit of Jesus; they therefore ally themselves together to cultivate brotherly love, enjoy Christian intercourse, and to promote such objects as they may agree hereafter to prosecute together.[6]

Almost any eighteenth-century Pietist would have been perfectly happy with the thoroughly Protestant and distinctively evangelical doctrinal basis adopted by the Alliance.[7] The new organization not only reflected evangelical convictions but it was also motivated by a strong sense of social justice. Its position in this respect erected an obstacle at the outset when an attempt was made to organize an American branch of the Alliance. The original constitution prohibited any slaveholder, who was such by his own choice, from holding membership in the body. The Alliance became and remained a unifying force in international Protestantism for over half a century.

---

[5]Bass, *Protestantism in the United States*, p. 246.
[6]Slosser, *Christian Unity*, p. 184.
[7]*Ibid.* "(1) The Divine inspiration, authority, and sufficiency of the Holy Scriptures; (2) The right and duty of private judgment in the interpretation of the Holy Scriptures; (3) The Unity of the Godhead, and the Trinity of Persons therein; (4) The utter depravity of human nature in consequence of the fall; (5) The incarnation of the Son of God, his work of atonement for sinners of mankind, and mediatorial intercession and reign; (6) The Justification of the sinner by faith alone; (7) The work of the Holy Spirit in the conversion and sanctification of the sinner; (8) The immortality of the soul, the resurrection of the body, the judgment of the world by our Lord Jesus Christ, with the eternal blessedness of the righteous, and the eternal punishment of the wicked; (9) The Divine Institution of the Christian Ministry, and the obligation and perpetuity of the ordinances of Baptism and the Lord's Supper."

London (1851), Berlin (1857), Geneva (1861), and New York (1873) witnessed huge gatherings of the Alliance with colorful parades and striking pageantry. After the turn of the century, both attendance upon the meetings and influence began to wane. But the Alliance had succeeded in opening up new vistas of Christian fellowship across denominational lines. It had also anticipated some interests and emphases of the World Council of Churches. Perhaps the Alliance's greatest contribution lay in the opportunity it afforded Christians of various communions to discover one another. In spite of differing traditions, doctrinal emphases, racial and national origins, the discovery brought new understanding among Protestants and created a climate for future ecumenical advance.

The modern mission movement.—Of greater significance to the rise of the ecumenical movement was the missionary movement of the nineteenth century. The missionary endeavor of the Protestant denominations from its very beginning has been closely related to ecumenical concerns. It has served somewhat as a catalyst, incubator, and goal, all at the same time, of the ecumenical movement. In other words, the cause of missions became both the cradle and the most effective apologetic of ecumenicity.

William Carey, in a letter to Andrew Fuller in England, proposed in 1806 a "general association of all denominations of Christians from the four quarters of the world."[8] Fuller felt the idea an impractical one with no promise of fruitful results. Yet the seed was sown and the conditions which prompted Carey to express the desire to his friend stimulated other missionaries in various countries to consider the advisability of interdenominational meetings on a less ambitious plane.

The first of these consultative meetings was held in Bombay, India, in 1825. Many such meetings were convened in various parts of the country. The third of the North India conferences which assembled at Lahore from December 26, 1862, to January 2, 1863, was by far the most ambitious and also the most significant. The conference heard carefully prepared papers, observed the Lord's Supper together, and quite frankly discussed the possibilities of union among Protestants. Seventy-one delegates were present for the deliberations.[9]

---

[8]Cited by Hogg, *Ecumenical Foundations*, p. 17.
[9]*Ibid.*, p. 21.

The third conference of the South India mission conferences, held at Madras January 2-5, 1900, proved to be the most important of all mission conferences, even surpassing that of Lahore in North India. A number of "firsts" were registered with this conference. For the first time in such gatherings, the delegates were the officially elected representatives of their denominations. Instead of gathering simply to hear papers read before the assembled delegates, Madras became a "work conference." The delegates were divided into committees and assigned subjects prior to the meeting. The committees then presented their reports, after which the entire conference of assembled delegates met in plenary session to discuss the reports.

India's lead was followed by other missions on every continent of the world. From Japan to Mexico the air was filled with strains of Christian hymns sung in many different languages by missionaries and nationals rejoicing in a newly awakened fellowship. "The most prominent motif through all these conferences was Christian unity—unity engendered by the situation, unity manifest by the experience itself. Where there had been no awareness of Christian unity, these meetings made it real. Where, in common purpose and effort, Christian unity had been recognized, these gatherings strengthened it."[10]

While missionary conferences of interdenominational nature were becoming increasingly frequent on the mission fields, Anglo-American missionary conferences of a similar nature were meeting from time to time in England and America. The first of these convened in London on October 12 and 13, 1854, at the close of the annual meeting of the British Organization of the Evangelical Alliance. Subsequently, international missionary conferences met in Liverpool (1860), London (1878 and 1888), and New York (1900). The most influential of these was the Liverpool meeting.

The dynamic for all such conferences was the missionary enterprise. The assembled delegates were irresistibly drawn to a discussion of the increasing ecumenical nature of their meetings. Hogg suggests that "here also may be a real clue to the twentieth-century renascence of the word 'ecumenical.' "[11] The last three conferences carried the term "ecumenical" in their titles. In spite of serious shortcomings in organizational structure and deficiencies of vision which characterized these Anglo-American conferences, they contrib-

---

[10]*Ibid.,* p. 31.
[11]*Ibid.,* p. 49.

uted significantly to the growing demand for a truly international and interdenominational missionary movement representative of all the missions, boards, and denominations of Christendom. By the end of the nineteenth century interdenominational mission conferences had become a rather common occurrence even on the continent of Europe.

Student movements.—A vital corollary to the missionary conferences in the mission fields and those of Europe and America were the international student Christian movements. The Student Christian Movement included four major youth organizations: The Young Men's Christian Association, the Interseminary Missionary Alliance, the Student Volunteer Movement, and the World's Student Christian Federation. Motivated from the beginning by a healthy missionary and evangelistic concern, the whole movement found immeasurable inspiration from the evangelistic efforts of Dwight L. Moody and Ira D. Sankey.

Through Moody, Henry Drummond was won; and Drummond exerted an incalculable influence on his student generation in both England and America. Among Moody's converts at Cambridge were C. T. Studd and Stanley Smith who soon became the nucleus of a band of mission volunteers reminiscent of the haystack prayer group of Williams College a generation before. One of the group, J. E. K. Studd, came to America on a speaking tour of American colleges and universities. At Cornell his message went straight to the heart of the vice-president of the Cornell YMCA, John R. Mott. No man was to mean more to the emerging ecumenical movement in the years ahead than John R. Mott.

The Student Christian Movement proved of inestimable value to Edinburgh, 1910. It also gave students of many different communions the opportunity to experience an ever deepening fellowship in spite of denominational barriers. Thus a leadership was prepared which was to bring to subsequent ecumenical conferences youth, enthusiasm for missions, and experience in interdenominational work that had been nonexistent before.

Denominational developments.—Of far less importance than the cause of missions to growing ecumenical concern, but by no means an insignificant factor, was the expressed concern for the reunion of Christendom on the part of various denominations. Among the earliest of these, if not the earliest, was the Protestant Episcopal Church in the United States. As early as 1853 a petition was introduced to the General Convention of the Episcopal Church asking for a statement of principles which would guide the Episcopal churches in the discussion of federation with other Christian bodies.[12] The request was repeated in 1880, accompanied by a number of signatures. This time the petition was not ignored. A report was brought which contained the now famous four points relative to the Scriptures, the Nicene Creed, the sacraments, and the historic episcopate.

As the inherent parts of this sacred deposit, and therefore as essential to the restoration of unity among the divided branches of Christendom, we account the following, to wit:

1. The Holy Scriptures of the Old and New Testament as the revealed Word of God.

2. The Nicene Creed as the sufficient statement of the Christian Faith.

3. The two sacraments—Baptism and the Supper of the Lord—ministered with unfailing use of Christ's words of institution and of the elements ordained by Him.

4. The Historic Episcopate, locally adapted in the methods of its administration to the varying needs of the nations and peoples called of God into the unity of His Church.[13]

The Anglican bishops, meeting at Lambeth in 1888, reaffirmed their commitment to and interest in a united Christendom. In 1908, the Anglican bishops actually issued a letter suggesting that ministers and laymen of all denominations meet in a centrally located place for the purpose of promoting a greater mutual understanding among the different denominations. A similar call was issued later by the Protestant Episcopal Church in the United States, which led eventually to the first World Conference on Faith and Order. In addition to the Anglicans, from 1888, Baptists, Reformed, Disciples, and Congregationalists all expressed a genuine concern over the divided state of Christendom.

Eventually all roads of cooperative concern were to converge on Edinburgh. Pietism, interdenominational organizations, the international student movements, and denominational concern for unity found their fruition in the international missionary convention at Edinburgh. Edinburgh became both the capstone of previous cooperative efforts and the foundation stone of the modern ecumenical movement. Here the International Missionary Council was born, and

---

[12]Haselmayer, *Lambeth and Unity*, pp. 3-4.
[13]*Ibid.*, p. 10.

the movement which was to give birth to the World Council of Churches was initiated.

Edinburgh, 1910

With Edinburgh, 1910, the ecumenical movement became articulate. There were many factors that gave Edinburgh, 1910, its unique place in ecumenical history. Unlike previous international missionary conferences, attendance at Edinburgh was limited to official delegates of the mission boards and societies prorated on the basis of income. Edinburgh, like Madras, 1900, was a work conference. Topics were assigned by a program committee for study some two years before the conference was to convene. Three of the topics were closely related to the growing ecumenical concern of the conferees. A higher percentage of nationals was present and deliberated in the proceedings than in any previous mission conference.

Edinburgh was much more representative than other such conferences had been. The Anglo-Catholics came and participated vigorously in the discussions. The fellowship in Christ assumed far greater realization than before. In spite of the wider representation racially, nationally, and ecclesiastically, barriers were transcended in the realization of the oneness of the redeemed. But that which gives Edinburgh its unrivaled place in ecumenical history was the formation of the Continuation Committee.

It was during the discussion of the report of the commission on "Cooperation and the Promotion of Unity" that the motion originated. Sir Andrew Fraser made the motion with the understanding that it was but a small step in the direction of the reunion of Christendom.[14] The motion was discussed and debated at length, for as Dr. Latourette suggests: "The idea of a permanent organ of international cooperation, to carry on the work which had been begun at Edinburgh, was still so new as to arouse deep anxieties and hesitations in the minds of many members of the Conference."[15] However, when the vote was taken, the action was unanimous in favor of the proposal.

Upon hearing the news, the delegates sprang to their feet and sang the Doxology. Then fittingly enough, the man responsible for the in-

---

[14]Gairdner, *Echoes from Edinburgh*, 1910, p. 47.
[15]Latourette, "Ecumenical Bearings of the Missionary Movement and the International Council," in Rouse and Neill, p. 362.

ception of the idea was chosen as the first chairman of the Edinburgh Continuation Committee. The choice was a fortunate one. John R. Mott was a man uniquely endowed for such a post.

In Mott, the foreign missionary enterprise acquired one of its most farsighted and resourceful leaders. He brought to his new position a combination of qualities which fitted him ideally for the place—youth, energy, evangelistic zeal, business ability, administrative capacity and initiative, a wide acquaintance with laymen, and mind peculiarly fitted to appeal to their practical common sense.[16]

This last action of the conference establishing the Continuation Committee helps to give Edinburgh of all mission conferences its precedent-setting position. It at once gave continuity and stability to the nascent ecumenical movement.

Geneva, 1920

The optimism that characterized the Edinburgh conference of 1910 was soon eclipsed by the misunderstanding, hate, and ill will engendered by World War I. The war disrupted plans which were already under way to hold another ecumenical conference. But in this instance the conference would concern itself with social issues confronting Christianity in a twentieth-century world. Even the outbreak of the war did not prevent the Archbishop of Uppsala, Nathan Söderblom, from sending out a worldwide appeal for unity and love. But it did postpone the first conference on Life and Work (social issues) until 1927.

However, a preliminary conference with highly beneficial results assembled at Geneva, Switzerland, August 9-12, 1920. Some ninety delegates from fifteen countries responded to the invitation to attend the Geneva meeting. A Greek delegation in Geneva at the time, attending a consultative meeting on Faith and Order (theology and ecclesiology), was personally invited to attend the Life and Work planning conference by Söderblom himself. Thus, there was initiated at Geneva a relationship of the Greek Orthodox Church with the ecumenical movement which has continued to the present.

The German Protestants were not officially represented but some leading German churchmen were present. And in spite of severe psychological problems, the German and French delegates managed

---

[16]William Adams Brown, *Toward a United Church,* p. 56.

to work together. Under the capable and energetic leadership of Söderblom, the conference did make progress. A committee on arrangements composed of twenty-five members, with power to enlarge itself, was appointed for Stockholm. It was agreed that all Christian bodies should be invited to the proposed Life and Work Conference, including the Greek and Roman Catholic churches. It was Söderblom's contention that failure to invite any group for a priori reasons was to take a sectarian stance and thereby nullify the ecumenical nature of the movement.

Life and Work

Five years after Geneva, in the Cathedral of Stockholm the Universal Christian Conference on Life and Work finally convened on August 19, 1925. Many more difficulties than those first anticipated at Geneva were encountered in planning for the first ecumenical conference on Life and Work. The Provisional Committee through meetings at Peterborough (1921) and Hälsingborg (1922) succeeded in recasting the entire organization.

The preparation for Stockholm was greatly aided by a British conference of similar nature held at Birmingham in April, 1924. Indeed, Copec[17] anticipated much of the agenda of the first ecumenical conference on Life and Work, but it could not rival Stockholm in importance. For here there were assembled more than six hundred delegates from ninety-one participating denominations and thirty-seven countries.

The Stockholm conference studiously avoided any topic which was considered too theological for consideration by the Life and Work movement. The only action of the conference subject to a vote was the "Message." Its acceptance by delegates was viewed by some as the one solid achievement of the conference. Some felt that the conference failed to face up to the divisive issues with candor, choosing rather to avoid that which should have been open for frank discussion and careful appraisal.[18] In this respect, according to Stockholm's critics, the conference showed no advance over Edinburgh and revealed an innate weakness in the Life and Work movement.

Perhaps the very failures of Stockholm made possible the more

---

[17]Copec is an abbreviation for the Conference on Christian Politics, Economics, and Citizenship.
[18]Brown, p. 86.

realistic stance of Oxford (1937). The attendance was smaller but the representation larger than Stockholm. Of the 425 persons present, there were only 300 delegates, but these represented 120 denominations and 40 countries. The Germans were barred from attending by the Nazi government. All who attended were made painfully aware of the Third Reich's attempts to use religion in its program of hate and conquest.

Against such a backdrop, Oxford called the church back to its basic task.

> The primary duty of the Church to the State is to be the Church; namely, to witness for God, to preach His Word, to confess the faith before men, to teach both young and old to observe the divine commandments, and to serve the nation and the State by proclaiming the Will of God as the supreme standard to which all human wills must be subject and all human conduct must conform. These functions of worship, preaching, teaching, and ministry the Church cannot renounce whether the State consents or not.[19]

Before the conference adjourned, the proposal to merge with the Faith and Order Movement in forming the World Council of Churches was approved with only two dissenting votes. Thus, the Universal Christian Council for Life and Work transferred its responsibilities and functions to the new Provisional Committee of the World Council of Churches in Process of Formation on May 13, 1938.

Faith and Order

On August 3, 1927, 394 delegates from 108 denominations met together at the University of Lausanne to take part in the First World Conference on Faith and Order.[20] Invitations for such a conference were originally extended by the Protestant Episcopal Church of the United States. Plans for the proposed conference, however, did not actually materialize until after the war. Initial postwar preparations were made at Geneva, in 1920, where a Continuation Committee was appointed and charged with the responsibility of working out the necessary details. Six commissions were organized and topics were assigned for preliminary study before the conference

---

[19]Cited by Karlström, "Movements for International Friendship and Life and Work, 1925-48," in Rouse and Neill, p. 591.
[20]Brown, p. 101.

convened. At last, vision and plans merged; Lausanne took its place
in ecumenical history.

Bishop Charles Henry Brent of the Protestant Episcopal Church
of the United States, former missionary and longtime ecumenical
stalwart, was elected president. Lausanne became the crowning
achievement of his life. His arduous efforts, in spite of failing health,
made the conference possible. He died some two years later in
Lausanne.

The report of the commission on "The Unity of the Church,"
of which Bishop Brent was the chairman, was unanimously received
without comment. However, some of the other commissions did not
fare so well. The difficulties which they encountered within the sectional meetings and on the floor of the assembly arose out of a
misunderstanding of the task at hand, as well as the nature of the
reports. There seems to have been considerable confusion in the
minds of the conferees regarding the purpose of the assembly. Some
were convinced that the conference was to make definite plans for
the immediate reunion of Christendom.[21] Consequently, the Evangelical Lutherans and subsequently the Greek Orthodox felt constrained to read statements before the conference, clarifying their respective positions relative to church union. Others joined the rising
chorus, advising caution against a precipitate move toward corporate
union. Bishop Brent, whose personal desire was for union—the
quicker the better—attempted in vain to allay fears and quiet the
rising tumult. Repeatedly he assured the assembled delegates that
the purpose of the conference was not unitive but exploratory, in
which the discussion of differences was quite as important as areas
of agreement, with, of course, the hope that a way to eventual union
might be found.

The differences were certainly discovered and discussed. In fact,
one of the most encouraging features of Lausanne was the frankness
with which widely differing viewpoints were presented and discussed.
Even though the report of Section VII on "The Unity of Christendom
and the Relation Thereto of Existing Churches" was committed to
the Continuation Committee for further study, it received serious opposition from some of the Anglicans present. It was their fear that
the report might encourage the position of those who felt that union

---

[21]Tatlow, "The World Conference on Faith and Order," in Rouse and Neill,
p. 423.

and collaboration could take place along lines of Life and Work at the expense of Faith and Order. One thing was quite clear.[22] Matters of Faith and Order were of vital importance to the delegates and would likely remain an integral part of ecumenical conversations for some time to come.

The report, "The Church's Message to the World—the Gospel," which was largely the work of Professor Adolf Diesmann, met with unanimous approval.[23] It proved to be one of the most far-reaching actions of Lausanne, echoing and reechoing through the corridors of ecumenical history.

A Continuation Committee of ninety-five was appointed to carry on the work of the Faith and Order movement in consultation with the participating communions. The committee met annually, with the exception of the years 1932-33, between the Lausanne and Edinburgh meetings. By 1929, the leadership of the Life and Work and the Faith and Order movements had come to the realization that the work of the two movements covered much the same ground. The result was the appointment of a small committee from each movement to coordinate activities and avoid overlapping. This was the beginning, even though possibly no one realized it at the time, of what was to become the World Council of Churches.

The Second World Conference on Faith and Order convened August 3, 1937, at Edinburgh. There were 344 delegates with 84 alternates and 15 Continuation Committee members from 123 denominations. Additional guests and youth representatives swelled the total to 504 persons in attendance. The backlog of some seventeen years' experience in ecumenical conversation relative to matters of Faith and Order gave the delegates a definite advantage over Lausanne. Even though the German Lutherans were prohibited from attending by the Nazi controlled state, and the Orthodox felt constrained to issue a statement setting forth their opinion on the best method of achieving unity, the conference closed with a genuine sense of accomplishment.

The only disruptive note at Edinburgh arose concerning the approval of plans for the formation of the World Council of Churches. The opposition, strangely enough, came from an Anglican, the Bishop of Gloucester who made two attempts to defeat the proposal. One

[22]*Ibid.*, p. 422.
[23]*Ibid.*, p. 424.

explanation for the harmony that prevailed in the Edinburgh meeting was the realism that characterized the approach of the delegates to topics considered in the meetings of the sections.

The illusion of a cheap or easy union, if it ever existed in some minds, was noticeably lacking. There was the customary frankness concerning divisive issues but there was more—respect born of an attempt to understand one another that represented a real advance in the maturing ecumenical movement. Canon Hodgson put it this way: "It had been what those who had planned it hoped it might be—'a genuine *Conference*' where there had been 'a genuine interchange of thought.' "[24]

The accomplishments of the Faith and Order movement have been succinctly summarized by one who was an active participant at Edinburgh, Bishop Yngve Brilioth:

> It may be described as a sincere willingness to speak the truth in love—to take differences seriously, but at the same time to see to the motives rather than to their expression, to look for the hidden unity in the apparent diversity, to honour all genuine forms of Christian thought and practice. It has been the conviction of the leaders of the Movement that theological work is certainly worthwhile, although the practical results may be slow to emerge. This peculiar temperament has been in a certain sense academic, but the scholars' task has been illumined by the vision of the one Church, holy, catholic and apostolic, a vision that has convinced us of its eternal reality although its external realisation may recede into a distant future.[25]

The International Missionary Movement

The International Missionary Council found itself in an interesting position relative to the emerging World Council of Churches. Since Edinburgh, 1910, the International Missionary Movement had pursued what William Adams Brown has described "its own independent and important course."[26] Until the New Delhi assembly of the World Council of Churches, 1961, the International Missionary Council remained the separate organizational expression of the movement. However, the separateness of this ecumenical organization was more apparent than real, as its history clearly indicates.

---

[24]Cited by Tatlow, p. 435.
[25]*Ibid.*, p. 441.
[26]*Op. cit.*, p. 118.

After World War I, the International Missionary Council replaced the Continuation Committee which had preserved the continuity of the movement through ten tumultuous years. It formally ceased to exist by 1921, but actually had failed to function as an international organization from the beginning of the war, losing the confidence of the Germans completely by 1917.

It did succeed in preserving a kernel of ecumenical interest and hope through a most difficult time. At Crans, Switzerland, near Geneva, from June 22 to 28, the leadership of the Continuation Committee and the Emergency Committee met to discuss the next step in the organizational life of the International Missionary Movement, since it was obvious to everyone that the Continuation Committee was quite defunct and the Emergency Committee, organized in 1918, had served its purpose. It was agreed to form an International Missionary Committee based upon the national missionary councils with power to act. The proposed organization would "function as an international co-ordinating council through its secretaries and biennial meetings."[27] The conference also recommended that Mott be made chairman and Oldham, secretary.[28] Plans reached their fruition at Lake Mohawk, New York, in the fall of 1921, when the International Missionary Council was officially organized.

The newly formed International Missionary Council, even though the heir of Edinburgh, 1910, and the Continuation Committee, was forced to make its place in the postwar era, just as did the Life and Work and Faith and Order movements. One of its most important meetings was in Jerusalem in 1928.

Full of apprehension, the continental delegates, especially the Germans, Dutch, and Swedish, met with the chairman of the council two days before the beginning of the conference. They were given an opportunity to express themselves freely, and Jerusalem was the better because of it. Altogether there were 231 members at the sessions, held during the Lenten season, March 24 to April 8.

The accommodations were exceedingly primitive, but neither the tents in which the delegates slept nor the candles by which they read were indicative of the progress in ecumenical adventure which marked Jerusalem as one of the great conferences in ecumenical history.

---

[27]Hogg, p. 197.
[28]*Ibid.*

Some of the accomplishments of Jerusalem may not be as apparent as others. That which was most obvious was the wider representation given to those referred to in ecumenical parlance as "younger churches." Nearly one fourth of those present represented denominations on the "mission fields of the world." Jerusalem chose deliberately not to speak with a western accent. Theologically, this conference identified itself with Lausanne and the Faith and Order movement when it made the "Message" of Lausanne its own.[29]

The conference addressed itself to a number of pressing social problems, but the first and last concern was Christian unity. The closing sentences of the last report, "Cooperation Through National Christian Councils," illustrate the point: "Only as we come back to the place called Calvary can we see the hindrances of our divisions and the failures of our Christian expression throughout the world. Only in penitence for the past and in a new sense of our oneness in Christ can we go forward in the task of the days to come."[30]

Jerusalem's accomplishments were such that John R. Mott, writing some ten years later, said that it had "already exerted a greater influence than that at Edinburgh in 1910. Jerusalem symbolized uniquely the emergence within Protestant Christianity of a world church in process of achieving spiritual unity through devotion to a common commitment."[31] Doubtless, the influence of Jerusalem was quite extensive. Hogg suggests that "Jerusalem's insistence upon the centrality of Jesus Christ, its emphasis upon partnership, and its recognition of the universality of secularism stimulated an evangelistic impulse in the churches of Asia and resulted there in several movements of great power."[32] Whatever else may be said of Jerusalem, it must be understood that Jerusalem and the International Missionary Council were still in the mainstream of the ecumenical current.

Just as the world was about to be plunged afresh into another global conflict, the International Missionary Council made plans to hold its first conference in Asia. The question of the propriety of holding such a conference at such a time was uppermost in the

[29]*The World Mission of Christianity, 1928* (New York: International Missionary Council, 1928), p. 37. Messages and Recommendations of the Enlarged Meeting of the international Missionary Council held at Jerusalem, March 24-April 8, 1928.
[30]*Ibid.*, p. 79.
[31]Cited by Hogg, pp. 253-54.
[32]*Ibid.*

minds of every concerned person. The answer to that question is now history. For just as Jerusalem made its contribution to ecumenical history, so did Madras.

Actually the conference was held in a small village by the name of Tambaram, fifteen miles from Madras. Here there gathered 471 men and women from 69 countries of the world on the campus of Madras Christian College during the Christmas season, 1938. The representatives of the younger churches numbered more than half of the assembled delegates. Few conferences have been more representative.

Madras followed the plan which by this time had become standard procedure for such conferences. Sections were organized for the careful study of prearranged topics. Later the reports were read and discussed by the entire assembly. The theme of the conference was the church, with special emphasis on the mission of the church. Hendrik Kraemer's *The Christian Message in a Non-Christian World* provided a stimulus for the entire conference. His name and his thesis of "radical discontinuity" became frequent topics of conversation were both formal and informal.

The worship experiences of Madras were particularly significant to the participants, leaving an indelible impression upon their lives. Madras also demonstrated the interdependence of the International Missionary Movement upon other organizational expressions of the ecumenical movement by borrowing rather heavily from the Oxford Conference of 1937. But to the insights of Edinburgh and Oxford, it added its own.[33]

Madras made many contributions. Its careful analysis of the problems of the indigenous church was balanced and stimulating. It opened up a new area of great importance, hardly touched upon by ecumenical conferences since the days of the World's Evangelical Alliance, when it launched into a discussion of religious liberty. Of great practical value to the entire missionary endeavor was the rather thorough examination of Christian literature. Its most significant contribution, however, lay in the sense of comradeship which it so graphically demonstrated at Madras. The ties of fellowship thus strengthened, even though strained during the long years of conflict in World War II, were never severed.

---

[33]*Ibid.*, p. 297.

After Madras, the International Missionary Council continued to go its own way. But the path it followed was no deviating one. Eventually it would converge with that of the proposed World Council of Churches. For the present there was work to be done which only the International Missionary Council could do.

4

The World Council of Churches (A.D. 1938-61)

The formation of a Provisional Committee for the organization of the World Council of Churches at the Oxford and Edinburgh conferences of 1937 represents a culmination of ecumenical thought as well as a new beginning. The concept of an international league of churches seems to have been entertained by a number of churchmen during the early twenties. Undoubtedly the newly organized League of Nations provided the early stimulus for such thinking. However, it was the advent of a second world war, the rise of the modern totalitarian state, and the prostitution of Christianity for its demonic purposes which hastened the crystallization of ecumenical thought.

Nationalistic distortions of the Christian faith made a mockery of its claims of universality. Influential leaders of both the Faith and Order and the Life and Work movements felt that neither of these movements, nor other interdenominational expressions of Christianity, adequately conveyed the universal nature of the church—a church which is not subject to the state, the pressures of a secular society, or the provincialism of a parochially segmented religion. Fragmentation, they argued, must be replaced with a new ecumenical structure which could speak effectively for all of "non-Roman Christendom."[1]

It was also a growing conviction on the part of the aroused leadership that the distinction between the Life and Work and Faith and Order movements was not so much artificial as impossible. In both conferences it had become increasingly evident that Faith

---

[1] William Temple as cited in Rouse and Neill, p. 703.

and Order and Life and Work were inseparable and that any consideration of the one inevitably involved the other. Therefore, it had become increasingly obvious that the two movements could not long maintain a separate existence. The most logical development in ecumenical organization was the formation of a world council of denominations which would embrace the aspects of both movements and become even more representative of non-Roman Christianity.

The actual groundwork for this new step was laid by four ecumenical stalwarts: William Temple, J. H. Oldham, William Adams Brown, and Samuel McCrea Cavert. During a visit to the United States in 1935, Archbishop Temple, in an informal consultation with a number of interested persons in the home of Dr. J. Ross Stevenson at Princeton, first urged the consideration of a world council. He asserted that "the time had come for an interdenominational, international council representing all the Churches, with committees to carry on various projects now forming the objectives of the distinct world movements."[2]

Dr. J. H. Oldham, in a paper prepared for the summer meeting (1936), proposed that Life and Work, in consultation with other ecumenical movements, appoint a committee to make preliminary plans for the formation of the World Council "prior to the conferences at Oxford and Edinburgh and present a report to the conferences."[3]

The proposal met with immediate approval by the respective conferences, including the International Missions Conference and the World Alliance of YMCAs. William Adams Brown had previously spent a considerable amount of time in Europe, attempting to create a favorable climate for just such a development. But it was Dr. Cavert of the Federal Council (USA) who first suggested the name "World Council of Churches."

A committee of thirty-five actually began to implement the Oldham proposal at Westfield College, London, in July, 1937. The members of the committee were drawn from the leadership of the various organizational expressions of ecumenical Christianity, including the YMCA, the YWCA, and the World's Student Christian Federation. The committee, in record time, reached the conclusion to recommend to the conferences of 1937 that the World Council of

---

[2] *Ibid.*, p. 701.
[3] *Ibid.*, p. 702.

Churches be formed which would be "a body representative of the Churches and caring for the interests of Life and Work and Faith and Order respectively."[4]

The Westfield meeting also "emphasized the principle, later adopted in the Constitution, that the Council should have no power to legislate for the Churches or to commit them to action without their consent."[5]

The basic concept of a new ecumenical organization was adopted by both the Life and Work and Faith and Order conferences meeting in 1937. However, since there were a number of questions regarding the nature of the proposed World Council of Churches, it was agreed that a committee of seven delegates and seven alternates from the Life and Work and Faith and Order conferences would form the committee of fourteen to perfect plans for the formation of the proposed World Council. This committee convened in Utrecht May 9-12, 1938, to draw up the constitution of the World Council.

In Process of Formation

The Utrecht meeting parallels in importance better known ecumenical gatherings. Here the basic nature and structure of the World Council were determined. The conference was careful to dispel fears that a superchurch was in the making.

Archbishop Temple, in a memorandum delivered to the conference, spelled out the limitations of the World Council. "It is not a federation as commonly understood, and its Assembly and Central Committee will have no constitutional authority whatever over its constituent churches. Any authority that it may have will consist in the weight it carries with the churches by its wisdom."[6]

Utrecht had difficulty in arriving at a creedal basis for the proposed council. The overwhelming opinion of the conference asserted that the "churches were gathered together by the divine Lord of the Church."[7] The Faith and Order doctrinal basis was then adopted which stated: "The World Council of Churches is a fellowship of Churches which accept our Lord Jesus Christ as God and Saviour."[8]

---

[4]Ibid.
[5]Ibid., p. 703.
[6]Ibid., p. 704.
[7]Ibid., p. 705.
[8]Ibid.

It commended itself to the assembled delegates because it was brief, and on the surface said what many believed, but could also be interpreted to include those who could not accept the traditional Trinitarian formula or who rejected the doctrine of the incarnation.

At Utrecht provision was actually made to put the World Council of Churches in operation until a general assembly could be held. A Provisional Committee was formed. It included the committee of fourteen and their alternates, with some members from the parent organizations. On May 13, the newly created Provisional Committee made Archbishop William Temple chairman. Dr. Visser 't Hooft was asked to become general secretary. The Administrative Committee of Life and Work transferred its responsibilities to the newly formed Provisional Committee. To all intents and purposes what some feared would happen did. The Life and Work movement lost its identity in the emerging World Council.

Utrecht's task was accomplished when the completed plan for the formation of the World Council was approved by the Continuation Committee of Faith and Order at Clarens, Switzerland, in August, 1938. This procedure was proscribed by the Faith and Order Conference at Edinburgh the previous year. Once the plans were approved, the committee of fourteen sent out invitations to all the denominations represented at Oxford and Edinburgh in 1937 to become charter members of the World Council of Christian Churches.

Even though the leadership of the International Missionary Council had been deeply involved in the ecumenical movement from the beginning, the International Missionary Council felt that the purpose of world evangelism could best be served by maintaining a separate existence. The Madras conference (1938) declared "that the International Missionary Council has no meaning except in so far as it is a constant reminder of the Christian obligation to the evangelisation of the world." [9] However, the conference determined to maintain close ties with the World Council and asked Dr. William Paton, one of its secretaries, to give part-time service to the World Council.

The Provisional Committee and the paper organization of the World Council were forced to serve throughout the duration of the war. Offices were set up in Geneva, London, and New York. Contact was not only made possible through the work of these offices but ecumenical ties were strengthened among widely separated contin-

---

[9] *Ibid.*, p. 706.

gents of Christendom. And, in spite of numerous obstacles, including the deaths of such ecumenical notables as William Temple, William Adams Brown, and Dietrich Bonhoeffer, the World Council lived. Its survival brought new opportunities as well as problems.

Amsterdam, 1948

The process of formation of the World Council, which had taken eleven tumultuous years, came to an end on Monday, August 23, 1948, in Amsterdam. "One hundred forty-seven Churches in forty-four countries were represented by three hundred fifty-one official delegates. With these were hundreds of alternates, consultants, accredited visitors, youth delegates, and representatives of the Press." [10] Altogether, when the World Council was officially organized, there were no less than fifteen hundred persons present.

The emotion-packed event, which actually constituted the World Council of Churches a historical reality, found expression in the "Message" of this first assembly: "Christ has made us His own, and He is not divided. In seeking Him we find one another. Here at Amsterdam we have committed ourselves afresh to Him, and have covenanted with one another in constituting this World Council of Churches. We intend to stay together."[11]

To those who had struggled so long through the frustrating war years, this appeared to be an achievement only attributable to providential guidance. The number of communions accepting the Committee's invitation had grown from 50 in 1939 to 90 in 1945, and finally to almost 150 on the eve of Amsterdam. Actually, if one were to include the churches [12] which had unofficial visitors of the denominational bodies that failed to join the World Council, this figure would have been exceeded. There were more churches represented than many expected but not as many as some had hoped.

The Roman Catholic Church, the Russian Orthodox Church, the Southern Baptist Convention, and the Missouri Synod of Lutherans were the larger bodies of Christendom not officially represented. However, the newly organized Council of Evangelical German Churches made possible the attendance of German Christians who had fared

---

[10]*Ibid.*, p. 719.

[11]Visser 't Hooft (ed.), *The First Assembly of the World Council of Churches, Official Report, Amsterdam Assembly Series*, V, 55.

[12]The term "church" is used here to refer to various national denominational groups. This is the usage followed in ecumenical literature.

so terribly during the war. Representing the Greek Orthodox were delegations from Constantinople, Greece, and "of the emigration." The attendance of the last two groups named was no accident. The Provisional Committee had been diligently seeking a rapprochement with the German Protestants and the Greek Orthodox since the cessation of hostilities in 1945. Stuttgart (1945) and Geneva (1946) were two indispensable milestones along the way. In spite of suspicion, misgivings, and fear, Amsterdam was reached at last.

The two and a half years preceding Amsterdam were years of intensive preparation on the part of the Provisional Committee. A committee on arrangements, headed by Dr. Cavert, was largely responsible for the planning. Confronted with a world devastated by the most costly of all wars, the theme selected was "Man's Disorder and God's Design." The suggested treatment of the theme was broken down into four sections, the approaches of which had been predetermined by guidelines supplied by the three historic streams of ecumenicity. An international symposium was prepared on each of the four themes. It was clear from the outset that the Amsterdam agenda was designed for serious study.

John R. Mott, who called the first assembly of the World Council of Churches to order, was one of the few living links between Edinburgh, 1910, and Amsterdam. J. H. Oldham and Ruth Rouse were also ecumenical pioneers who enhanced the Amsterdam conference.

The schedule of activities adopted at Amsterdam was reminiscent of the earlier gatherings. The first two days were given to introductory addresses, orientation into the program of study, and the assignment of delegates to sections and committees. The next four days were spent in study and discussion in the sections during the morning and in a large variety of committee meetings during the afternoon. The last five days were spent in discussing, amending, and revising the reports on the floor of the assembly.[13]

The assembly honored John R. Mott, "the grand old man of the ecumenical movement," by making him honorary president. Six other ecclesiastical statesmen of differing communions and countries were elected to the office of president. The organizational aspects of the World Council were further strengthened by the formation of a ninety-member Central Committee. George K. A. Bell, bishop of

[13]Kennedy, *Ventures of Faith,* p. 47.

Chichester, was made chairman and William A. Visser 't Hooft, secretary. Thus with only minor changes, the structure hammered out at Utrecht was allowed to stand.

Actual decisions of the assembly were enunciated with reference to two types of reports: committees and sections. While the committee reports were concerned with subjects of practical nature which gave very little room for fundamental disagreements, the sections brought reports which at times became highly controversial. These reports represent some of the best efforts and most careful study accomplished before and during the conference on the respective subjects.

Section I, "The Universal Church in God's Design."—The report of Section I was discussed in the plenary session and returned to the section for revision. It was finally adopted with two additional changes, suggested from the floor. In its final form the report emphasized the following points:

1. All Christians have a basic unity in Christ.
2. Separation has been due to a Roman Catholic view of the church with its emphasis on visible continuity and *apostolic succession*. The evangelical view of the church with its emphasis upon the initiative of the Word of God and the idea of faith as seen in the Reformation doctrine of justification have also made their contribution to the divided state of Christendom.
3. Common beliefs and common problems were said to indicate that the church was founded by Christ and preserved by the Holy Spirit. The function of the church was described in terms of the promotion of the worship of God, the proclamation of the gospel, and the service of humanity.
4. The report asserted that "the glory of the Church is wholly in her Lord," and the shame of the churches in "worldly standards of success, class division, economic rivalry, a secular mind," and "churches segregated by race and colour."[14]

Section II, "God's Design and the Church's Witness."—Under the chairmanship of John A. Mackay, Section II presented a report which was unanimously adopted after little discussion. The heart of the report read:

All that we need to know concerning God's purpose is already revealed in Christ.

[14]Visser 't Hooft, 51-56.
[15]*Ibid.*, 64.

It is God's will that the Gospel should be proclaimed to all men everywhere.

God is pleased to use human obedience in the fulfilment of His purpose.[15]

In view of the above truths, the duty of the church was defined in terms of faithfulness to the gospel and to its own nature as the church. Only by such faithfulness, it was held, could the church maintain the intimate connection between worship and witness which is so vitally necessary for an effective witness.

Section III, "The Church and the Disorder of Society."—The report of Section III met with the severest treatment of all the reports. It attempted to focus the Christian conscience on the injustices, corruptness, and disorder of contemporary society, particularly with its emphasis on the subjugation of human personality to the techniques of modern industry and the regimentation of totalitarianism. Its task was a difficult one.

Its treatment of communism and capitalism met with the most opposition. The report condemned communism and capitalism almost on equal terms, on the basis that both ideologies were false. The report declared as an alternative, "It is the responsibility of Christians to seek new creative solutions which never allow either justice or freedom to destroy the other."[16]

A second part of the report discussed racial problems and Christianity. In the area of racial problems, the report declared, the church has failed most miserably. Yet, in this field of racial relationships, the delegates were told, the will of God is most clear. Therefore, the church "must call society away from prejudices based upon race or color and from the practice of discrimination and segregation as denials of justice and human dignity, but it cannot say a convincing word to society unless it takes steps to eliminate these practices from the Christian Community because they contradict all that it believes about God's love for all His children." [17]

Section IV, "The Church and the International Disorder."— The last report, the report of Section IV, met with a mixed response also. However, the opposition was not due so much to what was said as to what was left unsaid. The two most important elements of the

---

[16]Kennedy, p. 101.

[17]*Ibid.*

report discussed the two major problems confronting Christianity on a world scale; namely, war and religious liberty.

War was branded in the clearest terms "as contrary to the will of God."[18] And in no case, it was emphasized, could it ever receive the approval of Christians. However, three possible Christian positions were recorded in the report:

Position 1: Even though entering a war may be a Christian's duty in particular cirumstances, modern warfare . . . can never be an act of justice [majority opinion].

Position 2: Military action is the ultimate sanction of the rule of law . . . and . . . citizens must be distinctly taught . . . to defend the law by force if necessary.

Position 3: Christians must refuse military service of all kinds, convinced that absolute witness against war and for peace is for them the will of God, and they desire that the Church should speak to the same effect.[19]

The declaration on religious liberty, as innocuous as such a report could be and without spelling out possible implications, was presented in four statements.

1. Every person has the right to determine his own faith and creed.

2. Every person has the right to express his religious beliefs in worship, teaching, and practice, and to proclaim the implications of his beliefs for relationships in a social or political community.

3. Every person has the right to associate with others and to organize them for religious purposes.

4. Every religious organization formed or maintained by action in accordance with the rights of individual persons has the right to determine its policies and practices for the accomplishment of its chosen purposes.[20]

The last official action of this First Assembly of the World Council of Churches was the drafting of the "Message" for the benefit of fellow Christians who were not at Amsterdam and to "all who are willing to hear." It was presented by the committee chosen for the purpose of its formulation as "a modest document." In substance, the "Message" stated that although not of one faith or of one baptism, those meeting at Amsterdam did confess one Lord, who is the basic principle of unity. Upon that basis, they told the world, "We have

---

[18]*Ibid.*
[19]*Ibid.*, pp. 102-3.
[20]*Ibid.*, pp. 103-4.

met together and *intend to stay together."* The message condemned
war and divisions among Christians. It emphasized the fact that the
task of reconstruction had just begun, and it called upon the Christians
of the world to join in this task by implementing those decisions
reached at Amsterdam.[21]

With a simple service at the Wester Kirk, which featured sermons
in three languages, the First Assembly of the World Council of
Churches was brought to a close. The benediction was pronounced
by Marc Boegner.

To some, the most significant achievement of Amsterdam was the
survival of the World Council of Churches. The only important action
of the assembly which received unanimous approval was the
adoption of the "Message."

But the determination to "stay together" in spite of the most serious
differences on matters of both Faith and Order and Life and
Work was a genuine achievement, without which the movement could
hardly have survived.

Evanston, 1954

Most Americans first became aware of the Second Assembly of the
World Council of Churches in Evanston, Illinois, through information
carried by the nation's news media describing the gigantic Festival of
Faith, held at Soldiers' Field in Chicago on Sunday evening, August
15. The Festival of Faith provided some unforgettable moments
for the 125,000 assembled witnesses.

Hymns and pageantry, light and liturgy served to dramatize the
theme of the assembly and focus attention of the thousands present
and millions who were not there upon the ecumenical movement.
This was the first time that such a gathering had convened in the
United States since the inauguration of the modern ecumenical movement,
and it was something to shout about. Actually, a far more
significant drama took place during the following sixteen working
days of the Second Assembly's life.

The assembly, contrary to some misconceptions, was not a convention
of frolicking glad-handers; it was a body of 502 carefully
chosen delegates from 132 of the 163 communions in the World
Council. With the addition of consultants, fraternal delegates, ac-

---

[21]Visser 't Hooft, 9-11.

credited visitors, official staff, wives, husbands, and press, the number of regular attendants swelled to something like 2,400 persons.[22]

Sessions were held on the campus of Northwestern University in Evanston, Illinois, but the plenary meetings were conducted in Mc-Graw Memorial Hall. For the actual formulation of the message of the assembly, the reports of the sections and committees of all the participants, except accredited visitors, were divided into groups, sections, and committees. The assembly's steering committee supervised and coordinated the entire organizational structure.[23]

Without such careful preparation, the Assembly could not have begun to accomplish what Evanston actually achieved within the brief span of seventeen days. Echoes of the First Assembly had hardly died out in the Nieuwe Kirk in Amsterdam when conversations were launched at Woudschoten, Netherlands (1948), looking toward the Second Assembly.

Serious consideration of the main theme was first begun in Toronto in 1950. The Central Committee and the Executive Committee of the World Council discussed and reviewed every facet relative to the proposed theme, almost to the very eve of Evanston. The most comprehensive work was done at Lucknow, India, 1952-53. The Third World Conference on Faith and Order at Lund, in 1952, laid the groundwork for the Faith and Order Commission's published survey and the preliminary working paper for the study of the first two sections at Evanston.[24] The Commission of the Churches on International Affairs took the responsibility of setting forth the guidelines for the four remaining sections on evangelism, social questions, intergroup relations, and the laity.[25]

In the United States the host denominations were involved in extensive preparation for the Second Assembly. In addition to the rather routine matters of public relations, accommodations for delegates, and the equipment of designated worship centers, an attempt was made to acquaint American ministers more intimately with the ecumenical movement. A summer ecumenical institute was sponsored by ten seminaries in the Chicago area. Prominent ecumenical leaders from

---

[22]*The Christian Century, LXXI* (Sept. 22, 1954), 1158.
[23]Visser 't Hooft (ed.), *The Evanston Report,* pp. 11-12.
[24]See surveys in *The Christian Hope and the Task of the Church* (New York: Harper & Bros., 1954).
[25]*Ibid.,* p. 7.

Europe and Asia comprised the faculty, and Dr. Visser 't Hooft brought the closing address held in Chicago's First Methodist Church. Total attendance of the institute numbered 1,785.[26]

Opinions differ in evaluating the overall impact and specific achievements of Evanston. *The Christian Century* reflected a rather pessimistic appraisal when the editor wrote:

Always at Evanston, and not far below the surface, there were grim disunities which the World Council may at limited times and to limited degrees transcend, but which it has hardly even begun to dissolve. The personal fellowship at Evanston, such as it was and grateful as the participants were and will continue to be for it, was not the kind of fellowship that can reach out beyond a meeting to bring divided congregations and denominations together. It will not have much if any effect on the scandal of denominational competition in our American towns. It will leave the Greek Evangelicals as insecure as ever. It will do little to end the bewilderment of African natives over the conflicting claims of various church ordinances. Evanston will not be remembered for having carried forward the cause of Christian unity. It might possibly (though we hope not) be remembered for having shown how far off and blocked off the goal of unity is.[27]

The displeasure of the American old-line liberals, whose opinions *The Christian Century* reflected, was indicative of a theological stance which seemed to be threatened by the increasingly popular neoorthodox movement of the Continent.[28] It was due to the influence of continental theologians that the theme was selected in the first place. And it was a neoorthodox interpretation which Professor Edmund Schlink of the University of Heidelberg and Professor Robert L. Calhoun of Yale gave the theme in their opening addresses.

But in the opinions of the liberals, they convinced no one but those convinced already. They were quite sure that not only had such theologians failed to carry the day against the "social gospelers" but that the social gospel had saved the assembly from complete failure. This viewpoint was stated quite bluntly: "Evanston made the surprising disclosure that the social action, which the church has been so nervous about lately, stepped forward confidently to save the day.

---

[26]The author attended the institute at McCormick Seminary.
[27]"Evanston Retrospect", LXXI, 1124-25.
[28]*Ibid.*, 1127.

And the theology which has recently been so sure of itself got absolutely nowhere at all."[29]

The position vocalized by *The Christian Century* reflected dismay over the apparent reassertion of sectarianism before and during the assembly. Prior to Evanston, the Presbyterians, Anglicans, Disciples, Lutherans, and Methodists held preliminary meetings. In fact, the Lutherans adopted a definite policy of action which they were accused of attempting to follow during the assembly.[30] The greatest shocker of all, however, was the bombshell dropped into the assembly by Archbishop Michael, on behalf of the Orthodox representatives, when he presented as a separate declaration the Orthodox statement on Faith and Order.

After analyzing the report on Faith and Order, the Orthodox delegates told the assembly that "the whole approach to the problem of reunion is entirely unacceptable from the standpoint of the Orthodox Church."[31] The Orthodox position was based upon what was termed a "twofold agreement." By this statement, Archbishop Michael, speaking for all Orthodox delegates, explained:

The whole of the Christian Faith should be regarded as one indivisible unity. It is not enough to accept just certain particular doctrines, basic as they may be in themselves, e.g. that Christ is God and Saviour. It is compelling that all doctrines as formulated by the Ecumenical Councils, as well as the totality of the teaching of the early, undivided Church, should be accepted.

One cannot be satisfied with formulas which are isolated from the life and experience of the Church. . . . On the other hand, the Orthodox Church cannot accept that the Holy Spirit speaks to us only through the Bible. . . . The Bible is given to us within the context of Apostolic Tradition in which in turn we possess the authentic interpretation and explication of the Word of God.[32]

Furthermore, the archbishop informed the assembly, "The Episcopal Succession from the Apostles constitutes an historical reality in the life and structure of the Church and one of the pre-suppositions of her unity through the ages." [33] From the twofold premise regarding tradition and the episcopate, the Orthodox spokesman proceeded to

---

[29]*Ibid.*, 1125.
[30]*Ibid.*, 1129.
[31]Visser 't Hooft, *The Evanston Report*, p. 93.
[32]*Ibid.*
[33]*Ibid.*, 93-94.

dismantle the entire Report on Faith and Order by concluding: "We are bound to declare our profound conviction that the Holy Orthodox Church alone has preserved in full and intact 'the faith once delivered unto the saints.' " [34]

The most ardent ecumenists were taken aback by the forthright declaration of the Orthodox delegation. In fact, some expressed their bewilderment publicly over the continued presence of the Eastern Orthodox Church within the World Council.[35] But the assembly assured the adamant Orthodox that they were still wanted.

Ardent ecumenists had evidently expected a great impetus toward the union of denominations from Evanston or even a mandate from the assembly that could be used as a catalyst in this direction. But the only statement remotely resembling such an expectation in the "Message" was altered before its final adoption. In the preliminary draft, it read, "To stay together is not enough. We must grow together." In the final draft the last sentence was changed to read, "We must go forward." [36] However, the phrase, "to grow together," did find expression in the last paragraph of the Faith and Order Report in spite of the protests from both the Bishop of Durham and a Baptist layman.[37] Apparently few, except the protesters, felt that the statement was either a directive to unite or that it was offensive on other grounds.

The general secretary of the World Council sided with those who wished a redraft of the last paragraph. Perhaps this was due to the often repeated position of Visser 't Hooft, who decried the desire of the World Council to become a "superchurch." Clarifying his position, or rather that which he envisioned for the World Council, the general secretary declared, "It is therefore a sign of confused thinking to speak of the World Council itself as the World Church. And it is completely erroneous to suggest that the World Council is or has any ambition to become a Super Church, that is, a centre of administrative power." [38] However, he went on to indicate that this did not mean that the World Council had no interest in union of the denominations. To the contrary, he insisted that "the Council can

---

[34]*Ibid.*, p. 95.
[35]"Evanston Retrospect," 1129.
[36]Visser 't Hooft, *The Evanston Report*, p. 2.
[37]*Ibid.*, p. 97.
[38]*Ibid.*, p. 25.

and must work to create a situation in which there is so much in common between the churches, that there is no adequate reason for them to remain separate from each other." [39]

Doubtless Visser 't Hooft was disappointed with the progress of Evanston toward this goal.

However, the Second Assembly of the World Council was not altogether fruitless. Even *The Christian Century* conceded this. The genuine accomplishments, it maintained, were all in the realm of social action. Specifically, it singled out the reports of Sections III, IV, and V for commendation. Of these, the pronouncement on race evoked the highest praise. "Perhaps only one of them, that dealing with racial tensions, rises to heights of impressive eloquence and has a chance to become a document of historic importance in church history." [40] Undoubtedly the writer had in mind paragraphs 12 through 15 of the report of Section V on "Intergroup Relations: The Churches Amid Racial and Ethnic Tensions." A portion of this report is of such nature and importance as to merit quoting here:

> The great majority of Christian churches affiliated with the World Council have declared that physical separation within the Church on grounds of race is a denial of spiritual unity, and of the brotherhood of man. Yet such separations persist within these very churches, and we often seek to justify them on other grounds than race, because in our hearts we know that separation solely on the grounds of race is abhorrent in the eyes of God.
>
> We seek to justify such exclusion on the ground of difference of culture, or on the ground that a residential pattern of segregation necessitates it, or on the ground that the time is not yet ripe. . . . We often make use of the unregenerateness of the world to excuse our own.
>
> The Church is called upon, therefore, to set aside such excuses and to declare God's will both in words and deeds. "Be not conformed to this world, but be ye transformed by the renewing of your mind, that ye may prove what is that good, and acceptable, and, perfect, will of God." We believe it to be the will of God that such proof in word and deed now be given.[41]

The report of Section III, entitled "Social Questions: The Responsible Society in a World Perspective," emphasized some pertinent Christian insights with a genuine ecumenical accent. Among other

[39]*Ibid.*, p. 26.
[40]"Evanston Retrospect," 1131.
[41]Visser 't Hooft, *The Evanston Report*, 153-54.

things the report declared: "There can be for the Christian no ultimate authority but very God."[42]

Again, it reminded the delegates: "No one form of government has a universal claim on Christians, but any political system must include some elements without which it tends to become an oppressive tyranny. For these, Christians should work by active participation in political affairs." [43] But in paragraph 15 there was interjected a warning of the possible dangers of the welfare state.

The state is not the source of social justice, but it must be its guardian, ready if necessary to accept responsibility to counteract depression or inflation and to relieve the impact of unemployment, industrial injury, low wages, and unfavorable working conditions, sickness, and old age. But in doing so the state remains the servant not the lord of social justice. Therefore we must warn against the danger that the union of political and economic power may result in an all-controlling state.[44]

With some additional censures of communism and capitalism the report concluded: "We are not called upon to shoulder the burden of this world, but to seek justice, freedom and peace to the best of our ability in the social order. The Church knows that in obedience and prayer our efforts will bear fruit. For God has called us unto liberty to serve one another by love. 'Faithful is he that calleth you, who also will do it.' " [45]

The assembly also took notice of the fact that religious liberty is an ideal not realized in many significant areas of the world when it adopted Resolution III, which in part said: "The Assembly also deeply regrets that in certain countries from which information can be gathered with reasonable accuracy, Christians are suffering many disabilities and even violence; and human rights and liberties, albeit acknowledged in official protestations, have in practice been denied." [46]

The resolution continued with assurances of prayerful concern and an expression of gratitude for both the fidelity of the brethren under fire and a fellowship with them which desolation and persecution could not break.

---

[42]*Ibid.*, p. 115.
[43]*Ibid.*
[44]*Ibid.*, p. 116.
[45]*Ibid.*, p. 126.
[46]*Ibid.*, p. 149.

Many delegates regarded the "Message" as the most constructive and promising result of the Second Assembly. Its doctrinal affirmation was Trinitarian; its vision, missionary; and its tone, ecumenical. Doubtless, few Christians are inclined to disagree with the paragraph which reads:

Here where we stand, Jesus Christ stood with us. He came to us, true God and true Man, to seek and to save. Though we were the enemies of God, Christ died for us. We crucified Him, but God raised Him from the dead. He is risen. He has overcome the powers of sin and death. A new life has begun. And in His risen and ascended power, He has sent forth into the world a new community, bound together by His Spirit, sharing His divine life, and commissioned to make Him known throughout the world. He will come again as Judge and King to bring all things to their consummation. Then we shall see Him as He is and know as we are known. Together with the whole creation we wait for this with eager hope, knowing that God is faithful and that even now He holds all things in His hand.[47]

Evanston is now history and in spite of all of its apparent weaknesses, its decisions, experiences, and resolutions entered the stream of Christian history and must be reckoned with.

New Delhi, 1961

Perhaps the full impact of Evanston upon Christianity has been further obscured by the rather conspicuous achievements of the Third Assembly at New Delhi. New Delhi immediately assumed a position of major importance in the annals of ecumenical history, more because of what was done than what was said. If the accomplishments of Evanston were largely intangible, those of New Delhi were quite evident from the opening days of the Third Assembly.

The contrast between the Third and Second Assemblies could hardly have been more dramatically highlighted by any other choice of location. Evanston and New Delhi represent two different worlds, as different as Asia from America or the mind of a Yogi from that of a Yankee.

The Third Assembly convened for worship on Sunday morning, November 19, in a vast tent (Shamiana) erected near the conference hall. The hangings of Indian design and the sound of hymns sung to the accompaniment of plaintive Indian instruments reminded the

---

[47]*Ibid.*, p. 1.

thousands gathered for the occasion of their Asian environment. The theme, "Jesus Christ, the Light of the World," found expression in hymn, prayer, and sermon directed by Metropolitan Juhanon of the Mar Thoma Syrian. Church of Malabar. He was assisted by a Presbyterian of Ghana, a Methodist of Argentina, a Baptist of Burma, who delivered the sermon, an archbishop of the Orthodox Church, and an Episcopalian from the United States. As the service ended, once again the sound of Indian music filled the air.

In the afternoon, Bishop Otto Dibelius, co-president of the World Council, called the first General Session of the Third Assembly to order. The assembly was composed of 577 voting members. The addition of 105 advisers; 100 youth participants; 59 fraternal delegates; 45 observers; and 120 guests raised the total number of participants to 1,006.[48] Among the participants were five official observers of the Roman Catholic Church. This at once gave New Delhi a status that had never been achieved previously by an assembly of the World Council.

The participants met to carry on the work of the assembly in three types of sessions—general, business, and deliberative. The more speculative theological subjects dealt with at Evanston were eliminated. Reports were formulated on Witness, Service, and Unity. There were numerous committees. Matters of Faith and Order were reduced to the "Report of the Committee on Faith and Order." Quite obviously, New Delhi was concerned with the more pragmatic aspects of the ecumenical movement. The developments in this area give New Delhi its significance in ecumenical history.

Among the first of these developments was the enlargement of membership in the World Council. Twenty-three different communions were added to the membership of the World Council of Churches. This group constituted the largest number received by the World Council since its organization. Confessionally they were as far apart as Eastern Orthodoxy and Pentecostalism and as geographically separated as Russia and Chile. The Orthodox Churches of Russia, Bulgaria, Rumania, and Poland comprised the largest confessional group to join. Two Pentecostal bodies from Chile were also received. Russian and Spanish were consequently added to the official languages of the World Council of Churches.[49]

---

[48]Visser 't Hooft, *The New Delhi Report*, p. 29.
[49]*Ibid.*, p. 9.

The entrance of the Eastern Orthodox bodies had been facilitated by a change in the confessional basis of the World Council, a development that appeared quite remote in 1948. This event was not an accomplished fact without vigorous protests on the part of those who objected to the dogmatic implications of the change either on the basis of the principle involved in adopting a "creed," or what was viewed as a trend toward ecclesiastical exclusivism. The final vote, however, registered 383 affirmative, 36 negative, and 7 abstentions.

The new basis reads: "The World Council of Churches is a fellowship of churches which confess the Lord Jesus Christ as God and Saviour according to the Scriptures and therefore seek to fulfil together their common calling to the glory of the one God, Father, Son and Holy Spirit." [50]

The Greek Orthodox Church was highly pleased with the new creedal basis. In discussing the issue, Professor H. Alivisatos, speaking on behalf of the delegates of the Orthodox Church of Greece, said: "The Orthodox Church of Greece therefore gladly accepts and votes for the proposed new formulation in the sense that it is in full agreement with the Trinitarian doctrine as formulated by the two first ecumenical synods of the old and undivided Church and in the so-called Nicaean-Constantinopolitan Creed." [51]

Archpriest Vitaly Borovoy, speaking for the Russian Orthodox Church, frankly admitted, "The expected acceptance of the New Trinitarian Basis played a very important role in the decision we made to join the WCC [World Council of Churches] and made our task much easier."[52]

The obvious influence of the Eastern Orthodox Church in bringing about this development reflects a basic change in Orthodoxy's approach to the ecumenical movement. The new stance was spelled out by Dr. Nikos Nissiotis of the Church of Greece, who spoke on Orthodoxy's concept of unity.

The Orthodox Church does not ask others to "come back to us" or to deny their own traditions but believes that its witness can help all the other historical churches "to recover their own true life." . . . This means in practice that Orthodoxy must give up its defensive, confessional-apologetic attitude, and, in the glory of the Holy Spirit, become a mighty

---

[50] *Ibid.*, p. 152.
[51] *Ibid.*, p. 155.
[52] *Ibid.*, p. 157.

river of life, filling the gaps, complementing opposites, overcoming enmities, and driving forward towards reunion.[53]

This doesn't mean that Orthodoxy has forsaken its concept of the Church since Evanston. A careful reading of the entire text of Dr. Nissiotis' presentation will doubtless validate this impression. It does mean, however, Orthodoxy intends to exert a greater positive force for the reunion of Christendom along Orthodox lines within the World Council. Since the Orthodox Churches now make up the single largest confessional block within the World Council, Orthodoxy is in a position of unprecedented influence.

Another action which helped to immortalize New Delhi in ecumenical history was the merger of the International Missionary Council with the World Council of Churches. First discussed while the World Council was in process of formation from 1938 to 1948, the decision to remain separate while maintaining a cooperative relationship had been sustained until 1958. Since 1958, negotiations between the two ecumenical councils had succeeded in working out the details and in resolving most of the anticipated difficulties. Dr. Franklin C. Fry presented the recommendation on behalf of the Central Committee to integrate the two organizations. The work of the International Missionary Council consequently became the responsibility of the newly created Commission on World Missions and Evangelism.[54]

The Third Assembly adopted the strongest statement on religious liberty yet set forth by the World Council of Churches. Even though no statement concerning the separation of church and state found its way into the report, the religious rights of the individual were clearly and unapologetically set forth. The amendment proposed by the Metropolitan of Carthage and adopted by the assembly that "the religious liberty defined in this Statement should be exercised in accord with the Report on Christian Witness, Proselytism and Religious Liberty" could in no way dim the lustre of the original statement.[55]

The events outlined above symbolize the end of one era and the beginning of another.

---

[53]*Ibid.*, p. 22.
[54]*Ibid.*, p. 59.
[55]*Ibid.*, p. 161.

5

Catholic Ecumenism and Vatican Council II

April 25, 1962, the General Secretary of the Baptist World Alliance, Dr. Josef Nordenhaug, received a letter from Monsignor J. G. M. Willebrands, secretary of the Vatican Secretariat for Promoting Christian Unity, in which he asked if the Baptist World Alliance would send an observer to the forthcoming ecumenical council if formally invited. The letter was referred to the Executive Committee of the Alliance on Wednesday, August 22, in session at Stabekk, Oslo, Norway.

After spending most of the day discussing the matter, a unanimity of opinion failed to materialize. Even those who personally longed to demonstrate a genuine interest in Roman Catholic renewal felt that no observer should be sent at the price of broken fellowship. In a formal reply to the Vatican correspondent, the Executive Committee registered appreciation for the letter and its inability to "encourage a formal invitation." However, the Alliance assured the "authorities of the Roman Catholic Church of its hopes and prayers that the forthcoming Council will contribute to an increasing understanding of the will of God and the unity of his people."[1]

Diverse reasons motivated those taking part in the discussion from arriving at a more positive position relative to the proposal of Monsignor Willebrands. Doubtless, the specter of rock-throwing mobs, burning churches, sealed church doors, and imprisoned ministers from Spain, Colombia, and other "Catholic countries" weighed heavily against the proposal. But Baptists around the world mani-

---

[1]Minutes of the meeting of the Executive Committee held at the Baptist School, Stabekk, Oslo, Norway, August 20-22, 1962, p. 15.

fest a lively interest in Roman Catholic ecumenicity. They are exceedingly grateful for the Council's statement on religious liberty.
Baptist scholars will continue to study carefully all the documents of
Vatican Council II and the basis of hope which they constitute for
a new day of improved relations between Roman Catholics and other
Christians. In spite of deeply rooted suspicion of Vatican policies
on the part of Baptists, there is evidence that a more positive attitude is developing. Baptist interest in and hopes for some authentic
change in Roman Catholicism call for a discussion of Vatican
Council II.

The Ecumenical Movement and Catholicism

Prior to John XXIII and Vatican Council II, Catholic ecumenism
was shaped by a centuries-old mold. It was reactionary and un-
changing. Before the ground swell of contemporary Catholic ecumenicity, to speak of Catholic ecumenism was to use contradictory
terms, as these words were commonly understood.

For the Roman Catholic, the terms "Catholic" and "Ecumenical"
have been synonymous. Therefore, when Rome has been most Catholic, that is, most aggressive in her missionary efforts, she has been most
ecumenical. The converse has also been true. For Rome to fraternize
with the ecumenical movement, as it has been generally understood,
was to promote schism and violate basic Roman ecumenical principles. Therefore the specific objective of Catholic ecumenism has been
to promote the return of "baptized dissidents to the unity of the Body
of Christ, which involves their acceptance of the faith and communion
of the See of Peter and the Catholic Church throughout the world."[2]

Pius IX (1846-78) condemned an organizational expression of the
Oxford movement as embodied in the Association for the Promotion
of Christian Unity. Founded by an Anglican priest, Frederic George
Lee, in 1857, it proposed to work toward the organic reunion of the
Anglican Church, the Orthodox Church, and the Church of Rome.[3]
In addition to condemning the new ecumenical venture, the pontiff
reiterated the traditional view that outside the Roman Church not only
is there no salvation but there can be no unity as well.

It is known that Catholic dogma states that nobody outside of the

---

[2]Hanahoe, *Catholic Ecumenism*, p. 52.
[3]Tavard, *Two Centuries of Ecumenism: The Search for Unity*, p. 36.

Catholic Church can be saved and that those who defy the authority of the Church and its definitions and are divided from the unity of the Church and the successor of Peter, the Roman pontiff, to whom the custody of the vineyard was committed by the Saviour (as the Council of Chalcedon says), cannot gain eternal life.[4]

From time to time visionary ecumenists, Anglicans, Orthodox, and Romanists continued to work toward the reunification of Christendom, but always without Rome's blessing.[5] Such efforts, as Tavard reminds us, are destined for disaster. "There will be no universal reunion without the Bishop of Rome, since there can be no Catholic unity without Roman Catholicism." [6] "A Catholic reunion," Tavard adds, "must recognize the permanent infallibility of the Church, which is the Body of Christ and the Spouse of the Holy Spirit." [7]

The first pope of the modern era to address himself seriously to the problem of Christian unity was Leo XIII (1878-1903). Leo is better known to most Protestants for his encyclical, *Christian Constitution of States (Immortale Dei)*. However, Catholic scholars such as Hans Küng view the first twentieth-century pontiff as a precursor of John XXIII and the herald of a new day.

The man of the new era was Leo XIII. The Church of the preceding period had been built a fortress. . . Leo XIII certainly did not demolish the fortress, but he threw open its gates and its windows, even in his very first encyclical.[8]

There was an apparent ambivalence in the pronouncements of Leo on ecumenism. While he inaugurated prayers for the reunion of Christendom and continually addressed himself to various bodies of Christians such as the Orthodox, the Anglicans, and the Scotch Presbyterians, he held the party line with an implacable obstinacy.[9] Some attribute Leo's rejection of the validity of Anglican orders to the Curia.

It is, of course, a known fact that Leo felt individual conversions from Protestant communions did not help the cause of reunion but only served to further alienate those denominations from which the

[4]Fremantle, *The Papal Encyclicals*, p. 132.
[5]See Tavard, p. 65.
[6]*Ibid.*
[7]*Ibid.*, p. 66.
[8]Küng, *The Council, Reform and Reunion*, p. 89.
[9]Tavard, pp. 67-74.

converts came. He favored the approach that John XXIII adopted
and made his own, which is that of rapprochement with various
ecumenically minded communions, particularly the Orthodox and the
Anglicans.

On the other hand, while moderating the terms of reproach which
the Roman Church had used of Protestants since the Reformation,
Leo's price of reunion remained the same as that of his predecessors—
capitulation on the part of the "separated."

Gregory Baum indicates that Leo addressed himself to the problem
of reunion in some thirty-five encyclicals of his twenty-five-year
reign.[10] Even though the attention given to unity in these encyclicals
varies, his fundamental position never changes. Reiterated by Pius
XI and others, its basic thesis was first enunciated by Leo XIII, the
father of Roman Catholic ecumenism.[11]

Benedict XV, who occupied the papal throne during war years
(1914-22), assumed a more rigid stance toward other denominations
than even his predecessor, Pius X. Benedict's position was not immediately evident, since his first response to the proposed conference
on Faith and Order was apparently cordial and positive. However,
there was no mistaking his attitude or the official position of the
Church regarding the proposed Faith and Order Conference to which
he gave voice when replying to the official invitation issued by a
deputation which visited His Holiness in Rome. According to the
deputation,

> The contrast between the Pope's personal attitude towards us and his
> official attitude towards the Conference was very sharp. One was
> irresistibly benevolent, the other irresistibly rigid. The genuineness of
> the Pope's personal friendliness towards us was as outstanding as the
> positiveness of his official declination of our invitation. His Holiness
> himself emphasized the distinction.
>
> The Holy Father, after having thanked them for their visit, stated
> that as successor of St. Peter and Vicar of Christ he had no greater
> desire than that there should be one fold and one shepherd. His Holiness
> added that the teaching and practice of the Roman Catholic Church
> regarding the unity of the visible Church of Christ was well known to
> everybody and therefore it would not be possible for the Catholic Church
> to take part in such a Congress as the one proposed.[12]

---

[10]Cited by Tavard, p. 67.
[11]Tavard, p. 74.
[12]Cited by Rouse and Neill, p. 416.

The practical-minded Pius XI (1922-29) manifested ecumenical concern by directing his attention to a project which promised the most immediate results, rapprochement with the Orthodox. Several factors prompted this course of action.

Eastern Orthodoxy was in great distress due to the rise of communism and its antireligious policies. It was beginning to show a new openness to non-Orthodox bodies. For example, the Orthodox Church was closer to Rome doctrinally, ecclesiologically, and historically than the Anglicans.

If the Orthodox were going to unite with anybody, Pius reasoned, they should unite with Rome. To pave the way for such an eventuality, the pontiff ordered all of the seminaries under the jurisdiction of Rome to establish courses of study on Orthodox Christianity. However, there was no thought of any genuine concession on Rome's part to facilitate such a development. This was made perfectly clear in a papal encyclical of 1927 entitled *Mortalium Animos*. In this famous document, Pius XI declared that the Roman Church was the only true church. Therefore, he asserted, the only way to a reunited church is for all non-Roman Christians to become obedient to the See of Peter and accept everything the Roman Church teaches. In light of this immovable stance, the pope defined Rome's attitude toward the ecumenical movement:

> This being so, it is clear that the Apostolic See can by no means take part in these assemblies [conferences of Life and Work and Faith and Order], nor is it in any way lawful for Catholics to give to such enterprises their encouragement or support. If they did so, they would be giving countenance to a false Christianity quite alien to the one Church of Christ. Shall we commit the iniquity of suffering the truth, the truth revealed by God, to be made a subject for compromise? These pan-Christians who strive for the union of the Churches would appear to pursue the noblest of ideals in promoting charity among all Christians. But how should charity tend to the detriment of faith?[13]

It is Neill's opinion that, "from the attitude expressed in *Mortalium Animos*, the Vatican has never really receded. Yet at one or two points there has seemed to be a certain softening of the decisions of Rome in practical matters." [14] Facts to substantiate Bishop Neill's contention are not difficult to come by.

---

[13]Cited by Neill, *Men of Unity*, p. 172.
[14]*Ibid.*

One of the most irenic of Rome's scholars, Stephen C. Gulovich, addresses himself to the problem of the Orthodox Church. It is Gulovich's thesis that the major barriers between the Eastern and Western churches are mistrust and suspicion. Rome has never been at fault, she has been misrepresented and misunderstood. Wherefore the task to which Rome must give herself, according to Gulovich, is mainly one of public relations. "Toward what shall we labor and for what shall we pray? Toward removing suspicion and reestablishing mutual trust and love." [15]

The position enunciated by Gulovich, even though in perfect harmony with the policy defined by Pius XI and reaffirmed by his successor Pius XII, 1939-1958, hardly attempts to cut the Gordian knot of Roman and Orthodox differences as Sydney Smith admits in *The Catholic Encyclopedia.*[16]

The question of Anglican reunion from Rome's viewpoint presents even a greater problem, especially since Leo XIII refused to recognize the validity of Anglican orders. From the High Church Anglican viewpoint, the longed-for reunion with Rome is frustratingly easier on paper than in actuality.

"A Memorandum by a Canonist" is considered by some the outstanding document on the subject. Cardinal Mercier, archbishop of Malines, felt it was a masterpiece and the long-sought answer to the problem of Anglican and Roman reunion. It states that the one indisputable price which Rome demands is submission to the authority of Rome.

It would be necessary, then, if the Anglican Church wished to belong to the unique and visible society of Christ, for her to establish herself and the Roman Church a link of dependence and submission to the successor of Peter. In other words she must become not Latin but Roman, while preserving all her internal organizations, all her historical traditions and her legitimate subordination to the universal Church whose centre of unity is in Rome.[17]

The ablest Roman Catholic writer, in defense of the position as enunciated by Pius XI, is M. J. Congar. At times his critique of the

---

[15]Gulovich, *Windows Westward,* pp. 36-37.

[16]Sydney F. Smith, "Union of Christendom," *The Catholic Encyclopedia: An International Work of References* (New York: Robert Appleton Co., 1912), pp. 147-48.

[17]Bell (ed.), *Documents on Christian Unity,* p. 32.

ecumenical movement is so caustic and his analysis of the theological weaknesses so devastating that the ecumenist despairs of any possibility of rapprochement with Rome. But Congar leaves the door slightly ajar when he admits the possibility of Rome's lending some assistance to the movement through the presence of her theologians at various conferences.

Catholic co-operation will certainly not take the form of official membership, but more probably that of theological assistance, and some more or less permanent advisory contact of Catholic theologians. Such a share, so far from being contrary to the doctrinal position of the Church, would be in complete accord with her mission to impart to all who will give heed to her the tradition and the wealth of her interior life.[18]

Even though the official position of the Church remained the same during the reign of Pius XII, who contented himself with pious platitudes deploring the sinful divisions of Christendom and urging a return to the Mother Church, much thinking and extensive writing on the ecumenical movement have marked the last two decades. European Roman Catholic scholars such as Canon G. Thils, Maurice Villain, Cardinal Bea, Hans Küng, Abbe Couturier, and Americans like Edward Duff, Gustave Weigel, John Courtney Murray, and George H. Tavard have prepared the ground for a new day in Roman Catholic ecumenical relations. However, it remained the task of John XXIII to dramatize Rome's change of pace by calling for an ecumenical council, the first council in a century.

John XXIII, 1958-63

The obstacles to another council in the Church of Rome seemed insurmountable. Sheer numbers and distances involved, as well as formidable objections raised by the Curia, militated against the mere proposal of a council in the twentieth century. Theologically, the role of a council since the Vatican Council of 1869-70 was called into serious question. Such problems would have stymied a lesser man. But Pope John was not to be denied. His long career in the diplomatic service of the Church had made him aware of the Church's needs and had equipped him with the skills necessary in attempting to overhaul the Church to meet the challenge of a hostile world.

---

[18]*Divided Christendom*, p. 143.

Angelo Roncalli was born November 25, 1881, in the village of Sotto il Monte near Bergamo on the Lombard plains. His parents were devout peasants. That the College of Cardinals chose an Italian was not surprising. The Church had chosen Italians exclusively to serve as popes for the last 417 years.

But perhaps no Italian pope had been as cosmopolitan in outlook as the patriarch of Venice. He had served the church faithfully throughout an eventful life. For some time he was papal nuncio in Bulgaria, Turkey, and France. In Bulgaria and Turkey he came into direct contact with the Byzantine Church as well as the Armenians, Copts, and various Uniates. In France he was introduced to some of the most progressive Roman Catholic scholars on the Continent. Here he was impressed with how little the Church really mattered to the vast majority of Frenchmen.

Rocked by postwar tribulations, France went on an antireligious binge that saw communism make serious inroads into Roman Catholic ranks, even among the clergy. Thus it was a chastened Italian, who had brooded long over the ills of a materialistic age that refused to take the Church seriously, who assumed the papal crown and the pontifical name of John in October, 1958.

Angelo Roncalli was the first pope in more than five centuries to take the name of John. This action was significant. The last John was designated XXIII. He called the Council of Constance which later deposed him and then made him a Cardinal Bishop. He was subsequently dubbed an antipope. Therefore, in a sense, Angelo Roncalli began his papal career by attempting to rewrite an all but forgotten turbulent page in Roman Catholic history. It was a bold stroke which opened for modern scrutiny a fifteenth-century closet full of Vatican skeletons, relics of the Great Schism (1378-1419).

The man who arose to the papacy as a compromise candidate continued to surprise his colleagues with unprecedented and unexpected acts.[19] The most astonishing of all was his expressed desire to call a council, which was voiced early in his pontificate to his secretary of state, Cardinal Tardini. Undoubtedly the suggestion sounded preposterous to the Curia. There were good historical grounds for questioning the place of a council in the structure of the Church.

Since the Vatican Council of 1869-70, and the subsequent one-man

---

[19]See Rynne, *Letters from Vatican City*, pp. 7-9.

rule of the Church by a succession of pontiffs from Pius IX to Pius XII, there appeared to be no room for a council. What could it do that was not already being done by the pope and the Curia?

John's answer was, "Plenty." The aged pope had not forgotten the impressions received during his extensive travels and his diplomatic missions, nor had he lost any of the skill that was his to win friends and influence people on behalf of the Church.

The Purpose of the Council

A cardinal is reported to have asked Pope John to explain the purpose of the proposed council. Whereupon the newly elected pontiff went to a window and threw open the shutters and exclaimed, "To let a little fresh air into the Church." The graphic figure used by John caught the fancy of news media around the world. As a result, this rather insignificant act has become one of the most widely known of John's numerous symbolic gestures. But what did he mean? In the encyclical, *Ad Petri Cathedram,* of June 29, 1959, he set forth the goal of the ecumenical council as he envisioned it.

"There will be one fold and one shepherd." (John 10:16). This irresistible assurance was the compelling motive which led Us to announce publicly Our resolve to call an Ecumenical Council. Bishops will come together there from every corner of the world to discuss important matters of religion. But the most pressing topics will be those which concern the spread of the Catholic faith, the revival of Christian standards of morality, and the bringing of ecclesiastical discipline into closer accord with the needs and conditions of our times. This in itself will provide an outstanding example of truth, unity and love. May those who are separated from this Apostolic See, beholding this manifestation of unity, derive from it the inspiration to seek out that unity which Jesus Christ prayed for so ardently from his heavenly Father.[20]

The term "ecumenical" must be understood within the Roman Catholic context. Strictly speaking, the council was not ecumenical in the modern use of that term. It could be spoken of as ecumenical in this sense only as it looked toward the reunion of Christendom and, therefore, constituted a necessary step in this direction. The Roman Church, however, has considered all of the councils, even when called only by a pope and not representative of the whole of

---

[20]In Küng, pp. ix-x.

Christendom, as ecumenical, that is, with the exception of the Council of Pisa, which it no longer recognizes as a council. According to the scheme, Nicaea, 325, becomes the first such council so designated and the Second Vatican Council called by John XXIII becomes number twenty-one.

The purpose of this council, in John's mind, was ecumenical in the sense that it proposed to provide for all of Christendom an example of Catholic unity which would stimulate a desire for reunion with Rome.

Three goals were spelled out rather carefully in the papal encyclical calling for the council: (1) spread the Catholic faith; (2) revive Christian standards of morality; and (3) update ecclesiastical discipline.

Pope John summed up the purpose of the council with these words: "See, this is what the Church is, what she does, what she looks like. Only when she appears thus healthily modernized and rejuvenated can she say to those separated brethren 'come to us.' "

The purpose of the council has been even more succinctly summarized by the Italian word *aggiornamento,* which means to bring the church up to date. Thus, the movement to which the Council has given expression is a movement for the renewal or the reform of the church. As Küng has demonstrated, the word *"renewal"* is to be preferred to the term *"reform."*

Pope John carefully avoided the use of the term *"reform."* He specifically declared the council was not to discuss theological matters nor was it an attempt to overhaul Catholic dogma. Of course, he hardly had a choice in the matter. For how can the pastoral function of the church be discussed without involving theological issues? From the traditional viewpoint championed by the Curia, how can reform in the church be justified? Exactly how do you go about criticizing a church that is virtually deified, said to be without error and incapable of sin? In the light of what is now termed Vatican Council I and the dogma of papal infallibility, is there room for a council at all?

Vatican Council I seemed final enough when it proclaimed the popes infallible.

Moreover, that the supreme power of teaching is also included in the Apostolic primacy, which the Roman Pontiff, as successor of Peter, Prince of the Apostles, possesses over the whole Church, this Holy See has always held, the perpetual practice of the Church confirms, and oecumenical Councils also have declared, especially those in which the East with the West met in the union of faith and charity. . . .

Therefore faithfully adhering to the tradition received from the beginning of the Christian faith, for the glory of God our Saviour, the exaltation of the Catholic religion, and the salvation of Christian people, the sacred Council approving, we teach and define that it is a dogma divinely revealed: that the Roman Pontiff, when he speaks *ex cathedra*, that is, when in discharge of the office of pastor and doctor of all Christians, by virtue of his supreme Apostolic authority, he defines a doctrine regarding faith or morals to be held by the universal Church, by the divine assistance promised to him in blessed Peter, is possessed of that infallibility with which the divine Redeemer willed that his Church should be endowed for defining doctrine regarding faith or morals; and that therefore such definitions of the Roman Pontiff are irreformable of themselves, and not from the consent of the Church.

But if any one—which may God avert—presume to contradict this our definition: let him be anathema.[21]

The solution to the rather formidable problem of the finality of Vatican Council I is suggested in Küng's *The Council, Reform and Reunion*. Küng argues that Vatican Council I was closed prematurely on September 20, 1870, because of a seige of Rome by the Italians, who took away the papal rule of the city of Rome. Its declarations on papal infallibility were never meant to be final. The Council had intended to proceed to a definition of collegiality which never materialized.

Vatican Council II was called to complete the work which Vatican Council I was forced to leave undone. Küng finds the precedent for reform by council in a long line of ecumenical councils. The Church then can be reformed if one understands correctly what is meant by reform. The Council then attempted to reform its human appearance, not its divine appointments. The eternal doctrine remains the same but must be reformulated in order for the Church to speak effectively to the modern world.[22] In other words, the progressives are attempting to change the church without really changing it. They are determined to maintain a continuity with that which is termed "essentially Catholic."

The motives which prompted John XXIII to call Vatican Council II may have been somewhat different from the stated objectives. Subilia expresses the opinion that Rome, as she has often done

---

[21]Estep, *John XXIII and the Papacy*, Appendix C.
[22]Küng, pp. 88 ff.

with other movements in the past, after having condemned the ecumenical movement, determined to grab the "ecumenical ball" and run with it.

Now that the Ecumenical Movement is a historic fact and has gathered to itself all non-Roman Christendom, Protestant, Orthodox, Anglican, Old Catholic, i.e, practically two-thirds of Christianity, Rome could not continue left in the minority, a passive spectator, running the risk of being by-passed by history. Hence she feels it necessary to initiate a grandiose process of bringing Catholicism up-to-date and improving its efficiency, with a spectacular playing up of the ecumenical theme.[23]

According to Subilia, Rome, stimulated by the ecumenical movement, has now decided to capture the imagination of the Christian world and advance the cause of Catholicism by playing a dominant role in the movement. This, he calls the ecclesiastical motivation. Subilia believes the Vatican is motivated by political aims as well. It is suggested that Rome feels the necessity of presenting some semblance of a united front against the common foes of communism, secularism, materialism, and paganism. Subilia sees evidence for both the ecclesiastical and the political motives in the encyclical *Ad Petri Cathedram*.[24]

The writers who go under the pseudonym of Rynne ascribe still another motive to John. Many of the Church's leaders, according to Rynne, especially in the Curia and in the United States, were in need of an education in modern Catholic thought of the intellectual centers of Europe. John chose the method of a council as the quickest possible way of accomplishing so difficult a task.

In the end what seems to have convinced Pope John of the necessity for calling a Council was not only the parochial outlook of most of the men about him in the Vatican, but the backward attitude of so many bishops in the stabilized dioceses of the Old and New World. Though good men and hard-working administrators of both the spiritual and corporal works of the Church, they knew nothing of the new spirit fermenting in the minds and hearts of many of the clergy, young and old, and made manifest in the writings of the more advanced theologians, lay intellectuals, and church scholars.[25]

Regardless of purpose or motivation, Vatican Council II con-

---

[23]*The Problem of Catholicism*, p. 21.
[24]*Ibid.*, p. 23.
[25]Rynne, p. 29.

vened on October 11, 1962, in St. Peter's Basilica. The beginnings of the Council, thoroughly covered by press, radio, and television, brought to the attention of the world a colorful medieval spectacle that only Rome could stage. More than twenty-five hundred bishops, cardinals, patriarchs, *periti* (experts), and observers from every sector of the Church assembled in St. Peter's for the initial mass and opening address by the pope.

At eight o'clock sharp two papal gendarmes "resplendent in parade uniform of white trousers and black top boots, coats, and busbies, slowly swung the great doors open, exposing to a portion of the crowd row upon row of bishops, clad in flaming white damask capes and mitres, descending Bernini's majestic *scala regia* from the papal apartments."[26]

The bishops were followed by the scarlet-clad college of cardinals. Finally, the pope, on the *sedia gestatoria,* was carried in traditional papal splendor to the entrance of the basilica.

Amidst all the grandeur of the Roman pageantry, the first session of Vatican II was ushered in, accompanied by the strains of the traditional hymn *Veni Creator Spiritus.* After the music had subsided, mass was celebrated with certain sections chanted in both Greek and Latin. The cardinals made their obeisance to the see of Peter.

From an improvised throne erected directly in front of the ostentatious centuries-old papal throne with its high canopy, the rotund and aged pontiff addressed the assembled throng. His opening remarks were pointedly negative as he indicated the displeasure he felt with the "prophets of doom." In this forthright disclosure, the pontiff exposed the dour-faced Curia with unprecedented frankness. This became the launching pad for a very positive challenge to bring the church up-to-date. The pope declared that "the substance of the ancient doctrine of the *depositum fidei* is one thing; the way in which it is expressed is another."[27] He then repeated the major objectives of the Council which had been previously publicized. Herein lies the key to an understanding of the nature of the Council's task as envisioned by John and the progressives. It is a matter of interpreting the Church and its teaching to a new age.

The deliberative sessions began on Saturday, October 13. To the

---

[26]*Ibid.,* p. 68.
[27]*Ibid.,* p. 72.

Protestant observers, accustomed to Protestant assemblies, matters moved at a snail's pace. Finally, with the presentation of the schema on the liturgy on Monday, October 22, debate actually got under way. It is impossible to even attempt a summary of the debates on the various schemata. However, an attempt will be made to present some of the results of the first session.

The First Session

It was quite evident from the opening day that the Council was divided into two opposing camps, a fact known for some time by knowledgeable participants. On one side were the obscurantists and on the other, the progressives. Leading the Curia block of obscurantists was Alfredo Cardinal Ottaviani, secretary of the Congregation of the Holy Office and chairman of the Theological Commission. He was flanked by Archbishop Enrico Dante, the papal master of ceremonies. Cardinals Siri, Ruffini, and Pericle Felici, Pietro Parento, and Dino Stoffa, all influential figures in the Curia, were solidly within this camp.

The progressives, whose numbers were far greater than those of the obscurantists, were largely outside the Curia and without comparable standing in the power structure of the Roman Church. They counted in the forefront of their ranks Cardinal Leinart of Lille; Cardinal Bea, the newly appointed secretary of the Secretariat for Promoting Christian Unity; Cardinal Alfrink, archbishop of Utrecht; and Leo Joseph Suenens, cardinal of Belgium.

It was also quite evident that the Americans had precious few prelates among the progressives and not a few vocal supporters of the obscurantists. The Americans also looked bad when compared with their North European counterparts from their inability to handle the Latin and their rather superficial theological orientation.

In fact, the whole Council revealed how hopelessly outmoded Latin was as a vehicle of communication within the church in the twentieth century. This fact did much to make possible the acceptance of the liturgy schema which advocated the limited use of the vernacular, celebration in both kinds, and concelebration. Ottaviani arose to denounce all three, and went much overtime. He was called down by the president of the day and subsequently absented himself from the council for two weeks.

A most interesting clash between obscurantists and progressives developed during the debate on the schema, *De Revelatione*. The schema had been prepared by the Holy Office and was presented by Cardinal Ottaviani. It set forth the view that there were at least two sources of authority—the Bible and tradition. To this assertion, Ottaviani added, "Our teaching is traditional and will and must ever remain the same."

Cardinal Leinart arose at once in opposition. This *schema* does not please me. It is not adequate to the matter it purports to deal with, namely Scripture and tradition. There are not and never have been two *sources* of revelation. There is only one fount of revelation—the Word of God, the good news announced by the prophets and revealed by Christ. The Word of God is the unique *source* of revelation.[28]

This schema, along with other schemata, was sent back to their respective commissions for reworking. Ottaviani and company met with further rebuff when the schema, *De Ecclesia,* prepared by the Theological Commission of which he was chairman, was also referred to the commission for further revision.

The presence of officially elected Protestant observers represented an ecumenical breakthrough for the Vatican. The cordiality of the pope and terms of affection such as "our beloved separated brethren," used in reference to the observers, were indicative of the graciousness of the most popular pontiff in many a generation. But it is difficult to measure accurately the actual accomplishments of the Council under John. Perhaps his encyclical *Pacem in Terris* was the most significant formal utterance of his brief reign.

The Second Session

John XXIII, the "pope in a hurry," died on June 3, 1963. His death, although deeply felt throughout the world, came as no great surprise. The pontiff's health had deteriorated rapidly during the closing days of the first session. In fact, all during his brief pontificate, from his very first address as pope, he had indicated his expectations of a short reign.

He was succeeded by Cardinal Montini of Milan on June 21, who took the title of Paul VI. If the choice of the name was based upon admiration for his predecessors who bore that name, the Church not only had a new pope but one with basic principles

---

[28]*Ibid.,* p. 143.

that ran counter to those that motivated John to call the Council in the first place.

Outwardly, at least, Paul attempted to walk in John's footsteps. He apparently impressed many informed theologians with his devotion to his predecessor's objectives when on September 21, shortly before the second session began, he addressed the Curia as "the Pope who today has made the legacy of John XXIII his own, and has made it a program for the entire Church."[29] However, his first encyclical, *Ecclesiam Suam,* betrayed, in the eyes of many, his true perspective. *The Christian Century* editorialized:

We awaited this encyclical with confidence but we read it with sorrow and dismay, detecting behind it the creaking of closing windows, the silencing of dialogues and the shuffling feet of "open door" churchmen reluctantly retracing the steps which took them into a crusade the present pope appears unwilling to lead.

Ecclesiam Suam is the product of a man who has not made up his mind, who hangs in intellectual suspension between tradition and progress, ecclesiastical democracy and papal autocracy, unifying charity and divisive dogma. Consequently he offers in his first pastoral letter a kind of encyclical supermarket in which everyone can find what he wants if he has the patience to look for it. Pope Paul VI is for reform in the church, but reform "is not to be understood in the sense of change" and the church's reform and renewal "cannot concern either the essential conception of the church or its basic structure." In one word he attributes authority to the council fathers as they return for the third session of Vatican Council II, yet in other, more subtle words he makes it quite plain that though the assembled bishops may deliberate he alone will decide the policy and program of the church.[30]

The subsequent turn of events has not entirely substantiated the rather pessimistic appraisal which *The Christian Century* gave Paul's first encyclical.

Perhaps the most significant action of the second session was the strong support which the bishops gave the concept of collegiality. This idea undoubtedly had been greatly encouraged by John XXIII, who never forgot for a moment its importance as a preliminary step for any fruitful discussion of reunion with the Orthodox Church. A month after the second session had begun, on October

---

[29]Brown, *Observer in Rome,* p. 17.

[30]"A Venture in Ambivalence," *The Christian Century,* LXXXI, No. 35 (August 26, 1964), 1051.

30, the Council voted overwhelmingly to send the schema, *De Ecclesia,* back to the Theological Commission with the request that it be revised according to the clearly expressed wishes of the bishops on the "five questions," which included approval of the concept of collegiality and its ramifications in three of the five questions.

Collegiality means, according to Brown, "the supreme power of the pope to that of the other bishops, who share rule with the pope by virtue of the fact that all are members of the episcopal college."[31] This day, in Brown's mind, was the most encouraging day of the entire Council. At the close of the day he wrote, "This is beyond doubt the most important day in Roman Catholic history since 1870."[32]

Another victory came for the progressives when they defeated an attempt by the curialists to present a separate schema on Mary. Thus, the plan to further emphasize Mariology at the expense of ecumenical relations with Protestants was for the moment forestalled. Another action which caused the hopes of Protestant observers to rise to unprecedented heights was the favorable response with which the first three chapters of *De Oecumenismo* and the introduction of the chapter on religious liberty by Bishop DeSmedt of Bruges were received by the bishops. However, the bright days of the second session were soon overshadowed by the dark days.

During the sixth week the atmosphere began to change. Cardinal Ottaviani's bold-faced refusal to accept the Council's action on collegiality as binding on the Theological Commission was the first in a series of setbacks which began to shatter the rising hopes of the younger bishops. The feeling was accentuated when a strong majority voted for the schema "On Instruments of Social Communications," which reflected a "hard-nosed" policy of traditional Romanism.

The greatest disappointment of the session resulted from an increasing awareness of the Vatican's hand in Council politics. It became quite apparent that the pope was manipulating the agenda of the final days of the session to prevent any debate on the religious liberty schema.

---

[31]*Observer in Rome,* p. 58.
[32]*Ibid.,* p. 122.

The dramatic change in emotions felt by the oscillating prospects of the Council during the second session is reflected by Brown.

As I hear the speeches pro and con, and note that the forces favoring collegiality seem very much in the ascendancy, I sometimes have the feeling that we are witnessing the beginnings of a revolution of incalculable magnitude—a revolution that slowly and quietly will transform the whole face and structure of the Catholic Church.[33]

Again, when the "five questions" received the approval of the Council, Brown wrote, "This is beyond doubt the most important day in Roman Catholic history since 1870." But his optimism turned to abject pessimism by the close of the session.

Without resorting too dramatically to the "good-guys-bad-guys" way of interpreting the Council, it must be said that the last ten days of the sessions demonstrated that the progressives were not so much in control of things as might have been assumed after their strong victory in the "collegiality" vote. The conservatives somehow rallied, and thwarted conciliar acceptance of statements on religious liberty and the Jews. They obviously hope to tone down any subsequent statement on "collegiality" so that it will lose its significance.[34]

The only consolation that his bishop friends were able to give their affable Protestant observer was, "Remember, the Church moves slowly." This was little consolation to one who had expected so much and repeats, " 'I will *continue* to expect much more.' "[35]

The Third Session

Two actions by the Council mark the high-water mark of the third session: the strong affirmative vote on collegiality and the acceptance of the schema on the Jews. The sentiment as expressed by the majority of the bishops from the beginning of the Council had been strongly in favor of collegiality. The vote on the "five questions" in the second session and the reaffirmation of this concept in the third should have surprised no one. The schema on the Jews was a gesture of goodwill that rejected the anti-Semitic posture often associated with Rome.

While it is highly questionable whether the Council, the Church,

---

[33]*Ibid.*, p. 59.
[34]*Ibid.*, pp. 249-50.
[35]*Ibid.*, p. 220.

the pope, or anyone else can absolve anyone of anything, at least the Council fathers were trying to say—and they said it by a vote of 1,770 to 185—"We refuse to blame the Jews with the death of Christ." A questionable action on historical grounds, it was an attempt to reverse a centuries-old stance which had spawned anti-Semitism and brought untold suffering to millions for ages.

With these two actions, Vatican Council II, 1964, ground to a halt.

Paul VI had left many of the bishops wondering just where he stood on numerous issues before the Council by the end of the second session. Concerned theologians within and without the Roman Church hoped against hope that Paul would continue with the same open ecumenical approach that had so distinguished his predecessor. Session III almost completely shattered these hopes.

There is no doubt that Paul possesses a similar gift for symbolic action that characterized John—but is the sincerity there? His kiss for Athenagoras is a case in point. It was perfectly timed to take the spotlight off of a most embarrassing play in the eyes of the Church. *The Deputy* was playing to full theaters all over Europe. Was that kiss, as it now appears, a consummate bit of play acting in the light of Paul's clearly demonstrated views on collegiality? The much publicized trip to Bombay and its sequel, the story of the golden rose, an age-old symbol of papal honor which was sent to the shrine of Our Lady of Fatima to calm the irate Portuguese, leaves one asking questions that will not continue long unanswered.

The press has not taken kindly to all of Pope Paul's dramatics. Joseph Roddy caustically describes one of the pope's acts which backfired toward the close of the third session. The event took place the day after the pope attended a Shakespearean reading in Rome in which Cardinal Wolsey, in recalling his political downfall, says:

"For God's sake let us sit upon the ground
And tell sad stories of the death of kings"
were the lines from Richard II,
". . . for within the hollow crown
That rounds the mortal temples of a king
Keeps Death his court. . ."
Paul consigned his own gold crown to the world's poor at a solemn High Mass in St. Peter's the very next morning. With him on the altar

at the time were two crowned Byzantine Rite bishops who thought at once of uncovering and following the Pope's lead, especially since their crowns happened to be borrowed. Had they done so, their gesture might have been less hollow than the Pope's. Only days later, the crown Paul gave to the poor turned up as the property of New York's Cardinal Francis Spellman, head of the world's richest Catholic archdiocese. Even uncritical Catholics were hardpressed to speak kindly of the Cardinal's catch, on exhibit between two poor boxes in St. Patrick's Cathedral until it moves to the World's Fair.[36]

The last days of the third session of Vatican Council II were reminiscent of the Council of Trent, which was led during some of its sessions by other Pauls; namely, Paul III (1534-49) and Paul IV (1555-59). Then, as now, the major issue resolved itself into a power struggle between the council and the pope. The papacy won out, with the help of the Jesuits.

At Vatican Council II, the papacy's victory was not so clear-cut. However, he did appear to have the edge over the exponents of collegiality. The pope and the council found themselves at cross-purposes a number of times. The mission schema was rejected by a vote of 1,601 to 311. This would have had no significance had Paul not positionized himself on the schema. It is a purile and mediocre document at best.[37] But Paul chose for some reason to appear on the council floor and speak for its acceptance. The vote revealed that the bishops were taking to heart collegiality. They dared to reject the personal appeal of the pope to accept an inferior schema.

Subsequent actions by Paul revealed just as clearly how lightly he viewed the opinions of his bishops, collegiality or no collegiality. Acting within the traditional context as defined by Vatican Council I, he gave a "crushing No to meaningful collegiality,"[38] according to *The Christian Century.*

When, on the pope's authority, Eugene Cardinal Tisserant canceled the bishops' procedural vote on religious liberty and Pope Paul upheld this action despite the signed plea of 1,400 bishops, one Protestant observer said: "We have seen the naked face of what we have always

---

[36]Joseph Roddy, "Catholic Revolution," *Look,* Vol. 29, No. 3 (February 9, 1965), 27.

[37]See Abbott and Gallagher, pp. 584-630.

[38]"Do We Have a Council?" *The Christian Century,* LXXXI, No. 49 (December 2, 1964), 1483.

feared in Rome." Douglas Horton, former dean of Harvard Divinity School and an observer at Vatican Council II, commented: "What is collegiality going to mean if the college of bishops is run by its president (appointed by the pope)? If the pope is going to let the presidents run it, it does not mean a thing." Though their reaction was not so open and vocal, the response of many bishops to the pope's intrusion was one of similar dismay.[39]

Finally, the schema on ecumenicity was accepted but not as it had been prepared and debated by the council fathers. Paul VI sent nineteen "suggested emendations" or amendments. They were presented at such a time when debate was impossible. The Council had no other live option, unless the bishops chose to scrap the whole schema, than to accept the schema as amended. It seems that Paul was arbitrarily setting a precedent which deliberately ignored the principle of collegiality. If this is true, one-man rule will remain the norm for the Roman Church.

A third time, in proclaiming Mary as the "Mother of the Church, that is of the whole people of God—of the faithful as of the pastors," the pope once again flaunted his authority in the face of the Council. The Council had studiously avoided giving Mary any additional title. The delegates had spent weeks debating whether to give her a separate schema or not before finally voting the proposal down by a narrow margin. Paul VI, in conference with the Protestant observers, announced his intention to give Mary the new title, once again demonstrating how little he was concerned with true dialogue or rapprochement with the Protestant world.

What is the significance of these actions by the newly elected pontiff? Has the pontiff been judged too harshly by Protestant critics? The Roman Catholic journalist Michael Novak, expresses the opinion that Paul VI was attempting to identify himself with Latin Catholicism.

Moreover the bestowing of a new title on Mary at a time when so many in the Catholic world no longer feel any need for such additional titles and when so many other Christians can only be repelled seems to find its rationale in the pope's references to the Portuguese nation—that is to say, in his identifying himself with Latin Catholicism at the expense of the rest of the church.[40]

---

[39]*Ibid.*
[40]"Ecumenical Sadness and Hope," *The Christian Century*, LXXXI, No. 50, (December 9, 1964), 1518.

Whatever else the actions of Paul may mean, he appeared at the close of the third session to be "hand in glove" with the obscurantists of the Curia. Instead of emerging as one who has made the legacy of John his own, some Catholics and Protestants tend to categorize him as a "prophet of doom."

The Fourth Session

In spite of all the superlative gestures Pope Paul seems capable of producing from an endless repertoire, he has appeared to some candid observers as a reluctant reformer.

The Christian Century (September 22, 1965, p. 1147) editorialized: "But we have also come to see Pope Paul as a half-hearted participant in the church's changes, a man whose gloomy vision of church-and-world has become clear from his habit of issuing a warning-of-the-week. At least weekly, it seems to us, he is cautioning some element of Catholicism against moving too rapidly or too vigorously."

This impression was further enhanced by a papal encyclical released on the eve of the Fourth Session entitled *Mysterium Fidei.* The new encyclical reasserted the traditional Roman Catholic view of the eucharist with a ringing affirmation of the "real presence." *The Christian Century* (September 29, 1965, p. 1181) saw in this action an attempt to apply the brakes on conciliar progress. "Apparently Pope Paul purposed to spin about the council's fourth session a conservative mood, a restrictive web of orthodoxy and tradition."

However, the fourth session of Vatican Council II achieved much more than some Protestants and Catholics alike expected.

The Council's "Declaration on Religious Liberty" was delayed from session to session. When the fourth session began on September 14, some feared the bishops would never have an opportunity to vote on the preliminary draft. But the contemplated visit of Paul VI to the United Nations Assembly and the United States increased the pressure upon the Council to do something about the much talked-about religious liberty pronouncement. The papal image before the United Nations Assembly and the American people would have suffered considerably without some positive action on the declaration prior to his visit. In record time for conciliar action, the bishops, by a vote of 1997 to 224, adopted the preliminary draft, which was actually the fifth corrected version prepared since 1963. The document was then referred to the Vatican Secretariat for Promoting Christian Unity for revisions in light of debate on the schema.

The document, in its final form, delineates the principle of religious liberty not only for the individual but also for religious bodies. On biblical grounds it argues against coercion in any form that would force a person to adopt a faith contrary to his conscience.

Therefore, the right to religious freedom has its foundation, not in the subjective disposition of the person, but in his very nature. In consequence, the right to this immunity continues to exist even in those who do not live up to their obligation of seeking the truth and adhering to it. Nor is the exercise of this right to be impeded, provided that the just requirements of public order are observed.

On his part, man perceives and acknowledges the imperatives of the divine law through the mediation of conscience. In all his activity a man is bound to follow his conscience faithfully, in order that he may come to God, for whom he was created. It follows that he is not to be forced to act in a manner contrary to his conscience. Nor, on the other hand, is he to be restrained from acting in accordance with his conscience, especially in matters religious.

However, the social nature of man itself requires that he should give external expression to his internal acts of religion; that he should participate with others in matters religious; that he should profess his religion in community. Injury therefore, is done to the human person and to the very order established by God for human life, if the free exercise of religion is denied in society when the just requirments of public order do not so require.[41]

The practical implementation of these principles has not as yet measured up to the rather clear enunciation of principle in the schema. Perhaps, the gate which has been left open for possible exceptions is indicated by the phrase which recurs repeatedly "provided that the just requirements of public order are observed." But some American Catholics feel the Roman Church has at last spoken an unambiguous word for religious liberty. Father John B. Sheerin, C.S.P., editor of the *Catholic World* said that the Declaration on Religious Liberty would bring Roman Catholics "up-to-date with Roger Williams."[42]

---

[41]Abbott and Gallagher, pp. 679, 681.
[42]Cited in *The Christian Century*, LXXXII, No. 40 (October 6, 1965), 1214.

After Pope Paul's return, the "Declaration on Religious Liberty" was amended by an overwhelming vote to reaffirm that the Roman Catholic Church is the "one true Church," and all men have a moral duty "to profess and embrace the Catholic faith insofar as they are able to know it." The acid test of the sincerity of the Roman Church in the application of the principles of religious liberty will come in future actions that Rome may take in regard to her privileged status in countries where she is the established church. Then history will disclose just how deeply the principle of religious liberty has taken root within the Roman Church. Perhaps one of the most constructive acts of the fourth session may prove to be Vatican Council II's decree on the Jews. It is far more balanced than its earlier versions.

True authorities of the Jews and those who followed their lead pressed for the death of Christ (cf. Jn. 19:6); still, what happened in His passion cannot be blamed upon all the Jews then living, without distinction, nor upon the Jews of today. Although the Church is the new people of God, the Jews should not be presented as repudiated or cursed by God, as if such views followed from the holy Scriptures. All should take pains, then, lest in catechetical instruction and in the preaching of God's Word they teach anything out of harmony with the truth of the gospel and the spirit of Christ.[43]

Pope Paul VI, in his address before the United Nations Assembly, assumed the traditional Roman Catholic position of opposition to artificial means of birth control. If the Church eventually advocates a new position on this issue it will be contrary to the pope's public stand. Since the Council, the pope has announced a relaxation of Catholic regulations regarding mixed marriages. This action will undoubtedly help to ease the tension between Catholics and non-Catholics.

Evaluation

Years will elapse and volumes be written before the full impact of Vatican Council II may be known. Any evaluation at this point cannot escape the weakness inherent in a partial view. However, evaluations are being attempted and have some value. These run the scale all the way from those who feel that nothing has hap-

---

[43]*The Christian Century*, LXXXII, No. 45 (November 10, 1965), 1373.

pened, because nothing could, to those who feel that the one great church to which all Christians will give allegiance is actually in sight. These are the extremes.

What is the truth of the matter? Before attempting to answer this question, we are reminded that any evaluation can only approximate the truth. Yet, some conclusions do seem justified at this time.

Positively stated, they are:

1. Vatican Council II has destroyed the illusion that all Roman Catholics think alike on every theological issue.

2. The new interest in and emphasis upon the Bible as the one unique source of revelation will doubtless stimulate biblical studies in all levels of Roman Catholic life.

3. The change in terminology with reference to other Christians as "separated brothers" instead of "heretics" should provoke more sincere efforts at understanding one another on both sides of the fence.

4. The emphasis on the liberty of the individual to worship and serve God free of coercion should bring about a cessation of Roman Catholic discrimination and persecution in Roman Catholic dominated countries.

5. The abandonment of Triumphalism, a view of the Church which holds its history to be always and only a series of victories, and its replacement with the concept of a Church which both suffers and serves did find verbal expression during the Council sessions.

Negatively stated, they are:

1. The Council with its sixteen schemata issued a charter for reform. But it did not reform the Church. Only the future can determine to what extent this charter will be followed.

2. The schemata do not always speak an unambiguous word. Nor are they by any means of equal value; i.e. those on the Church, revelation, ecumenism, and religious liberty are of major significance. Whereas, those on communications and mission are quite disappointing.

3. The structure of the Roman Catholic Church has not been changed. It is still run by the Curia and the pope. Given the wrong combination of pope and curialists, reform may never come.

4. During the sessions of the Council, Rome did not appear to abandon the ancient dictum *extra ecclesiam nulla salus* (outside of

the Church there is no salvation). Instead, once again the Council affirmed Rome's conviction that she alone is the "one true Church."

5. The "Declaration on Religious Liberty" is by no means an unequivocal document. Grateful as we are for the basic principles of religious liberty which it enunciates, there is still a great gulf between it and the historic Baptist position.

The Basic Problems

While every concerned Christian cannot cease praying that Rome may truly be reformed and made conformable to the revelation of God in Christ, one must not ignore the basic differences which still divide Rome from Baptists and other evangelicals. There is no doubt that Rome has lessened tensions and attempted to halt overt acts of persecution in many instances. The situation in Colombia is greatly improved. The same thing may be said of Spain.[44] Some Roman Catholic churches have joined local councils of churches in various parts of the nation but, as Emil Brunner has observed, the basic doctrines of Catholicism have not been altered.

The Roman Catholic concept of the church remains unchanged. Excerpts from various papal documents during the pontificate of John XXIII demonstrate this fact. Speaking of the ecumenical nature of the Vatican Council II, John stressed the invitation for the "great return."

By the grace of God we shall then hold the Council, and we mean to prepare for it with an eye on those points where our Catholic family environment most needs reinforcement and reinvigoration, in the light of the pattern left by our Saviour. Then, when we have achieved that high endeavour, and when the road has been cleared, for our human part, of all that impedes its rapid passage, we shall hold up the Church in all her brightness, "without spot or blemish," and say to all who are separated from us, "orthodox," protestants, etc.: Behold, brethren, this is the Church of Christ. We have striven to be faithful to her, to ask from the Lord the grace that she might ever remain what He has wished her to be. Come! Come! This is the open road to encounter, to return. Come, take (or retake) your place, which for many of you is the place your fathers occupied years ago. And from such religious peace, from such a reunited Christian family, what joy, what prosperity—even of a political and social sort—may we not expect for all the world![45]

---

[44]See *Inquisicion, Tolerancia e Idea Ecumenica* (Bogota: Centro Mariano Nacional de Colombia, 1959).

[45]Cited by Subilia, p. 29.

On another occasion, John said, "Where Peter speaks, you know it is Christ who speaks, where the pastor who is Peter's successor holds the place of him who is called *Bishop of our souls.*"[46]

Paul VI has been even more direct than John—as his many utterances, actions, and particularly his encyclical *Ecclesiam Suam* have shown—in identifying the Roman Church as the only true church outside of which there is no salvation. Salvation still comes through the Church, which, according to Subilia, claims to be a continuation of the incarnation. Thus an institution is deified.

This incarnational ecclesiological myth of an inerrant institution is perpetuated at the expense of historical understanding of the revelation of God in Christ. However, the traditional view of the Bible in Roman Catholic life is being overhauled.

Instead of stressing the twin principles of the Council of Trent, Scripture and tradition, the progressives emphasize that the revelation of God in Christ contained in the Scriptures alone is normative. But, they maintain it must always be interpreted in light of the tradition and the teaching authority of the church. While these theologians now admit that the Bible, because of its nature, takes precedence over tradition, the Church does not really permit this to happen. For Roman theologians of all stripes, the Scriptures, sole valid interpreter is the Church. Thus, some Catholics feel that by a greater emphasis on the role of the Bible in the life of the church, "Protestant requirements would be met, without—as Father Boyer says so candidly—this introduction of the practice of using the Bible making any substantial difference."[47]

While evangelicals will rejoice at the new emphasis on the Bible in Roman Catholicism, they realize that Rome is still attempting to wrap the Word of God in Latin swaddling clothes.[48] The Church is still over the Scriptures, as Hans Küng admits. Baptists assert that the Scriptures are always over the church.

It is an age-old Baptist conviction that the emperical church must always be judged by the eternal Word of God, the Word which was historically mediated in the person of Jesus Christ. Even

---

[46]*Ibid.,* p. 30.

[47]Subilia, p. 37. See: G. C. Berkouwer, *The Second Vatican Council and the New Catholicism* (Grand Rapids: William B. Eerdmans Publishing Company, 1965). This is a most perceptive treatment of Vatican II.

[48]Abbott and Gallagher, p. 115.

though Vatican II demonstrated an awareness on the part of Rome of the historical revelation of God in Christ, Catholicism still lacks a proper regard for the testimony of the Scriptures. This was the unique contribution of the Reformation that is commonly over-looked.

Roland Bainton has focused attention upon this difference in Protestant and Catholic thought when in referring to the one unique element in Luther's contribution, he writes:

As for the claim that Luther was in no sense original, there is no better reply than that to be found in the recent work of Erich Hassinger, who finds Luther's contribution to have been his rediscovery of the historical core of Christianity. The claim of the Christian religion is that God did something unique in history. In the year that Caesar Augustus ordered all the world to be taxed, the Word became flesh. The Incarnation, the Crucifixion and the Resurrection constituted a unique self-disclosure of God in Christ. To Him the ages lead up, and from Him the centuries lead out. By faith in His redeeming work man is forgiven and remade. The assertion of the unique historical role of Christ is an offense because it assumes unevenness in the work of God, who, if this be true, declared Himself more manifestly to the men of the first century than to those in any other. There are various ways of escaping from the historical singularity of Christ. One is mysticism: God is accessible at all times equally to the waiting heart. Another is moralism: man is saved by his own good deeds done here and now. And still another is institutionalism: the church is the custodian and continuator of the revelation once and for all given. Luther asserted unequivocally the historical uniqueness of the work of God in Christ. Its continuance in the present is mediated through Scripture, which is the record of the event. And though it must be interpreted by the Spirit, yet the Spirit can never be dissociated from the outward Word.[49]

The council refused to draw up a separate schema on the virgin Mary. There are other indications that in Latin America there is a deliberate attempt to play down Marian aspects of Roman Catholic worship. Yet John XXIII in numerous addresses has paid the highest homage to Mary. Paul VI added another title to the long string which she already possesses. Some Protestants seem willing to rationalize their thinking sufficiently to accept with qualifications the Mariology of Rome.

Frederick C. Grant gives Mariology essentially the same status

---

[49]*Studies on the Reformation,* pp. 107-8.

as New Testament Christology.[50] However, for the most part, evangelicals are far more inclined to agree with Giovanni Miegge when he writes,

> It is perhaps fatal that in Catholicism there are entrusted more and more completely to the cult of the Virgin Mary those Christian values of humaneness, compassion, inner aspiration, of which it still feels itself to be the trustee. Of course Christ will not be forgotten. He will continue at the centre of official honours. Mary will still be conceived as the Mediatrix between Him and men. They will continue to say that one ascends from Mary to Christ. But the real diffusive and persuasive force, the real religious fascination, the real function of effectively focusing the faith and love and devotion of the masses will be exercised by the Virgin Mary. On that day it will be said that within Catholicism Christianity has given up the field to a different religion.[51]

It now appears that the dogma of papal primacy, so long an obstacle between the East and the West, instead of being ameliorated by the principle of collegiality, has not only survived the Council unscathed but has become, if anything, even more firmly entrenched. Evidently Rome is not prepared to forsake in the foreseeable future the papacy. In spite of the more obvious weaknesses of the Council, Baptists, along with many other Protestants, will take advantage of every opportunity of witness and dialogue which Rome's new stance may offer, while maintaining the integrity of their faith in humility and love.[52]

---

[50]*Rome and Reunion*, p. 177.

[51]Miegge, *The Virgin Mary*, p. 191.

[52]Baptist views of *aggiornamento* run all the way from the very optimistic reports of W. Barry Garrett in *Report from the Capitol*, January, 1965, p. 4, to the pessimistic appraisals of E. S. James in the *Baptist Standard*. The most recent work on Roman Catholic views of religious liberty is the excellent work by A. F. Corrillo de Albornoz, *Roman Catholicism and Religious Liberty* (Geneva: The World Council of Churches, 1959).

6

Competitive Protestant Councils

Even though the World Council of Churches is the most prominent embodiment of the modern ecumenical movement, it is the form with which most people in the United States are least familiar. The National Council of the Churches of Christ in the United States of America and its competitive councils are the more familiar expressions of cooperative Christianity. In order to understand the nature of the American Council of Christian Churches and the National Association of Evangelicals, some attention must be given to the National Council at the risk of repetition. However, there is still a measure of confusion as to the nature and function, as well as purpose, of the National Council among Baptists and other evangelicals which calls for clarification.

The National Council of Churches

The National Council of Churches finds its historical roots in the American Sunday School Union of 1824. From this early period numerous interdenominational organizations loosely related to the denominations came into existence to sponsor a variety of interests which defied a strictly denominational approach.

By 1905, a number of interdenominational organizations united in calling for a conference looking toward the formation of a nation-wide interdenominational federation that would correlate efforts which were frequently overlapping and, at times, competitive. Twenty-nine denominations responded to the call, sending 436 delegates to the Interchurch Conference on Federation which convened in Carnegie Hall on November 15, 1905. Ninety-three alternates and 16 honorary members completed the officially registered members of what Robert Handy terms "the most officially representative gathering of the Protestant forces (in America) up to that time."[1] Three years later the Federal Council of Churches was formally organized in December of 1908 by 33 participating denominations.

The enthusiasm generated by the actual formation of the national body led to an accelerated drive for the organization of local councils in every major city in the country. A Commission of Federated Movements was set up under the energetic leadership of Roy B. Guild, who served as its first secretary. The Commission's work was so effective that Dr. Guild could report, after only a year's effort, the existence of councils in at least forty cities. Beaming with enthusiasm, he declared, "There are fewer than a score of large cities without a federation or council of churches."[2]

The prewar optimism that characterized numerous enterprises in the first decade of the twentieth century came crashing down amidst the rubble of World War I. The federative movement was threatened with extinction. That it survived at all is remarkable. Thoughts and energies of ministers as well as laymen were turned in the direction of the war effort. Consequently, cooperative Christianity suddenly found itself devoid of leadership and funds. Inadequate finances and the failure of voluntary leaders to carry through effective programs of action brought a premature end to the work of numerous councils.[3]

The collapse of the grandiose scheme of church union embodied in the Interchurch World Movement dealt a near fatal blow to American interdenominationalism. Shortly afterwards, however, a resurgence of ecumenical feeling became manifest through the International Missionary Movement and the series of conferences set in motion by Geneva, 1920. The formation of the League of Nations supplied an additional stimulus for churchmen to think ecumenically.

By 1940, in spite of the ominous rumblings of a fresh international conflict, the ecumenical movement within the United States had completely recovered its equilibrium and promised to continue unabated. A program of unification of local, state, and federal

---

[1] Cited by Sanderson in *Church Cooperation in the United States*, p. 57.
[2] *Ibid.*
[3] *Ibid.*, p. 159.

councils provided the necessary coordination for the evolving National Council.

The next year saw the birth of the United Council of Church Women, as delegates from all sections and major denominations of the nation met in Atlantic City. An ambitious program was launched which envisioned a local council of churchwomen in every community in the United States. Nine years later, the United Council became an integral part of the new National Council.

The National Council of the Churches of Christ in the United States of America, after many years of planning and growing anticipation, actually crystallized by December, 1950, at Cleveland, Ohio.

Eight interdenominational organizations merged to create the new council: (1) Federal Council of the Churches of Christ in America, (2) Foreign Missions Conference of North America, (3) Home Missions Council of North America, (4) International Council of Religious Education, (5) Missionary Education Movement of the United States and Canada, (6) National Protestant Council on Higher Education, (7) United Council of Church Women, and (8) United Stewardship Council.[4]

Altogether some twenty-five Protestant and four Eastern Orthodox denominational organizations cooperated in the formation of the new council. "Subsequent to the formation of the National Council, four additional agencies have merged with it: (1) Church World Service, Inc., (2) Interseminary Movement, (3) Protestant Film Commission, and (4) Protestant Radio Commission."[5]

Such a vast and complex organization presents many functional problems. A studied attempt has been made to keep the leadership of the movement within close touch with the grass roots. A General Assembly of the National Council meets every two years and is composed of 694 officially elected representatives. Of these, 443 are clergy and 251 laymen. A general board composed of 256 members (166 clergy and 90 laymen) establishes the policies and supervises the work of the Council between meetings of the General Assembly.

The work of the Council is organized under four divisions:

---

[4]*Twentieth Century Encyclopedia of Religious Knowledge* (Grand Rapids: Baker Book House, 1955), II, 783-84.
[5]*Ibid.*, 783.

Christian Education, Christian Life and Work, Home Missions, and Foreign Missions. Joint departments exist to correlate the work where two or more divisions engage in an area of common interest, such as evangelism, religious liberty, family life, Christian vocation, and stewardship. Central departments render common services in the fields of Public Relations, Publication and Finances, Research and Survey, Broadcasting and Films, and Field Administration.

The National Council is affiliated with a vast complex of some 892 local and 50 state councils of churches. It also works closely with local Councils of Churchwomen and interdenominational ministerial associations. The Council's sponsoring denominations now number 34 with a total constituency of 40,000,000 (1957). Four Baptist bodies, the American Baptist Convention, the National Baptist Convention of America, the National Convention, U.S.A., Inc., and the Seventh Day Baptist General Conference are members of the National Council.

Numerous other denominations, including the Southern Baptist Convention and four other national Baptist bodies, participate through one or more of their agencies with some organization related to the work of the National Council. In fact, some Southern Baptist churches have belonged to local councils of churches for years. Therefore, with the help of its affiliate organizations, the National Council claims to serve directly or indirectly denominations which number approximately 50,000,000 members.

The nature of this service ranges from mammoth relief operations to the promotion of objectives on the ecumenical calendar. Millions witness through television and radio the work of the Council throughout the year.

Baptists often find their interest centered on the Council's activity in the field of religious liberty. They are at times irritated by the comity agreements which arbitrarily divide vast areas of a city, assigning to a particular denomination exclusive franchise. In the eyes of some Baptists, this is nothing other than an attempt to perpetuate the Old World *Landeskirche* in the name of ecumenicity, for it virtually denies to many residents a choice in the matter of religious preference.

While the National Council disavows any intention of becoming a superchurch, its program nevertheless parallels that of a well-organized and functioning denomination. Therefore, to give the Council one's unqualified cooperation and support would mean the substitution of the Council's program for a major portion of that of the cooperating denomination. Few communions within the National Council are prepared to go this far. The fact remains that the National Council is based upon the denominations, without which it could not exist. Its limited budget also prohibits the Council from assuming the full-orbed characteristics of a denomination.

Baptist criticisms of the National Council have their counterpart from within the Council. It is the Council's position that the strength of responsible criticism would be much better expended from within the Council than from without. Baptists and others are continually the recipients of invitations from the Council whose terms of admission are extremely broad. They read:

New members are received from time to time. Membership is open to communions which are constituted as autonomous church bodies, possess a history that demonstrates permanency and stability, have an established order of government and ministry, and acknowledge Jesus Christ as Divine Lord and Savior.[6]

The American Council

Fundamentalism expresses its own ecumenical outreach within the framework of a number of different organizations. Among these, the American Council of Christian Churches is the smallest of the competitive councils. But for its size, it is by all odds the loudest. The roots of the American Council are deeply embedded in an older fundamentalist movement. Fundamentalism as a distinct phenomenon in American Christianity arose in the first two decades of the twentieth century.

In an attempt to counteract what was viewed as the increasing corruption of Christianity through the leaven of the "Sadducees" (Modernists), a group of prominent ministers, in 1918, formed the World's Christian Fundamentals Association. Among the pioneers of the movement, the fundamentalists could claim the support of such stalwarts as W. B. Riley, A. C. Dixon, and G. Campbell Morgan. The organization almost from the beginning was torn by internal dissension. Just a decade after its beginning, the decadent condition was much in evidence. In its last meeting two resolutions

---

[6]*Working Together Through the National Council of Churches* (New York: The National Council of the Churches of Christ in the United States of America, n.d.), p. 2.

were passed that are indicative of the spirit of the movement and those matters which had become the burden of its existence. Cole highlights these in *The History of Fundamentalism:*

> Only two of the resolutions carried pertinent value—the delegates decided the Federal Council of Churches of Christ in America was their chiefest foe in organized Christianity; also, they approved of citizenship military training as a patriotic measure, for were not wars inevitable until the return to earth of the Prince of Peace?[7]

On these two notes, an anti-Federal Council stance and an ultra-conservative attitude in economic, political, and social matters, the emergent American Council of Christian Churches based its call for a new council. Actually organized in 1941, it envisioned its role as that of a competitive council, directly opposed to the policies of the Federal Council.

Doubtless other factors aided the fundamentalist cause. Among these was the growing dissatisfaction within Baptist and Presbyterian ranks over what was termed "the inclusive policy" of the respective foreign mission societies. Among the Northern Baptists the protests figured prominently in the rise of the General Association of Regular Baptists (1933). Simultaneously a similar development was in progress among the Presbyterians which led to the formation of the Orthodox Presbyterian Church and Westminster Theological Seminary.

A prominent figure in the Presbyterian phase of the evolving struggle was J. Gresham Machen, a professor of Princeton Theological Seminary, who came to the front ranks from 1923 to 1938. He and his Princeton colleague, Robert Dick Wilson, were among the most able scholars of the fundamentalist movement.

The familiar pattern of dissent also developed among the Congregationalists. As a result, the Independent Fundamental Churches of America was formed. The proliferation of splinter groups continued among other denominations with varying success. The Methodists and the Dutch Reformed Church were particularly affected.

All of the newly organized fundamentalist denominations, without exception, were small. Therefore they felt more intensely the need of a united witness than did the larger denominations. They also felt themselves hopelessly outnumbered and the hapless victims

---

[7]Cole, *The History of Fundamentalism,* p. 314.

of discrimination inspired by the Federal Council and the parent denominations. They complained that they were overlooked by the government in its chaplaincy program, discriminated against by various governments when their missionaries sought for the visas necessary for mission service, and denied a fair share of the radio and television time.

The fundamentalist protest found its resurging expression in the formation of the American Council of Christian Churches in 1941 and a few years later, its international counterpart, the International Council of Christian Churches. For the first time since the organization of the Federal Council, fundamentalism had found a voice that could be heard. J. Oliver Buswell, Jr., describes this development from the viewpoint of a participant.

It was then that the American Council of Christian Churches was formed of denominations of sound evangelical faith not in the Federal Council. By grace and hard work we broke the council's monopoly on the chaplaincy and supplied a large number of patriotic, courageous, Bible-preaching, soul-winning chaplains for the armed forces.

As the war drew to a close, the missionary agencies of our ACCC denominations found that the World Council of Churches had a virtual monopoly over visas for foreign missionaries in many parts of the world. Moreover, through this near-monopoly pressure was exercised to keep from the foreign mission fields missions and missionaries who stood for the purity of the Church and against inclusivistic ecumenism.[8]

Whether one agrees with Buswell's evaluation of the American Council and its accomplishments or not depends upon his sympathies. However, there is little room for disagreement in the role played by Carl McIntire. More than any other one individual, he was responsible for the formation of the American and International Councils. He was selected to serve as the first president of the American Council and now serves as president of the International Council. Since the American Council's formation, he has pretty well determined its policies and directed its energies through a number of media, the most important of which is his weekly paper, *Christian Beacon*.

McIntire's base of operations for many years has been Collingswood, New Jersey, where he serves as pastor of the Bible Pres-

---

[8]"The American and International Councils of Christian Churches," *Christianity Today*, IX, No. 9 (January 29, 1965), 10.

byterian Church. A disciple of Professor Machen, McIntire left Princeton with his teacher in 1929. He was also defrocked along with Machen and the other fundamentalist preachers in 1936. Shortly afterwards, McIntire broke with the small Presbyterian Church in America (Orthodox Presbyterians) that Machen had founded and formed his own Bible Presbyterian denomination, which now calls itself Evangelical Presbyterian. At present it has no relationship with Carl McIntire and the American Council.

As McIntire's grip upon the American and International Councils tightened, responsible leaders who earlier supported the new organization deserted the cause. As a result, the McIntire wing of fundamentalism has gone from one extreme to another. Following a pattern established by a well-known Texas fundamentalist, J. Frank Norris, McIntire seems to glory in his role as an irritant. Just prior to the World Council of Churches' first assembly in Amsterdam, he announced his own international congress of Christians to meet shortly before the World Council Assembly to organize the International Council of Christian Churches. Donald Grey Barnhouse, editor of *Eternity,* graphically describes the McIntire meeting.

In Amsterdam, the main event was the great meeting of the representatives of a vast proportion of organized Christendom. Before this main event there was a side show that finished in fiasco. The American Council of Churches, whose general history has been one of bitterness and negation in the United States, sought to extend its divisive work in Europe. A little group, less than fifty, of whom half were Americans, plus a small group of "observers," met for a few days before the World Council of Churches in order to form the International Council of Churches. So that there might be as large a number as possible, the American Council took several men from various parts of Europe who should not have been at any Christian meetings, men who had been fired from work, one at least on moral grounds. The Americans of course, were ignorant of this; it is so easy for a man to raise a flag of fundamentalism in order to hide deficiencies in other phases of life.[9]

The tactics of the McIntire organizations were vividly demonstrated in Miami Beach, Florida, during the 1965 Baptist World Alliance. They distributed handbills which carried attacks against the Russian delegates and the Alliance for seating them. They reasoned that since the Russian nation is an atheistic and communistic nation

---

[9]Cited in Roy, *Apostles of Discord,* p. 192.

then the Russian Baptists must also be Communists. Many pickets carried signs in front of the convention hall which read: "Russian Baptist Church not truly Christian"; "BWA Supporting One World Church Movement"; "Communists Go Home"; and "This Protest Is Sponsored by American Council of Churches, International Council of Churches, and International Christian Youth." Placards on top of cars carried such signs as, "Communists Go Home" and "Russian Baptist Church Is Communist Controlled."

Undoubtedly many of these people are sincere, but such tactics and spirit raise numerous questions. Eyewitnesses were left wondering just in what way the McIntire movement differs from other hate organizations that claim to serve a Christian purpose? McIntire, according to the press, made much of the alleged Communist infiltration of the Alliance. His irresponsible conduct and reckless charges have served to bring the fundamentalist cause into increasing disrepute.

The pages of the *Christian Beacon* reveal a number of interesting sidelights on the activities of the American Council and its leadership. In addition to its perennial attack on the National and World councils, it simultaneously bombards such prominent personalities as Billy Graham, Martin Luther King, and other targets, ranging from communism to the Supreme Court.

Much of the space of the *Christian Beacon* in 1964 was given to "Project America." This campaign, according to the *Beacon* (March 26, 1964), was a crusade by young Americans to reopen the doors of the public schools to God, the Bible, and the Lord's Prayer: "The purpose of the Crusade is to gather in forty-eight hours, a million signatures on petitions to Congress to let the people of the nation decide for themselves whether the Constitution ought to be amended to reverse the decision of the Supreme Court.

While many responsible churchmen were asking serious questions about the proposed Becker amendment, the McIntire-led fundamentalists were acting. Their actions, while diametrically opposed to the position adopted by many major denominations, including the American and Southern Baptist conventions, came perilously close to success among untutored congressmen, who almost always stand in awe of imposing petitions.

Program personalities featured during the summer of 1964 at the Christian Admiral, a hotel operated by the McIntire entourage, indicate the extremist nature of the movement. Noticeably lacking from the roster of speakers were fundamentalist leaders of previous years, with the exception of Robert T. Ketcham. Ketcham, a leader among the General Association of Regular Baptists from its beginning, apparently still supports McIntire and the American and International Councils.

Other speakers, who are better known for other reasons, were the controversial Major General Edwin A. Walker; Dr. Harvey H. Springer, "the cowboy evangelist" whose associations with Gerald Winrod and his own statements place him in the ranks of anti-Semitism; Major Edgar C. Bundy,[10] the avid anti-Communist lecturer; and Senator Strom Thurmond of South Carolina, who led the Senate fight for the Becker amendment.[11]

Quite obviously the American Council of Christian Churches has added an ultraconservative stance on political, social, and economic issues to the basic tenets of fundamentalism. It has apparently also become a superpatriotic organization, heavily tinged with racism. Thus, what might have emerged an effective witness to evangelical Christianity has become hopelessly dissipated.

Actual membership figures for the American Council are evasive. According to *Christianity Today* (Jan. 29, 1965), the total membership of the participating denominations and churches is 939,537. A footnote reads, "The ACCC states that it represents some 1,500,000 Christians throughout the United States. The ACCC also states that its Radio and Film Commission represents the Baptist Bible Fellowship, 1,000,000 plus; Southern Baptist Fellowship, 750,000 plus; and the National Fellowship of Brethren Churches, 25,000 plus."

The three largest contingents within the American Council are the American Baptist Association, 655,200; the General Association of Regular Baptist Churches, 154,767; and the World Baptist Fellowship. If one adds the 750,000 claimed by the Southern Baptist Fellowship (an organization of premillennialists from Southern Baptist churches), it is readily apparent that Baptists make up the bulk of the membership and supporters of the American Council.

The strong individualism, independence of local churches from any ecclesiastical authority, and militant conservatism which often

---

[10]Roy, p. 200.
[11]*Christian Beacon,* XXIX, No. 6 (March 19, 1964), p. 1.

characterizes Baptists, account for the show of strength within this organization.

Regardless of how one may juggle the figures, the American Council of Christian Churches still remains a relatively small and insignificant organization. However, like many other highly organized pressure groups of the right and the left, its voice and its influence reach far beyond the rather limited confines of its membership.

The National Association of Evangelicals

The National Association of Evangelicals arose out of the same religious milieu as did the American Council, but with a markedly different spirit. A preliminary organizational meeting took place April 7-9, 1942, at St. Louis, Missouri. In contrast with the American Council, with which it shares a common conservative theological stance, the NAE came into existence only after the widest possible consultation and carefully laid plans. Actually, its roots reach back to the New England Fellowship of 1929.

National Association leadership has felt from the beginning its organization was the true heir of the spiritual legacy bequeathed by the World's Evangelical Alliance. Indeed, there are many similarities between the two organizations to support such a claim. However, as yet, the NAE has not mustered the following that the Alliance at one time commanded. Of course, it could be pointed out that the Alliance existed before the "Great Apostasy."

The "Great Apostasy" is the term which the evangelicals use when referring to the rise of modernism within the Christian faith. Of the "Great Apostasy," Murch writes:

A new interpretation of Christianity commonly known as "liberalism" challenged the "faith once for all delivered to the saints." It refused to accept the authority of the Holy Scriptures and the historic creeds of Christendom, and began to project its heresies into every root and branch of the Christian Church.[12]

Even though obviously sparked by a reaction to liberalism and what was widely considered the organizational expression of liberalism, the National Council of Churches, the proposed evangelical organization was projected upon a more positive basis.

---

[12]*Cooperation Without Compromise,* p. 19.

The initial organizational meeting in St. Louis reflected both the negative and positive aspects of the NAE. At the same meeting a temporary executive committee and an advisory committee of twenty-five were formed. Officers of the new organization were then elected. Harold J. Ockenga of the Park Street Congregational Church of Boston, Massachusetts, was elected president. A national office was set up at O Park Street, Boston. J. Elwin Wright, who more than any other one individual was responsible for the crystallization of the new organization, was made promotional director. The following year a constitutional convention was held in Chicago with a representation from "some fifty denominations with a potential constituency of 15,000,000."[13] It was at this meeting that a "Statement of Faith" comprised of seven articles was adopted. The first three are indicative of the doctrinal position assumed by the new organization:

1. We believe the Bible to be the inspired, the only infallible, authoritative word of God.
2. We believe that there is one God, eternally existent in three persons, Father, Son and Holy Ghost.
3. We believe in the deity of our Lord Jesus Christ, in His virgin birth, in His sinless life, in His miracles, in His vicarious and atoning death through His shed blood, in His bodily resurrection, in His ascension to the right hand of the Father, and in His personal return in power and glory.[14]

From its beginnings the NAE manifested great interest in evangelism, missions, and religious liberty. After a clarifying statement on the noninterference of the church in political matters, the committee on Separation of Church and State declared:

On the other hand the state should never sanction nor support any legislation which looks toward the establishment of any form of religion or the abridgement of the free exercise of any that may be established. Likewise it should not use any public funds for the benefit of any sectarian institution. The state should have no voice in the doctrines that are taught by the church, neither should the state concern itself with the forms of worship that are observed by the church, nor with the personnel of the officiary of the church.[15]

---

[13]*Ibid.*, pp. 61, 64.
[14]*Ibid.*, pp. 64-65.
[15]*Ibid.*, pp. 69-70.

The NAE has continued to champion the cause of religious liberty with all the weapons at its command. Its record in this regard is commendatory. Particularly noteworthy have been the Association's efforts to secure the establishment of fair and equitable policies in allocation of radio time for all religious broadcasters and equitable representation for evangelical chaplains in the chaplaincy of the armed forces. The NAE has also been among the most vocal advocates of the persecuted evangelicals in such countries as Italy, Colombia, and Spain.[16]

A remarkable flexibility has enabled the organization to change its structure in accordance with the expressed will of the constituency and the changing needs of the times. Early in its history, the National Association expanded its operations in order to make the influence of evangelicals felt and to provide a needed stimulus in such areas as Christian education, foreign missions, social reform, and evangelism. By 1948, a working relationship had been established between the increasingly feeble English Chapter of the World's Evangelical Alliance and the NAE.

J. Elwin Wright, long a pioneer in unitive efforts among American evangelicals, was commissioned as early as 1946, the centennial year of the Alliance's existence, to lay the groundwork for a new international evangelical enterprise.

Other prominent churchmen on both sides of the Atlantic participated in the early talks. A plan of operation whereby national evangelical fellowships could be promoted ensued.

In the 1950 meetings of the NAE in Boston and the World's Evangelical Alliance in Hildenborough Hall the two organizations moved closer toward the formation of a newly structured international organization. The objectives at that time were: (1) To witness to evangelical and historic Christianity; (2) to encourage and promote fellowship among evangelicals; and (3) to stimulate evangelism and promote united evangelical action in every sphere of life.[17]

The final step in the formation of the international organization was taken at Woudschoten in the Netherlands, where representatives from some twenty nations convened during the month of August, 1951. The conference which began on Saturday, August 4, by

---

[16]*Ibid.*, p. 144.
[17]*Ibid.*, p. 183.

Wednesday had arrived at the decision to formally constitute the World Evangelical Fellowship along the lines of agreement on the bare essentials held fundamental to the faith. These articles, reminiscent of another list of fundamentals, were enumerated in a seven-point statement of faith to which all groups were to subscribe annually.[18]

The freedom and autonomy of denominations and national organizations were emphasized and guaranteed. In this way the newly formed World Evangelical Fellowship saved itself from an exclusivistic stance which could have placed it into direct competition with the World Council of Churches. Of course, the same action subjected it to denunciation and abuse from the McIntire-dominated International Council.[19]

Following the pattern of the World Council, the newly constituted World Evangelical Fellowship sent its message forth, announcing to the world the purpose which motivated its formation.

The World Evangelical Fellowship, in recognition of the unity in the Body of Christ of all who love our Lord Jesus Christ in sincerity, affirm their unity in the Spirit with, and express their fraternal greetings to, all our brethren in Christ the world over, whether individuals, churches or societies, who hold "like precious faith" with us. The hour has truly come when all the born again Bible believing Christians should unite in order to strengthen their fellowship in the Body of Christ, to bear wider witness to His infallible Word, and to better evangelize the world until He comes. We look to Him that we might be enabled "to speak the truth in love with all lowliness and meekness, endeavoring to keep the unity of the Spirit in the bond of peace."[20]

Commissions on Evangelism, Christian Action, Missionary Cooperation, and Literature were implemented. A theological discussion group was activated in the 1953 meeting at Clarens, Switzerland, and an International Radio and Television Committee was formed in an attempt to correlate the hundreds of evangelical efforts in broadcasting the gospel.

Whether or not the World Evangelical Fellowship will emerge a more rigidly structured organization is a question to which time alone holds the answer. At this point, both the NAE and WEF

---

[18]*Ibid.*, p. 187.
[19]*Ibid.*, p. 185.
[20]*Ibid.*, p. 189.

have carefully avoided usurping any functions of a church. The
NAE at present seems to be moving toward a more exclusivistic
policy, obviously motivated by the fear that with increasing dual
alignment on the part of sponsoring denominations with the NCC
that its own existence may be imperiled.

Perhaps the NAE and WEF would not exist today if there were
no National or World Councils. Although often in conflict with the
National Council, the NAE has refused to become a council or
take on the functions of a denomination. It has steadfastly adhered
to the original vision as expressed in the initial meeting at St. Louis:

We propose, therefore, to organize an Association which shall give
articulation and united voice to our faith and purposes in Christ Jesus,
while not considering ourselves as an executive or legislative body in any
wise controlling constituent members, nor proposing to initiate new
movements and institutions.[21]

With this purpose many Baptists are in agreement. Outstanding
among the early supporters of the NAE were R. G. Lee, the well-
known former pastor of the Bellevue Baptist Church, Memphis,
Tennessee, and Judge John McCall, prominent Baptist layman of
Memphis. Two leading Baptist ministers of the North also helped
in the initial stages of organization, namely, William Ward Ayer
of the Calvary Baptist Church, New York City, and John W.
Bradbury, editor of the *Watchman Examiner*. Among the ten million or more adherents of the NAE, Baptists possibly comprise half
the constituency. Many more Baptists, particularly in the Southern
Baptist Convention, are sympathetic supporters.

The Theological Basis of Conflict

Some of the theological issues which gave rise to the various
councils discussed in this chapter have been touched upon, but no
attempt has been made to deal systematically with the theological
currents and conflicts which account for the variety of "ecumenical"
structures. Serious study of the issues would be unnecessary if the
resulting competition were only the product of personality conflicts.

Even though personalities inevitably become a contributing factor
to any theological controversy, this phenomenon does not indicate

---

[21]*Ibid.,* p. 59.

that such controversies have no theological basis. There is little doubt that strong personalities possessed of equally strong opinions engender animosity on the one hand and elicit disciples on the other.

Two such leaders at opposite extremes of the theological spectrum are Charles Clayton Morrison and Carl McIntire. These opinionated prophets find it virtually impossible to separate themselves from their positions or to admit any validity in an opposing view. But objectivity, even though unattainable in the absolute sense, must not be abandoned if one is to rise above caprice or pure subjectivism. Nowhere is this more obviously necessary than in a historical examination of the theological issues underlying the rise of the competitive councils.

The Decline of Orthodoxy

The nineteenth century witnessed both the high tide of Protestant missionary advance and the beginning of the decline of traditional theological concepts associated with Protestantism since the Reformation. This decline, at first gaining momentum very slowly, became an avalanche just before the turn of the century. The effect upon the ecumenical movement has been far-reaching. It has affected the movement in two ways. Directly, it greatly de-emphasized and virtually eliminated the theological basis for union. Indirectly, through the social gospel, it gave the ecumenical movement a new dynamic. That there has been a widespread deviation from traditional orthodoxy, even those most ignorant of theological trends have been able to discern. The results have been felt from the smallest of communities to the most remote corners of the widespread mission enterprise.

The decline to which reference is made is not that set in motion by the transcendental philosophy of New England or the Unitarian and Universalist theologies and the subsequent humanism. These movements undoubtedly made their impression upon the Christian thinking of their day through such men as Bushnell and Channing, but the course of Christian history was not severely altered. The decline to which attention is given here is a later development. Its roots are found in the writings of Friedrich Ernst Daniel Schleiermacher and Albrecht Ritschl.

It would be erroneous to leave the impression that this decline was the result of the thinking of only a few outstanding personalities. Many other factors were involved. Indeed, the decline was a result, in part at least, of the very atmosphere of the age.

With the beginning of the twentieth century the full force of the philosophical revolution, i.e., the change from the authoritarian medieval mind to the scientific modern mind, began to exert an ever stronger influence on the theological thinking of the American ministry and educated laity.[22]

Schleiermacher and Ritschl were the theological pioneers of this new age. They breathed the spirit of a new day and helped to blow the shape of the hourglass for the twentieth century. Rauschenbusch early discovered the importance of these men to the new theology.

So far as my observation of doctrinal handbooks goes, it seems that those writers whose minds were formed before the eighties rarely show any clear comprehension of social points of view. . . . Those individuals of that era who did strike out into social conceptions of Christianity deserve the name and honor of prophets.
Among the earlier German theologians Friedrich Schleiermacher, Richard Rothe, and Albrecht Ritschl seem to me to deserve the title.[23]

It was perhaps inevitable that the new theology of the Continent and the humanism of New England Unitarianism and Universalism would sooner or later coalesce. Although of separate origin, New England liberalism and the rationalism of the Continent were basically akin.

Hopkins discovered in the older liberal movement the roots of the social gospel and the new theology. "Roots of a social gospel of brotherhood are to be found in Channing's Baltimore sermon, while the 'new theology' derived from Bushnell by Munger, Gladden, and other Congregationalists was itself inherently social."[24]

It is not at all strange that American Christianity should receive its new theology from the Continent. Unitarianism was in such disrepute in this country that an impartial examination of its theology was highly improbable. It had pretty well run its course. No one in the more orthodox circles cared to be branded a Unitarian.

---

[22]Heick and Neve, *A History of Christian Thought*, II, 312.
[23]*A Theology for the Social Gospel*, p. 27.
[24]*The Rise of the Social Gospel in American Protestantism 1865-1915*, p. 218.

Too, Rauschenbusch, as a good many other Americans, looked to the Continent and particularly to Germany for theological leadership. His knowledge of the German tongue made the difficult German works readily available. In this manner, Schleiermacher, Ritschl, Hegel, Rothe, Leibnitz, and other German theologians came to exert a wide influence on American theology.

Of these men, Schleiermacher was the pioneer and easily the most influential. Schleiermacher, "the father of modern theology," was by nature a skeptic. Brought up in the tradition of Moravian pietism, he early entertained serious doubts about his inherited faith. He read Spinoza and accepted much of what he read. He found aesthetic satisfaction in his friendship with Schlegel and the leading spirits of the Romantic movement. All of these elements exerted a lasting effect upon his developing theology.

In its final form Schleiermacher's theology rejected all objective references to faith. Religion was for him a "feeling of absolute dependence."[25] This statement became the unifying dogma of his new theology. Thus, Schleiermacher moved the point of reference from theology to psychology—from objective faith to subjective feeling. In spite of the change in his theology, Schleiermacher never forsook a warmhearted appreciation of Christ which had been a vital part of the religion of his childhood.[26] On the other hand, he reduced God to a "thing," not quite the pantheistic thing of Spinoza, but just one step removed, with love and wisdom added, to give God a more personal quality than Spinoza had been willing to give him.

Ritschl supplemented the contribution of Schleiermacher with that of his own innovation, known as "the doctrine of the historical Jesus." This historical Jesus of Ritschl took the place of the indefinable, mystical Christ of Schleiermacher. With the emphasis on the Jesus of history came a fresh emphasis on what was termed the religion of Jesus and interpreted to be a religion of doing rather than that of believing. In the new format, the supernatural was reduced to a minimum and the practical aspects of the Christian faith were significantly magnified.[27]

Thus, Schleiermacher and Ritschl in theology, and later Darwin

---

[25]Fisher, *History of Christian Doctrine*, p. 503.
[26]Heick and Neve, p. 104.
[27]*Ibid.*, p. 317.

in the field of science, Marx in economics, and Dewey in psychology created an atmosphere and furnished the source material out of which a new theology was evolved, or rather created, by Rauschenbusch. Advocates of the new theology declared that the central teaching of Christ was the kingdom of God. The concept of the kingdom immediately became the unifying doctrine in the formulation of a theology of the social gospel.[28]

Along with Strong, Rauschenbusch felt keenly the inadequacy of the older theology upon which he was reared. Discussing the view that sin is basically selfishness, he writes:

> This proposition gives a solemn and terrible importance to the fact that doctrinal theology has failed to cherish and conserve for humanity the doctrine of the Kingdom of God. Christ died for it. Theology has allowed it to lead a decrepit, bedridden and senile existence in that museum of antiquities which we call eschatology. Having lost its vision of organized righteousness, theology necessarily lost its comprehension of organized sin, and it set men to wrestling with their private doubts or sexual emotions by ascetic methods. But if sin is selfishness, how did that meet the case?"[29]

To study the works of Rauschenbusch is to study his conception of the kingdom. To him the social gospel and the doctrine of the kingdom were synonymous. Rauschenbusch held to the conviction that if one possessed an accurate concept of the kingdom, he was of logical necessity committed to the social gospel. It was for the purpose of a deeper understanding of the kingdom and for the implementation of its principles in the life of modern society that the Brotherhood of the Kingdom was first organized.[30]

Three effects of this new theology upon American Christianity may be discerned. First, it has supplied an "authoritarian foundation which social Christianity had previously lacked."[31] Second, it has helped to create a crisis in Christianity which set the fundamentalist against the modernist with a great many on both sides willing to deny the other a place in the kingdom.[32] Division, consternation, confusion, and widespread irreligion and doubt have been

---

[28]Strong, *The Next Great Awakening*, p. 21.
[29]Rauschenbusch, p. 47.
[30]*Ibid.*, pp. 127, 221.
[31]*Ibid.*, p. 203.
[32]Cf. Machen, *Christianity and Liberalism.*

accompanying results. Third, the decline of orthodoxy and rise of a new theology led the ecumenical movement at its outset to bypass a theological basis of union as too controversial in favor of a utilitarian one which would appeal more effectively to various Christian bodies.[33]

The Rise of the Social Gospel

It would not be too much of an overstatement to say that the modern ecumenical movement would not exist today without the social gospel. Indeed in its very inception, as preached by Schumacher in 1833, by Josiah Strong in the eighties, and by Walter Rauschenbusch ten years later, the social gospel proclaimed as one of its major aims the union of all Christian bodies.

The ecumenical movement has, in turn, paid its debt to these early pioneers by making the accomplishments of the aims of social Christianity the major reason for its existence. The decline of orthodoxy alone could not have created such a movement. There had to be a new nucleus around which the movement could be integrated. The social gospel supplied this center.

Even though the decline of orthodoxy has been considered prior to a discussion of the rise of the social gospel, the impression should not be left that the one preceded the other as one railway coach precedes another in a series, for this was not the case. Rather, as the wind precedes the storm and at the same time is part of the storm itself, even so the decline of orthodoxy preceded the social gospel and at the same time was so closely related as to constitute a part of the social gospel itself. The decline of orthodoxy and the rise of the social gospel took place simultaneously over an extended period of time, the one aiding the other by creating a need which only the other could supply.

The social gospel, with its insistent challenge of the status quo and with its new emphasis on the age-old ethical and social teachings of Jesus and the prophets, supplied a necessary anchor for intellects cast adrift on a sea of doubt. Many felt that at last they had discovered in the social gospel an eternal element in the Christian faith which would stand immovable amidst the growing avalanche of doubt.

On the other hand, there were those who embraced the social

---

[33]Tulga, *The Case Against the Federal Council of Churches*, pp. 12-13.

gospel first and then cut themselves loose from their former theological moorings. Such were those whose minds had been led into
the new arena of social Christianity, the contact with which made
them highly dissatisfied with the individualistic gospel of the orthodoxy on which, for the most part, they had been reared. Thus,
the converts to the social gospel were left to discover for themselves
an existing theological foundation adequate to meet the needs of
their new faith, but when failing in this to create one of their own.[14]

Undoubtedly, Christianity in every age has pulsated with feelings
prompted by the social implications of the gospel. It is true, however, that in some periods of history one must search extensively
for the slightest evidence of any emphasis on the social teachings
of the Bible.[35] Christianity was forced to wait until the latter part
of the nineteenth century for a newly awakened conscience on the
social implications of the gospel. Even the missionary enterprise
suffered a severe setback until the last decade of the eighteenth and
the early part of the nineteenth century, when a new interest was
manifested in the condition of the pagan world. Certainly, the nineteenth century had been an eventful century for Christianity and
for the world.

The antislavery movement, which had a large part to do with
bringing about the abolition of slavery through the Civil War, was
the result, in part, of an energetic application of the social teachings of Jesus on the race question.[36] With the close of the war the
interest of Christians was directed to other problems of growing
proportions in a rapidly developing industrial age. The eighties saw
many able voices raised on behalf of social Christianity.[37] It was
in this period that the social gospel began to take on the
characteristics of a well-defined movement.

From its inception the social gospel movement and the ecumenical movement have been closely related. This relation began when
both movements were in the embryonic stage of development. The
World's Evangelical Alliance, one of the most outstanding interdenominational organizations of the nineteenth century, possessed a
strong social interest from its initial organization. Indeed, because

---

[34]*Op. cit.,* p. 7.
[35]*Ibid.,* p. 8.
[36]Baker, *Relations Between Northern and Southern Baptists,* pp. 43 ff.
[37]Rauschenbusch, p. 27.

it was not willing to wink at slavery, the American branch was not organized until after the Civil War. After its organization the branch immediately became an effective unifying force in American Christianity.

One of the Alliance's best attended meetings was held in New York in 1873. Afterwards, however, the Alliance never commanded so great a following. The leadership sought to save the Alliance by choosing an able man to fill the office of general secretary. Josiah Strong, who had recently come into prominence through his book *Our Country* was selected for the office. Strong was highly successful. Under his leadership three of the Alliance's most important conferences were held.

Strong was an earnest advocate of social Christianity. He used the new position to inject his social views into the very life of the Alliance. Under his leadership the Alliance issued a call for all interested Christians to assemble at Washington in 1887 for a study of some of the most pressing social problems of the day.

This "call," sounding the note of crisis much as had *Our Country,* mentioned the major problems of the time and asserted that the Church had not yet fully recognized its "relations to the entire life of the community and the nation." The conference would study three questions: the "perils and opportunities of the Christian church and of the country," denominational cooperation to meet these, and means of securing such cooperation and of awakening "the whole church to its responsibility."[38]

Twelve to fifteen hundred delegates responded to the call. However, only five hundred delegates attended two years later in 1889 at the meeting of the Alliance in Boston. Again, under the leadership of Josiah Strong, the agenda was heavy with a consideration of the social problems of the times. Among other topics, much time was given to the discussion of crime, the relation of church and state, and methods of accomplishing church work. The progress of interdenominational cooperation was also discussed.

The last of these three conferences under the leadership of Josiah Strong was held in Chicago in 1893.[39]

Although under Strong's guidance, the Alliance virtually arose

---

[38]Hopkins, p. 114.
[39]*Ibid.,* p. 115.

from the dead, the innate conservatism of the organization proved
too much for him. His social convictions sought a wider and freer
expression than the Alliance would allow. He finally broke with the
Alliance to assume a place of responsibility in the newly organized
Federal Council of Churches of Christ in America.

The first definite organizational expression of the social gospel
movement came into existence in 1892 under the guidance of
Walter Rauschenbusch, Leighton Williams, and Nathaniel Schmidt.
The new organization was called the Brotherhood of the Kingdom.
Its purpose was to "bring together a group of like-minded Baptist
ministers for 'the better understanding of the idea of the Kingdom
of God.' " The program of the Brotherhood, which had been agreed
upon at the organizational meeting, was to "permeate modern social
movements with the social ideal, and to attempt this by emphasiz-
ing Jesus' teaching of the Kingdom of God, the central idea of the
Gospel."[40]

Early in the course of its life, the Brotherhood outgrew its
Baptist limitations to become an interdenominational body. This
was in keeping with one of the aims of the Brotherhood; namely,
the union of all divided Christendom.[41]

The spirit and ideals of Rauschenbusch have been carried bodily
into the ecumenical movement by Josiah Strong, W. A. Horton,
Shailer Mathews, Charles S. Macfarland, and a host of others. Perhaps nowhere can one observe how indissolubly the social gospel
and ecumenism have blended into one movement as in the works
of Charles S. Macfarland, militant former secretary of the Federal
Council of Churches. Waxing eloquent in a discussion of the waste
of natural resources, he proceeds to describe the far more serious
waste of the spiritual resouces in America.

While we have wasted the forests that make the mines, we have also
wasted by thousands our human brothers in the mines, have slaughtered
and despoiled our women, and have consumed our babies beyond the
count of Herod in our suffocated cities, while we had half a continent
of fresh air. . . .
But these are not an intimation of the worst of our dissipations, and,
indeed, these wastes have been largely because of a deeper and more
serious prodigality. We have let the very light within us become dark-

---

[40]Sharpe, *Walter Rauschenbusch,* pp. 116-17.
[41]*Ibid.,* p. 119.

ness, and the saddest of all has been the waste of our moral powers, our finer emotions, and our religious enthusiasms, through sectarian divisions, denominational rivalries, and unrestrained caprice often deluding itself as a religious loyalty.[42]

Through the years the National Council has continued to multiply its activities and enlarge its organization to cope with new social problems as they arise. The Social Service Commission of the Council has been extremely active in the investigation, consultation, and production of materials, looking to the solution of every problem confronting contemporary society.[43] Through the National and World councils, as well as through the influence of countless numbers of Christian leaders, the social gospel entered into and became a part of the ecumenical movement.

The Fundamentalist Reaction

As is quite obvious from the preceding discussion, there are widely divergent positions held by fundamentalists. Some, whose denominations are within the National and World councils are very close to the position of those whose loyalties lie in other directions. Yet there are points at which all fundamentalists concur in their opposition to ecumenical Christianity as embodied in the National and World councils.

Almost without exception, fundamentalist spokesmen attack what they consider an inadequate creedal basis of the NCC and the WCC. Tulga, of the Conservative Baptist Association, writes: "The doctrinal statement in the preamble of the Federal Council of Churches is actually without meaning since so many contradictory meanings are being assigned to these words in Federal Council circles."[44]

McIntire attacks the ambiguity of the term "divine" in the brief theological statement regarding Christ.

A wide range of views is covered by the term divinity of Christ. By it men mean that Christ was divine as we all are divine. By it men teach that His divinity differs from our own only in degree. By it men mean that His divinity places Him somewhere between God and man— and a lot of other things are taught. The sum of them all denies His unique eternal divinity or deity, places Him below God, and in most

---

[42]Macfarland, *The Progress of Church Federation,* pp. 11 ff.
[43]Cavert, *Twenty Years of Church Federation,* pp. 61-72.
[44]*The Case Against the Federal Council of Churches,* p. 15.

instances makes Him merely a man of like sinful passions with us, or at the most superman.[45]

Kik declares, "The NCC could not state less without losing any vestige of or resemblance to Christianity." Regarding the WCC, he writes:

> The World Council of Churches adopted a more direct and meaningful statement of faith. Not without opposition from those who felt that the meager sentence was too narrow and exclusive, the WCC adopted the following as its basis:
> The World Council of Churches is a fellowship of Churches which accept our Lord Jesus Christ as God and Saviour.[46]

Doubtless Kik would voice appreciation for the expanded statement of faith which the WCC adopted at New Delhi. Of all conciliar statements of faith, he likes the American Council statement best, which asserts belief in "the plenary divine inspiration of the Scriptures in the original languages, their consequent inerrancy and infallibility, and as the Word of God, the supreme and final authority in faith and life."[47]

A symposium edited by Mooneyham represents the NAE viewpoint. Without exception, the contributors to this volume stress the importance of a strong evangelical theology as a prime prerequisite for Christian unity. Clyde W. Taylor voices the unanimous opinion of the group:

> Our basic beliefs are important to us. We cannot give them up, not for any amount of union or united effort, if this be required of us. Rev. Jack Dain, missionary secretary of the Anglican Church in Australia, told evangelical leaders in India recently that above all else evangelicals must maintain their theological integrity.[48]

With the passing of the years and a growing maturity on the part of the evangelicals, criticism of the ecumenical movement has become better balanced. Evangelicals are not simply reacting, they are beginning to think and write creatively as they address themselves to the problem of Christian unity. There have also been

---

[45]*Twentieth-Century Reformation*, p. 13.
[46]*Ecumenism and the Evangelical*, pp. 123-24.
[47]*Ibid.*, p. 125.
[48]*The Dynamics of Christian Unity*, p. 79.

changes within the ecumenical movement. Its confessional basis is less ambiguous and more in keeping with the historic Christian affirmations than previously. However, there still remain unresolved contradictions between the confessional statements of the competing councils. G. W. Bromiley of Fuller Theological Seminary addresses himself to this problem in a recent work. He asserts that the solution to confessional conflict lies in a vital union with the Christ of the confessions and not in the confessional formulae which change from generation to generation and which more often than not divide rather than unite.

Unless we cling to the fact that unity is in Christ as the Truth and our confession of Him rather than in our statements of truth, there is obviously no possible way. All who think differently on important issues must be expelled or abandoned or denounced, and the fallibility of man defies the given unity in Christ in a riot of dogmatic disruption. But if we take seriously the fact that we are united in Christ, and therefore in the Truth, and therefore in our basic confession, there is a hard way that can be taken to overcome the doctrinal difficulties. It begins in humility, i.e., the recognition by each Christian and Christian body that it must be reformable under the Word and Spirit of God. It leads by way of evangelistic concern, namely, that Christ must be presented and souls won to Him, not only in our own Christianized lands, but also in distant continents, even though important points are still under dispute.[49]

After offering this basic premise, he then proceeds to present a six-point program for arriving at an acceptable confession which will truly unite. Such a program, he insists, must begin with a proclamation of Christ as Lord and include a concentration upon "the common preaching and teaching of positive biblical truth"; an acceptance, in substance, of the Apostles' Creed; continued open discussion of the creedal basis; and a willingness to examine objectively even contradictory confessions with an attempt at reconciliation under the guidance of the Word of God.

There are striking parallels between Bromily's position and that of Martin Marty, an avowed ecumenist. They agree on the absolute necessity of mutual recognition of all professing Christians and Christian bodies as in some sense belonging to Christ. This leads to a tacit, if not an overt, program of union which eschews proselytism.

Marty asserts that Christians possess enough "unity now to resume

---

[49] *The Unity and Disunity of the Church,* pp. 79-81.

their mission to the world."[50] Both Marty and Bromiley assert, in different ways, the necessity of a minimal confession of Christ as Lord, the catholic nature of the ecumenical movement, and a continual reformation. There seems to be more stress upon the determinative role of biblical authority in Bromiley than in Marty and a different understanding of the church's mission. Herein lie the major differences in the "new evangelical" stance and the "new ecumenical" position. They certainly are not as far apart as the two camps formerly were, but then their positions are not identical. Neither is Marty nor Bromiley truly representative of either the ecumenists or the evangelicals.

Fundamentalists commonly deplore the implicit theology of the ecumenical movement as embraced by the leadership of the World Council and the National Council of Churches. Despite its disavowals of a superchurch complex or ambition, Kik discovers much in the ecumenical movement that betrays just this characteristic. In a discussion of the Toronto statement of the Central Committee of the World Council, he points out that in the very statement denying any intention of becoming a superchurch, the WCC betrays itself.

At Toronto, the spokesman said, "The World Council cannot and should not be based on any one particular conception of the church. It does not prejudge the ecclesiological problem."

To this bland assertion, Kik replies acidly, "If concluding that existing divisions contradict the very nature of the Church is not prejudging the ecclesiological problem, we do not know what could be."[51]

The attack by certain ecumenicists on denominationalism is well known. Perhaps none has been more caustic in attacking the ends of a denominationally segmented Christianity than Clayton Morrison. Marty, although much more tame in his criticisms, reveals little appreciation for the denominations. Kik and many other critics of the ecumenical movement hold that the expressed goal of the movement, its condemnation of denominational divisions, and its growing structure predetermine its nature as a superchurch.

Actual evidence of a superchurch mentality and strategy seems much more evident in the literature, program, and organization of

[50]*Church Unity and Church Mission,* p. 20.
[51]*Op. cit.,* p. 127.

the National Council than in the World Council. Kik attacks what he considers a glaring weakness in the organizational structure of the National Council which lends itself to this kind of development.

The General Board, which accomplishes the real work of the Council through its divisions and committees, had a voting constituency of 169 at the September, 1957, meeting in New York. Only 91 (54%) directly represented denominations. A resolution was prepared for the General Assembly of 1957 that has the practical effect of further decreasing denominational representation by enlarging representation from state, city and local councils.[52]

Kik also accuses the National Council of attempting to dictate the policies of the denominations on missions, worship, evangelism, economics, religious education, social and moral responsibility, and community projects, amid other things. The National Council is charged with attempting to function as a superchurch when it tries to define dogma and when it declares its voice as the voice of the church.

Kik's charges arise from the basic assumption that "when councils become more than agencies for cooperative work and enter into the functions of the church, then they take on the nature of a superchurch despite disavowals."[53] With this judgment most members of the American Council and National Association would doubtless agree.

Again, Ford, after citing numerous quotations from Peter Brunner to Paul Griswold Macy, addresses himself to the superchurch problem.

There is no question but that the real thrust of the ecumenical movement is "one church for one world." For one who accepts the theory of the organizational nature of the church, there is hardly any other choice.

Frankly, I cannot accept this position. I cannot conceive that the true Church of Christ is synonymous with the sum total of all church organizational life.[54]

Tulga sees no alternative for the World Council other than that of a superchurch: "Given the status of the new catholicism to

---

[52]*Ibid.*, pp. 129-30.
[53]*Ibid.*, p. 131.
[54]In Mooneyham, p. 99.

which theological liberalism and European ecclesiasticism are committed and a hierarchy will not only be developed but it will be a necessity to administration."[55]

Clyde W. Taylor, long associated with the National Association of Evangelicals, echoes identical fears and accusations concerning the World Council's churchly aspirations. He contrasts the claims of the WCC to be nothing more than an international fellowship of national church bodies and often repeated goal of church union which continues to crop up in the addresses and writings of its leadership. "For example, a dispatch from the 1961 New Delhi meeting quoted Rev. Kenneth Slack, who is executive secretary of the British Council of Churches, as referring to "the coming great church."[56]

The charge that the WCC and the NCC have betrayed the Protestant heritage continues to appear among the criticisms of the ecumenical movement on the part of evangelicals. This accusation is based on a number of developments. Since 1920, some Orthodox bodies have participated in various ecumenical conferences. Consequently the joint worship services at times have followed the Eastern Orthodox liturgy with its invocation of blessings from the saints and the virgin Mary, "mother of God." This was more than fundamentalist observers could take.

In former days, Morrison and others called upon Protestants to unite in order to more effectively compete "with a formidable and aggressive Roman Catholicism."[57] At the same time there were others who felt that the ecumenical movement was only ecumenical in its claims but not in fact or desire as long as Rome was left out of its deliberations.

With New Delhi and the advent of Vatican Council II, it has become more apparent than ever that Roman Catholicism can no longer be ignored by the true ecumenist. Even though the path to reconciliation between Rome, the Greek Orthodox, and Protestant communions is by no means clear, some sentimentalists seem ready to stampede the "separated brethren" back into the "one true fold." Consequently, those outside the organizational expressions of the ecumenical movement are less and less inclined to consider favorably

---

[55]*The Case Against the World Council of Churches,* p. 31.
[56]Cited in Mooneyham, p. 83.
[57]*The Unfinished Reformation,* p. 35.

a movement that seems bent on self-destruction and an inevitable reversal of Reformation truth.[58]

Other Issues of Dissent

The basis of much fundamentalist displeasure with the National and World councils lies in the positions assumed by the councils on social, economic, and political issues.

McIntire in 1945 declared that "the Federal Council has repeatedly made a frontal attack upon what we speak of as the profit motive, which is the very heart of private enterprise and the soul of capitalism."[59]

Not all those associated with fundamentalism have taken the position assumed by the ACCC. To the contrary, the NAE has attempted, on a limited scale, to deal with certain problems of racial and social inequities. However, there is a wide gulf between the social action of the National Council and that of the National Association of Evangelicals.

Most evangelicals apparently put their emphasis on the personal aspects of the gospel. Even though not oblivious of the social implications of the gospel, there is evidently no disposition to make social action the sum total of the evangel. Therefore, the issue on the part of some fundamentalists with the National Council over its social stance is primarily one of emphasis rather than content. With others, there is the basic question of the Council's role as a political action lobbyist. Few evangelicals are prepared to accept uncritically the National Council's multitudinous pronouncements in these areas.

The ecumenical movement has been the recipient of some severe criticism at the point of its failure to stimulate a more vigorous missionary outreach. Criticism at this point is most keenly felt since ecumenists have continuously used the cause of missions for their rallying point. The missionary imperative, it was claimed, called for an ecumenical imperative. From Edinburgh to New Delhi, in "Message" after "Message," the Christian world has been challenged to disregard its divisions and unite, for it was assumed that world evangelism was dependent on a united church. It was commonly agreed, in ecumenical circles, that denominational divisions con-

---

[58]See Grant and Subilia.
[59]*Op. cit.*, p. 135.

stituted the scandal of Christianity. The church had erected a false stumbling block over which the heathen had to scramble to reach the Christ of the gospel. Fundamentalists, who are not only often divided from one another by traditional denominational lines but also by even finer distinctions in points of doctrine, refuse to accept this viewpoint as a valid judgment upon the failure of the Christian evangel.

Lindsell, in a national religious periodical, subjects this ecumenical presupposition to an incisive analysis. He points out that at one time "the vast majority of North American missionary personnel came from the old line denominations."[60] This, he explains, is no longer the case.

In 1956, 43.5 percent of North American foreign missionaries were related to the Division of Foreign Missions of the National Council of Churches; in 1958, the percentage dropped to 41.2 percent; and in 1960 to 38 percent (10,324). In other words, 62 percent of the North American foreign missionaries are not affiliated with the Division of Foreign Missions. Contrasted with the situation in 1911, 1928, and 1936, it becomes quite clear that the gap between missionary personnel and the ecumenical complex has widened steadily. More and more missionary work is being done outside rather than within the ecumenical framework. Even today if only one group—like the Seventh-Day Adventists with their 1,385 missionaries—were to withdraw from the Division of Foreign Missions, the Division's total missionary force would drop perceptibly (from 10,324 to 8,939). Furthermore, their withdrawal would leave under the direction of the Division of Foreign Missions less than one third of the total number of North American missionaries. If any observation is to be made from this summary, it is that the foreign missionary impulse of the ecumenical movement in North America today is far weaker percentagewise in overseas personnel than it was 50 years ago.[61]

By 1965, the missionary personnel affiliated with denominations associated with the National Council had dropped to 34.7 percent of the total.[62]

Lindsell then proceeds to examine every case of a church merger from the United Church of Canada to the United Church of South India. Without exception the missionary cause either made

---

[60]*Christianity Today*, VI (March 30, 1962), 3-7.
[61]*Ibid.*, 4.
[62]*Christianity Today*, IX (January 29, 1965), 8.

no significant advance or it actually suffered severe losses by all measurable standards. "Inclusive merger did not yield the kind of outreach that ecumenists envision" is his rather guarded understatement. By way of contrast, he then turns to evangelicals and non-ecumenical denominations. In every case these denominations showed a substantial increase in missionary personnel.[63]

Lindsell's research revealed that "faith mission agencies scored the most substantial increase of all in missionary personnel. Generally they represented small, isolated constituencies in Bible churches and fundamentalist groups. The roll call is impressive: Evangelical Alliance Mission missionaries increased from 95 to 807; Unevangelized Tribes from 48 to 211; Oriental Missionary Society from 36 to 198; Wycliffe Bible Translators from nothing to over 1,000."[64]

His conclusions are worth considering in this discussion.

With respect to missions and the fulfilment of the Great Commission, two generalizations seem to emerge. (1) Church mergers have as yet produced nothing that resembles a significant increase in foreign missionary witness so far as the number of missionaries is concerned. Actually, there seems to have been a general decline among those groups which have merged. (2) The increase of missionary passion and concern seems to have been stirred largely by faith boards and by the smaller and generally more theologically conservative groups. Therefore if church mergers are encouraged on the ground that "the divided state of the Christian Church is blocking its mission," there is little evidence to show that mergers do substantially improve the realization of the mission of the church. So far mergers just have not produced such results.[65]

Such a study tends to substantiate the evangelicals' contention that the missionary endeavor is primarily dependent upon an inner dynamic which alone furnishes the necessary vision and motivation for missionary service. This inner dynamic in turn is dependent upon a theological thrust which the ecumenical movement has apparently yet to discover.

Martin Marty's answer is perhaps the only one the convinced ecumenist could give to such an array of alarming statistics. He

---

[63]*Op. cit.*, 4-5.
[64]Ibid., 5.
[65]*Ibid.*

disparages the efforts of those who are apparently succeeding exactly at the point where the ecumenical movement has failed to live up to the expectations of its sponsors.

We have agreed that if missions mean snatching a number of souls away from the world into tightly organized ecclesiastical bodies, then the competitive principle is effective. Statistically, one will be productive in missions most of all if he proselytizes, disparages other Christian endeavor, undercuts other Christian workers, believes that he alone possesses the truth, cajoles people into accepting the advertisements of his confessions. While the ecumenical churches stand under judgment in comparison to the missionary zeal of the anti-ecumenical forces, they must be awakened to missions on a different basis and must resist the temptations to compete. For competition is a short-range exploitation of the Christian relation to the world.[66]

Doubtless the spirit of competition does enter into the conflicts between competing councils and denominations. It cannot be excused. It is sub-Christian. But is it not a part of the finiteness of man? It is just possible that this spirit is not the sole possession of the evangelicals or of the Baptists.

Can one really explain the sacrificial dedication of a Bill Wallace, who died at the hands of Communists in China, or a Ned Saint and his colleagues, who were martyred in the jungles of Ecuador, or of a Paul Carlson, who in an act of utter selflessness lost his life in the Congo, on any other basis than that of the love of Christ?

There perhaps are mixed motives in religious institutions, as in men, but the cause of Christ in single-minded devotion is hardly the sole possession of any council, denomination, or man.

Simply because one is associated with a denomination which belongs to some organizational expression of the ecumenical movement does not mean that he is simon-pure. Nor does it necessarily indicate that he has an ecumenical spirit. It certainly does not give him the right to impugn the motives of those who are not of his fold. Does not true ecumenicity arise above all this? Competitive councils and denominations there may be, but there is only one Christ. Does not the beginning of a scriptural ecumenicity lie in the realization that our unity is in him and our loyalty to him above institution, ceremony, or party?

---

[66]*Op. cit.,* p. 135.

7

Baptists Within the World Council

It has been quite evident in this study thus far that Baptists present no one uniform pattern of relationship to the ecumenical movement. There are Baptists in some degree of cooperation with the World Council of Churches, National Council of Churches, National Association of Evangelicals, and even the American Council of Christian Churches.

On the other hand, there are Baptist churches and bodies that cooperate with no interdenominational venture of any description. This variegated pattern is quite baffling to those outside the Free Church tradition. Even when Baptists are cooperating constituents of a given ecumenical body, they are often suspect. Doubtless there are valid reasons which underlie such suspicion and fear. However, the verbal abuse to which some Baptist organizations have been subjected in the ecumenical press has no justification within the context of a Christian fraternity.

What are some of the factors operative within Baptist life which have given rise to this ambivalent situation? The dynamic of Baptist life is part of the explanation. Vigorous growth in areas of relative freedom has produced a heady wine that has torn asunder the Old World wine skins. Proliferation and even fragmentation of the Baptist witness has been one of the results. Baptists rival the Holiness movement in the variety of their denominational structures. Baptist individualism, congregational polity, differing doctrinal emphases, strong personalities, geographical and cultural isolation, limited educational attainments, and strong conservative tendencies with some interesting liberal sidelights contribute their share in creating a rather confused picture.

One must be careful not to discount the influence of nontheological factors in shaping the character of contemporary Baptist organizations. Baptists have been subject to many of the same pressures as other denominations, yet with differing reactions. Therefore, it is virtually impossible to generalize about Baptist relations to the ecumenical movement. To condemn some Baptist groups for participation or nonparticipation in the organizational embodiments of the ecumenical movement without an understanding of their theology, ecclesiology, or historical development is manifestly unfair. Such a procedure is unjustified on both rational and Christian grounds.

It is impossible to discuss the relation of all Baptist groups to the ecumenical movement. The lack of literature on the subject is the first hindrance to such an undertaking. But there is an abundance of source materials available on the major Baptist bodies of the world, which will make possible a rather complete historical survey of Baptist ecumenical relations. This, in turn, should increase immeasurably an understanding of Baptists on the part of Baptists and non-Baptists alike. Doubtless some previously formed stereotypes will remain in the reader's mind, but those based on prejudice, partial information or misinformation should be discarded for a more accurate image.

British Baptists

Perhaps the most ecumenically-minded of all Baptists are the British Baptists. Very early in their history English Baptists fostered a spirit of interdenominational fellowship and cooperation. Several factors converged to produce this pattern.

Baptists were only gradually distinguished from Anabaptists on the one hand and Congregationalists on the other. In order not to force their newly formed convictions on others, baptized and unbaptized members were sometimes found in the same church.[1] Again, Baptists, as other English dissenters, have developed their denominational characteristics within a state-church environment.

Often companions in adversity, the free churches have quite naturally cultivated rather close ties.[2] Some early Baptist churches continued an open membership and open communion policy which

---

[1]The churches of Jessey in Southwork and John Bunyan in Bedford are two cases in point.

[2]Torbet, *A History of the Baptists*, p. 150.

tended to retard the growth of strong Baptist convictions. Even to-day there are members of English Baptist churches who have never received believer's baptism.[3]

Baptists in Great Britain have suffered heavy reverses in the present century. There has been a noticeable loss of vitality, conviction, and evangelism. It does not help a great deal to point out that this spiritual decline in England is a common malady of religion in general and of nonconformity in particular.

English Baptist ecclesiology is also undergoing something of a revolution. The Baptist Union of Great Britain and Ireland has developed such a centralized connectionalism that it has taken over many of the functions formerly belonging to the local church. In fact, British Baptists refer increasingly to the Baptist Union as "the Baptist Church."[4] It is not difficult to understand that appeal which the ecumenical movement has for those whose spiritual resources seem virtually depleted in the face of the twentieth-century theological breakdown.

Early Interdenominational Ventures

Interdenominational gatherings which were to lead toward the formation of the first free church council were held as early as 1892. The Baptists, led by Alexander Maclaren and John Clifford, were quite prominent in these informal meetings. In 1893 a Free Church Congress was held in Manchester. A communion service brought the Congress to a close. By 1896, the vague interdenominationalism had crystallized sufficiently to warrant the creation of the National Council of the Evangelical Free Churches.[5]

With the coming of John Howard Shakespeare to the Baptist Union as secretary in 1898, English Baptist life began to move with an accelerated pace toward the nascent ecumenical movement. During the earlier years of his administration, Shakespeare impressed his fellow Baptists with his dedication to the Baptist cause, his executive ability, and his preference for democratic procedure.[6]

Within a few years, however, English Baptists came to the pain-

---

[3]Payne, *The Fellowship of Believers*, p. 84.

[4] See *ibid.*, pp. 80-84, for confirmation of this description of English Baptist life.

[5]Payne, *The Baptist Union*, p. 150.

[6]Underwood, *A History of the English Baptists*, p. 252.

ful realization that they were either mistaken in their earlier estimate of Shakespeare or that he had changd drastically. He has been charged with duplicity. Described as "an autocrat to his fingertips," Shakespeare soon reached the conclusion that the free churches were too individualistic. He then proceeded to advocate a union of all free churches, visualizing a "United Free Church of England as the counterpart of the established church."[7]

In later years he even advocated union with the Church of England at the price of historic Baptist principles. His views were set forth in *The Churches At the Cross-roads* (1918) in which he declared that denominationalism is dead. Christianity's only hope in England, according to Shakespeare, was "a united church." In order to achieve this union, he expressed himself willing to accept the Anglican episcopacy and reordination.[8]

Shakespeare had apparently become so enamored with his dream of "reunion" that he lost touch with the rank and file of English Baptists. His proposals invoked a storm of protest in which the veteran Baptist leader John Clifford joined.

Clifford clearly spoke the mind of the majority when he advocated a basic unity of the spirit, while rejecting corporeal union based on compromise. He saw no conflict between a vigorous denominational life and spiritual unity which centers in the lordship of Christ and expresses itself in the love of the brethren. The opposition to Shakespeare's position was formidable. In the mounting crisis, his dream was shattered, and with it his health. He resigned his office in 1924 and died four years later.[9]

The autocratic rule of Shakespeare produced an inevitable reaction. Even though British Baptists were represented at Edinburgh in 1910 and at Geneva in 1920, they declined the invitation of the Faith and Order movement to participate in its conference at Lausanne in 1927. Instead, the Baptist Union sent a copy of its "Reply to the Lambeth Appeal" which had been adopted by the Union in 1926. Since the "Reply" is an official document of English Baptists relative to the ecumenical movement, it assumes unusual importance for this discussion.

The "Reply" was forged upon the anvil of historical circum-

[7]*Ibid.*
[8]*Ibid.*, pp. 252-53.
[9]*Ibid.*, p. 253.

stances growing out of the controversy over Shakespeare's proposals. At the height of his influence, the Anglicans felt it a particularly opportune time to press for reunion. They were assured of sympathetic cooperation from Shakespeare, who also wielded considerable power among other noncomformists through the Federal Council of the Evangelical Free Churches, which had taken the place of the more loosely organized National Council in 1919.

It was in 1920 that the bishops of the Church of England, attending the Lambeth Conference, issued the "Appeal to All Christian People." The "Appeal" contained nothing really new. It was a reaffirmation of the Lambeth Quadrilateral statement in 1888. The minimal basis for reunion, they declared, involved the acceptance of the Holy Scriptures as the Word of God, the Nicene Creed, the two sacraments "ministered with unfailing use of Christ's words of institution and of the elements ordained by Him," and the historic episcopate.[10] A presentation of the "Appeal" was made personally by the Archbishop of York before the Baptist Union Assembly in April, 1921. Baptists were quick to react. Courteously, but firmly, they rejected the Anglican overtures. However, the official reply was not forthcoming until 1926.

The "Reply" itself is a definitive document. It attempts to state in the clearest possible terms the Baptist position relative to both reunion with the Church of England and cooperative efforts among Christians in general. At the outset, the British Baptists affirm their faith in the universal church composed of all believers, "which He founded, of which He is the only Head, and in which He dwells by His Spirit, so that though made up of many communions, organized in various modes, and scattered throughout the world it is yet one in Him." The Assembly also declared that a particular church of Christ may be found "wherever companies of believers unite as churches on the ground of a confession of personal faith."

The assembled Baptists affirmed their primary allegiance to the Lord Jesus Christ "as the sole and absolute authority in all matters pertaining to faith and practice, as revealed in the Scriptures. . . . Moreover, it is plain to us that the headship and sole authority of our Lord in His Church excludes any relations with the State

---

[10]Haselmayer, p. 10.

as may impair its liberty. This view of the Church determines our attitude towards the special issues raised by the Lambeth Appeal."

The Assembly then proceeded to reject categorically the Anglican views of the sacraments and the ministry. "The baptism of infants," they asserted, "subverts the conception of the church as the fellowship of believers." About the ministry, the Baptists told the Anglicans:

Our doctrine of the Church determines our conception of the ministry. We hold firmly the priesthood of all believers, and therefore have no separated order of priests. The ministry is for us a gift of the Spirit to the Church, and is an office involving both the inward call of God and the commission of the Church. We can discover no ground for believing that such a commission can be given only through an episcopate, and we hold that the individual Church is competent to confer it.[11]

While rejecting union with the Anglicans as an impossibility for Baptists, the Assembly expressed its willingness to explore federation. "We therefore are prepared to join the Church of England in exploring the possibility of a federation of equal and autonomous Churches.[12]

The "Reply" was sent to Lambeth in lieu of official representation. However, the document was judged out of order, and the assembled delegates were never appraised of its existence. The position assumed by British Baptists as reflected in the "Reply" may still be representative of the Baptist Union. Writing in 1945, Underwood, an English Baptist historian, declared that the Baptist Reply to the Lambeth Appeal still represents the "convictions of the overwhelming majority of Baptists, not only in England, but throughout the world." He expressed a commonly held Baptist conviction when he wrote:

For them, spiritual unity is more valuable than corporate union. Corporate union might mean a dull uniformity, whereas spiritual unity is compatible with diversity. They do not believe that the world would be impressed by the spectacle of all Christians united in one ecclesiastical body, but they are confident that it would be moved by the sight of all Christians expressing their common life in Christ by loving one another

---

[11]Payne, *The Baptist Union,* pp. 280-81. The "Reply" is printed in full in Appendix IX.
[12]*Ibid.,* p. 282.

and co-operating together, in spite of differences of emphasis and organi-zation.[13]

The Baptist Union had sufficiently recovered from the unhappy days of the Shakespeare controversy to send official delegates to the next round of ecumenical conferences in Edinburgh and Oxford. In fact, the Secretary of the Union, Melbourn Evans Aubrey, was a member of the committee of thirty-five from which came the proposal to organize a World Council of Churches.[14]

In 1942 there was organized in the Council Chamber of the Baptist Church House a British Council of Churches with the Archbishop of Canterbury, William Temple, as president. The formation of the Council followed a period in which the free churches found themselves cooperating more closely than ever with the Church of England. Against the better judgment of some, in 1941 the free church leaders agreed to unite with the Anglicans in advocating religious instruction in the public schools and the ac-ceptance of government aid up to 50 percent of the cost on the construction of parochial school buildings. Following this unpre-cedented era of cooperation, Baptists, at the insistence of Arch-bishop William Temple, once again in 1947 entered into con-versations over reunion with the Anglicans. The talks were broken off in 1950 without any concrete achievements.

In the meantime, British Baptists took two significant actions on the ecumenical front. They participated in the formation of the World Council of Churches and one year later reaffirmed their position relative to union as set forth in the "Reply" of 1926. The Baptist Unions of Scotland and of Wales, as well as that of Great Britain, accepted the invitation to join the World Council of Churches. However, within each of the unions opposition to par-ticipation developed. It was strongest in the Baptist Union of Scot-land, where a one vote majority managed to champion the cause of ecumenical Christianity. Subsequently both the Baptist Unions of Scotland and Wales have withdrawn from the World Council. The Baptist Union of Ireland has never been affiliated with the World Council of Churches.[15]

---

[13]*Op. cit.,* p. 263.
[14]Payne, *The Baptist Union,* p. 200.
[15]Roberts-Thomson, *With Hands Outstretched,* p. 118.

However, the British Baptist Union is apparently firmly committed to the ecumenical movement, with certain reservations. Payne, secretary of the Baptist Union of Great Britain and Ireland, is a member of the Central Committee of the World Council of Churches and an ardent supporter of the ecumenical movement. Registering his appreciation for what membership in the World Council has meant to the free churches of England, he writes,

Recent decades have given the ecclesiastical situation in this country a far wider reference than a merely national one. Both the Free Churches and the Church of England are now communions of ecumenical range. The greatly improved relationships in this country have come in considerable measure from the opening up of world horizons and from the impetus of what is usually described as "the Ecumenical Movement," which in turn has been largely the product of the striking missionary expansion of the Church during the past hundred and fifty years.[16]

In spite of the glowing tribute which Payne offers the ecumenical movement, he admits the ecumenical era in England has been one of increasing decline and continuous setbacks.

Our special concern here, however, is with the situation in England, and it must be frankly admitted that the last forty years have seen a decline in the influence of the Free Churches. They have been badly hit by the general decrease in church attendance. Their impact on society has been less than in the previous fifty years. Almost all the Free Church bodies have become more centralized. . . There has been a growing sense of frustration and friction in many quarters, a loss of confidence, an uncertainty as to the future.[17]

Payne possibly reflects the thinking of English Baptists generally when he expresses his opinion on the possibilities of corporate union. In referring to union talks now in progress between the Presbyterians and Congregationalists, the Church of England and the Church of Scotland, and the Free Churches of Wales, he writes: "The Baptists are probably the community for whom recent developments create the greatest difficulties. Though theologians of various traditions, including Karl Barth and Emil Brunner, have criticised the current practice of infant baptism, there is little in-

---

[16]*The Free Church Tradition in the Life of England,* p. 133.
[17]*Ibid.,* p. 134.

dication that most Baptists believe that their convictions will allow them to unite organically with any other body."[18]

The American Baptist Convention

Baptists of the American Baptist Convention have a strong tradition of interdenominational cooperation. During the Colonial period there was little opportunity for Baptists to demonstrate this side of their character, since they were the victims of oppression. However, in Rhode Island and Pennsylvania their principles of religious freedom made possible a coexistence which was virtually impossible elsewhere.

When the Colonial authorities brought to the attention of the city council in Philadelphia that the Roman Catholics had erected a meeting house "wherein mass was openly celebrated by a Catholic priest, contrary to the laws of England," the Baptists and some others claimed that "Catholics and all other sects were protected by the laws which had been established by William Penn and that all were equally entitled to religious liberty."[19]

The first Jewish synagogue in the New World was established in Providence, Rhode Island, where the Baptist principles of separation of church and state made possible many divergent forms of religion without fear of persecution. Even the Roman Catholics were not denied this freedom. Roger Williams states this position in the clearest terms.

I confess in this plea for freedom to all consciences in matters (merely) of worship, I have impartially pleaded for the freedom of the consciences of the papists themselves, the greatest enemies and persecutors (in Europe) of the saints and truths of Jesus: yet I have pleaded for no more than is their due and right.[20]

When Baptists themselves were permitted to crawl out of the Colonial catacombs, they demonstrated their willingness to work with others. They were prominent in the first interdenominational mission society formed in the United States. Also they contributed liberally to the foreign mission enterprise through the American Board of Commissioners before the Triennial Convention was or-

---

[18]*Ibid.*, p. 137.
[19]Spencer, *The Early Baptists of Philadelphia*, pp. 63-64.
[20]Bainton, *The Travail of Religious Liberty*, p. 222.

ganized. Early Baptist educational institutions made ample provision for students, professors, and trustees of other denominations. Before 1845, this spirit of interdenominational cooperation comprised the heritage of all Baptists in the United States.

Three major factors predisposed Northern Baptists (American Baptists after 1950) to be favorably inclined toward the ecumenical movement.

The first of these was the population upheaval caused by the vast influx of European immigrants into areas where Baptists and other evangelicals had been predominant. Within a relatively short time the cities on the Eastern seaboard were transformed. The new citizens brought their Old World culture with its religion to their new homeland and rapidly succeeded in establishing enclaves of Irish, Italian, Polish, and German Catholics, which eventually affected the political and educational life of the community. Quite naturally, Baptists and other Protestants sought to cultivate closer ties with one another in face of the new challenge which they felt inadequate to meet alone.

A second factor, which has been far more determinative in the American Baptist Convention than in other Baptist bodies in the United States, is that of theological liberalism. Arising in the latter part of the nineteenth century, its full impact was not felt in this country until the early twenties.

Walter Rauschenbusch, Shailer Mathews, and Harry Emerson Fosdick personified among Baptists this liberal Christianity that appeared to threaten the very foundations of the faith. Certain seminaries became captive to the new theology. In the North, the University of Chicago, Crozier, Colgate-Rochester, and Andover Newton became centers of liberal agitation. Consequently, denominational walls were easily breached all along the line. Baptist seminaries and churches were merged with those of other denominations. The dual alignment of Baptist churches with Congregationalist as well as Baptist associations and the federation of weak Baptist congregations with those of other denominational affiliations became increasingly frequent.

The third factor affecting denominational life among American Baptists is that of connectionalism. Baptists of the North, out of suspicion for all extrachurch organizations, early in their history expressed a decided preference for the society method of denominational organization to that of the association. The society method had carried within itself the promise of freedom, for it left the churches free from any possible outside control, but it also freed the society of control by the churches.[21]

The door was cracked in the interest of an interdenominational outreach. When the Northern Baptist Convention first came into existence, it was little more than a loose federation of autonomous societies made up of interested individuals over which the denomination exercised little authority. The societies early sought alignment with various interdenominational bodies.

The members of the Northern Convention were informed at their annual meeting in 1910 of plans which the Foreign Mission Society had made to send representatives to the proposed International Missionary Conference at Edinburgh.[22] The society, in taking this action, was simply following a precedent already established by the Northern Convention relative to the organizational expressions of the ecumenical movement. In 1908, a year after the Convention was formed, it had become a charter member of the Federal Council of Churches of Christ in America. Since that time, Northern Baptists have had representatives at all major ecumenical conferences. However, the Convention's relationship to the ecumenical movement has not been maintained without opposition.

The Federal Council was the object of attack from within the Convention almost from the beginning. The Convention's allocation to the Federal Council budget was reduced in 1932 to $3,750. This was the year in which the fortunes of the Federal Council among Northern Baptists sank to their lowest level. The following year a special investigating committee, appointed for the purpose of examining the Convention's relationship with the Council, recommended that the representation be continued. However, as a sop to the discontented churches, certain guarantees were made concerning finances and representation on the Council.

Possibly due to Baptist criticism, the Federal Council was reorganized in 1933 and a Baptist, Dr. Albert W. Beaven, was made president. Some Baptists were still unreconciled to the trend of events within the Convention, of which Federal Council membership was viewed as symptomatic. These ultrafundamentalists left the Convention in 1933 and organized the General Association of Reg-

---

[21]Baker, *Relations Between Northern and Southern Baptists*, pp. 88 ff.
[22]*Annual of the Northern Baptist Convention*, 1910, p. 41.

ular Baptists. Many of those who remained within the Convention determined to exert all possible influence against continued affiliation with the Federal Council.

The Convention went on record in 1939 that Northern Baptists could continue their relationship with the ecumenical organizations only if "their unique and historic Baptist principles" were recognized.[23] For a decade thereafter controversy continued between the various factions within the Convention over liberalism and the role of the Convention in ecumenical Christianity.

In 1947 a Committee on Interdenominational Relationships was appointed to study the relationship of the Northern Baptist Convention to the Federal Council and the proposed World Council. A counter move by a vocal minority to lead the Convention to secure affiliation with the National Association of Evangelicals failed.

The duly appointed committee brought its "Report" to the Convention in 1948. The "Report" offered a compromise solution which it hoped would satisfy those who were reluctant to continue ecumenical relations without jeopardizing the Convention's full participation in the organizational life of the movement. The report was presented by its chairman, Edwin H. Pruden. Its temporizing nature is revealed by the opening paragraph.

> Your committee on Interdenominational Relations was assigned one of the most difficult and serious responsibilities imaginable, namely, the task of devising a means of preserving fully the absolute liberty and autonomy of the local church while maintaining our denomination's rightful place in co-operative Christianity.[24]

At the outset, the committee recognized the right of churches opposed to participation in the activities of the Federal Council to withhold financial support from the Council without affecting their own relationship to the Convention. A recommendation was made that the Convention meet its financial obligations to the Council by designated gifts for that purpose and from the distributable undesignated funds of the churches which had "voiced no objections to this arrangement." Provision was made for the churches which

---

[23]Torbet, "Baptists and the Ecumenical Movement," *The Chronicle*, XVIII (April, 1955), 91.

[24]*Year Book of the Northern Baptist Convention*, 1948, pp. 66-67.

so desired to register their opposition to the Federal Council in the denomination's *Year Book*.

The fourth recommendation quite clearly set the limitations of cooperation beyond which the Convention was unwilling to go. The Committee recommended:

That all our churches be assured that there is no thought of organic church union or the creation of an authoritarian ecclesiastical hierarchy in our support of the Federal Council, but rather are we seeking solely to give that measure of Christian co-operation which might rightly be expected of all Christians in a day like this.[25]

Four additional recommendations affirmed the continued cooperation of the Northern Baptist Convention with the Federal Council, and approval of the formation of the proposed National Council as well as the recently organized World Council of Churches. The recommendations also provided for a wider representation from the Convention in the deliberative meetings of the Federal Council with the traveling expenses of the representatives paid by the denomination, "in order that they may attend the meetings regularly and thereby make our Baptist position known and felt in the larger Christian fellowship."[26]

The "Report of the Committee on Interdenominational Relations" has the same significance for Northern Baptists as the "Reply" had for English Baptists. It meant that Northern Baptists were definitely committed to ecumenical Christianity with certain specified limitations. It also meant that a denomination with a strong congregational ecclesiology had worked out a modus operandi to the satisfaction of the majority whereby it could cooperate with the National and World Councils. The adoption of the "Report" by the Convention virtually closed the door on a large group of schismatic brethren known as the Conservative Baptist Association which had begun a withdrawal from the Convention in 1947.

It now appears that 1948 was the pivotal year for Baptists of the American Baptist Convention in the history of Baptist ecumenical relations. Even though no serious opposition has arisen to question the propriety of the Convention's participation in the ecumenical movement, the Convention has reaffirmed on four different

---

[25]*Ibid.*, p. 67.
[26]*Ibid.*

occasions the position taken in 1948. The last of these was in 1960 at Rochester, New York.

Some in the American Baptist Convention have interpreted "the overwhelming vote" at Rochester as a green light to corporeal union. This is the interpretation offered by George D. Younger, in an editorial on Baptists and the ecumenical movement:

Have we not, with the overwhelming vote at Rochester, finally reached the point where we no longer have to prove that "enlightened self-interest" is needed to justify our taking part in conversations about the unity of the church? Are we afraid of unity, or have we come to the place where we can serve our Lord by discussion of questions of co-operation, of mutual recognition and intercommunion, and even of corporate unity with other members of the Body of Christ?[27]

It would be a mistake to read too much into the 1960 action of the American Baptist Convention at Rochester. However, it does indicate that ecumenical Christianity in its present stage of development enjoys far more confidence among Baptists of the American Convention than it could command a decade ago.

This change in climate is the result of a number of interesting developments. First, the more adamant and vocal fundamentalists had left the Convention by 1951. Second, the merger talks with the Disciples, which had involved the Convention in continual controversy for some years, came to an end in 1950. And, third, the fears that the World Council of Churches was moving toward a superchurch, which appeared quite formidable in 1948, have largely disappeared.

John W. Bradbury in a report of the Second Assembly of the World Council of Churches at Evanston editorialized:

Since 1948, the voices which talked about "a world church," and which aroused outside opposition, have been silenced. Valid criticism, based on the suspicioned objectives, had the effect of producing corrective clarifications. At Evanston, Dr. Visser 't Hooft and other officials of the Council supported the published preparatory statement that "the World Council of Churches is not and must never become a Super-Church." [28]

Even though a few voices may be raised to the contrary, it is

---

[27]"Are We Afraid of Unity?" *Foundations,* IV (April, 1961), 101.
[28]*Watchman Examiner,* Vol. 136, No. 37 (September 16, 1954), 840.

quite evident that the majority of the American Baptist Convention has no interest in organic union. It is also apparent that most feel that they are not endangering their distinctive Baptist witness by affiliation with the various organizational expressions of the ecumenical movement.

Other Baptists Witness Within

The largest Baptist bodies to affiliate with the World Council of Churches are two major Negro Baptist conventions of the United States. The National Baptist Convention of America, numbering approximately 2,700,000 members, has belonged to the World Council of Churches since its beginning. The much larger National Baptist Convention, U.S.A., Inc., with some 5,000,000 members, has only recently joined. The very small Seventh-Day Baptist General Conference with a membership of approximately 6,000 completes the roster of Baptist denominational bodies of the United States within the World Council.

On the continent of Europe, out of the twenty-three national Baptist bodies, only three participate in the World Council. The Baptists of Denmark, the Netherlands, and Hungary now belong to the World Council. In addition, the Baptists of Sweden, Czechoslovakia, Poland, and Rumania belong to their respective national councils.

In the remainder of the Baptist world the rather small national conventions of Burma, New Zealand, and, most recently, the Cameroun are members of the World Council. Numerically this means that approximately 9,225,000 Baptists belong to national organizations which are a part of the World Council of Churches.

Perhaps these figures are not too signficant. In fact, they may be quite deceptive since they cannot present an accurate gauge of ecumenical concern. For example, the National Baptist Convention of America, which claims a membership of 2,700,000, sent no delegates to New Delhi. On the other hand, in spite of the official denominational positions of Australian, Canadian, and Southern Baptists, which for various reasons decline World Council membership, there is much interest in the ecumenical movement within these bodies. The Baptist Convention of Ontario and Quebec, in which ecumenical interest has been most evident, has run into difficulty. For some time the Baptists of this convention have been cooperating with the United Church of Canada in the production of Sunday School lesson materials. However, due to the widespread dissatisfaction with these materials and the increased pressure for corporate union, these Baptists have recently withdrawn.

Ecumenical interests in Australia seem to be on the decline. E. Roberts-Thomson, after writing a book on the ecumenical movement which constituted a vigorous plea for Baptist participation, has become a Presbyterian. This step followed his ouster as principal of the Baptist Theological College of New South Wales. The fortunes of ecumenicity within the Southern Baptist Convention are difficult to assess. Before such an evaluation can be projected, an attempt to understand the relationship of the Convention and its agencies with various ecumenical concerns will be made from the historical perspective.

8

The Baptist Witness
Outside the World Council

Of the approximately twenty-six million Baptists who comprise the Baptist world constituency, almost two thirds are affiliated with denominational bodies quite unrelated to the ecumenical organizations. Numbered among those still outside the World Council are the relatively large national bodies of the Latin American countries, the largest of which is Brazil with more than two hundred thousand members. Of Europe's twenty-three national bodies, twenty remain outside the World Council. Russia, with some half a million or more, and Germany with a hundred thousand are the largest of these. Canada, Australia, most of Asia and the Philippines, for various reasons, are not affiliated with the World Council. Within the United States the growing Conservative Baptist Association and the large and influential Southern Baptist Convention, numbering approximately eleven million members, are not directly related to either the National or the World Council of Churches. Because of its size and importance, the major portion of this chapter is given to a discussion of the Southern Baptist Convention and its relationship to ecumenical Christianity.

The Southern Baptist Convention

The position of the Southern Baptist Convention relative to the ecumenical movement continues to be misunderstood. It is often misrepresented even by Baptists. No clear understanding of the relationship of Southern Baptists and ecumenical Christianity is possible without some knowledge of the basic structure of Southern Baptist denominational life and its development within the historical vortex.

From 1814 to 1845, American Baptists worked together within

143

the organizational framework of the General Missionary Convention of the Baptist Denomination in the United States of America for Foreign Missions, better known as the Triennial Convention. The Triennial Convention was actually a society and not a convention.[1] Following a pattern of Baptist connectionalism generally preferred by Baptists of the North after unsuccessfully attempting to become an all-inclusive denominational organization, the Triennial Convention returned by 1826 to its original nature as a foreign mission society. With the formation of the Southern Baptist Convention, a more denominational and centralized national Baptist organization came into existence. W. B. Johnson was the chief promoter of the plan. Speaking in Edgefield, South Carolina, Johnson set forth the alternatives which Southern Baptists, who contemplated a new organization, faced.

I invite your attention to the consideration of two plans. The one is, that which has been adopted for years past, viz: Separate and independent bodies for the prosecution of each object. Your familiarity with the plan renders any remark upon it unnecessary. The other proposes one Convention, embodying the whole Denomination, together with separate and distinct Boards for each object of benevolent enterprise, located at different places, and all amenable to the Convention.[2]

The second of the two alternatives appealed to the majority of the members of the Consultative Convention meeting in Augusta, Georgia. A constitution was adopted which provided for one Convention with many functions. The new Convention, which embodied the associational method, lent itself to a far more centralized denominational development than would have been possible under the society plan. Thus a foundation was laid whereby churches with a strong congregational polity could work together effectively without violating the jealously guarded independence of the local church. The boards of the Convention, unlike the societies, could not act independently. Through duly elected messengers the churches would exercise authority over the Convention and the Convention could control the boards. The Convention was to have no authority over the churches.

Once created in the throes of a cultural and ideological con-

[1]Barnes, *The Southern Baptist Convention, 1845-1953*, p. 8.
[2]*Ibid.*, p. 27.

flict, there was some question as to whether the Convention would survive the crisis which brought about its formation. Serious threats to its continued existence came from the older societies. The Home Mission Society still pressed its claims in the South as well as in the rest of the nation.

Many of the Convention's churches felt more strongly tied to the Home Mission Society than to the Home Mission Board. Only gradually did the Home Mission Board of the Southern Baptist Convention displace the Society in the affections and loyalty of Southern Baptists. The American Baptist Publication Society continued to supply Sunday School literature for the majority of Baptist churches in the South until the turn of the century.

A series of organizations sprang up during the years to compete unsuccessfully with the Society. As late as 1892, the Society opened a branch house in Dallas for the distribution of its literature, as well as that of the recently organized Sunday School Board of the Southern Baptist Convention (1891).[3] Branch houses had long existed in Atlanta and St. Louis. Like the Home Mission Board, the Sunday School Board clung to a precarious lease on life in the face of rather formidable threats to its existence.

The Society commanded a large and loyal following in the South. As late as 1896 it appeared that it might yet win out over the newly created Board, but by 1897 the Board emerged from the struggle triumphant and the Society steadily lost ground until its literature was completely displaced by that of the Convention's own Sunday School Board. Doubtless, if the Convention had never been organized, Baptist denominational life in the South could not have developed as it did. And if either the Home Mission Board or the Sunday School Board had failed to displace their northern counterparts, it is questionable whether the division of Baptists into northern and southern conventions would have continued.

The struggles involved in the development of the boards of the Convention served to increase a sense of denominational integrity and destiny that continues to characterize the Southern Baptist Convention. This was evident as early as 1896, when someone for the Sunday School Board replied to the Society's offer to enter into a cooperative publication enterprise for the Baptist constituency of the nation:

---

[3]*Ibid.*, p. 93.

In conclusion, we venture to express the conviction that it is possible for you and us to mark out a plan for cooperation in which we could conduct each his respective work in a way that would render no injustice to either and be helpful to both. We have always held ourselves ready for this and are willing to make any concession toward it, provided always the Board itself be not marred as to its integrity, or weakened in its efficiency for meeting the great responsibilities God has laid upon us and attaining the great possibilities which God has opened to us here in the South.[4]

In the last half of the nineteenth century, sectional, cultural, and theological factors combined to create in the Southern Baptist Convention an aggressive, missionary, and evangelistic expression of Christianity that has known few parallels in history. One of the factors which helped to mold the theological and ecclesiological outlook of the Convention was the Landmark movement. The Landmark movement was not an isolated phenomenon limited to the confines of Baptist life in the South, as it is sometimes pictured. Rather, it was as Barnes has characterized it, a "Baptist type of high churchism."[5]

Landmarkism sprang up in the wake of a number of similar developments in other denominations. The Oxford movement was in full swing. The Mercersburg theology had become a divisive factor in the Evangelical and Reformed Church, and Alexander Campbell's movement which questioned the validity of all denominations was making vast inroads into Baptist ranks. In a sense, Landmarkism was a reaction to all of this. However, even though innovating in its tendencies, it was not entirely new.

As Barnes has suggested, the movement "precipitated the several elements of succession that had been held in solution in Baptist life."[6] No discussion of the Landmark movement can long omit the name of its greatest exponent and chief architect, J. R. Graves. In the very year of the Convention's birth, the young Baptist minister, originally a Congregationalist, born and reared in New England, moved from Kentucky to Nashville, Tennessee, where he joined the First Baptist Church of that city. For the next half century he became the storm center of a controversy that at times threatened

---

[4]*Ibid.,* pp. 95-96.
[5]*Ibid.,* p. 103.
[6]*Ibid.*

the life of the Convention itself. But the Convention survived, and while rejecting the more overt features of Landmarkism, could not completely throw off its influence.

The movement received its name from a tract written by J. M. Pendleton entitled "An Old Landmark Re-set." The tract presented a discussion of the third and fourth questions of five questions which Graves had offered for discussion to a group of interested Baptists at Cotton Grove, Tennessee, June 24, 1851. They are:

1st. Can Baptists consistently, with their principles or the scriptures, recognize those societies, not organized according to the pattern of the Jerusalem church, but possessing a different *government*, different *officers*, a different *class of membership*, different *ordinances, doctrines and practices*, as the Church of Christ?

2nd. Ought they to be called Gospel Churches or Churches in a religious sense?

3rd. Can we consistently recognize the ministers of such irregular and unscriptural bodies, as gospel ministers in their official capacity?

4th. Is it not virtually recognizing them as official ministers to invite them into our pulpits, or by any other act that would or could be construed into such a recognition?

5th. Can we consistently address as brethren, those professing Christianity who not only have not the doctrines of Christ and walk not according to his commandments, but are arrayed in direct and bitter opposition to them?[7]

If these questions are indicative of the major concern of Graves and his followers, it is obvious that ecclesiology was the major issue of the controversy. According to Landmark teaching, the word "church" in New Testament usage is always local. The church at Jerusalem was made up of those who also composed the kingdom of God. Therefore to be in a true church was to be in the kingdom of God. The aggregate of Baptist churches comprise the kingdom.

According to Graves's logic, only Baptist ministers were true ministers, and only the ordinances administered by them constituted valid ordinances. Certain characteristics began to distinguish the followers of Graves from ordinary Baptists. Only Baptist baptism administered by an ordained Baptist minister upon the authority of a Baptist church to a believer by immersion was a valid baptism. Any other baptism, even though of a believer and by immersion,

---

[7]*Ibid.*, p. 104.

was declared "alien." Local church communion for the members of
that particular church was vigorously championed. "But the members of no one church have a right to come to the table spread
in another church, though of the same faith and order."[8]

However, the "taproot" of Landmarkism was a theory of Baptist
succession. The documentary support for this theory was found in
Orchard's *History of Foreign Baptists,* which Graves republished
in 1855. Orchard, an English Baptist historian, proposed to show
that Baptist churches had existed from Jerusalem and the first
century in an unbroken historical continuity to the present. The
historical argument was deemed necessary to bolster the claim that
Baptist churches are the only New Testament churches. Since the
Jerusalem church was a local church and Christ had promised
eternal perpetuity to his church, then a succession of local churches
was guaranteed by Christ himself, according to the Landmarkers.

Contrary to popular opinion, the Landmark movement did not
spring out of the fertile minds of Graves, Pendleton, and Dayton,
de novo.

Certain elements of the system had long been present in Baptist
life, perhaps from the beginning of the modern Baptist movement.
The emphasis on the local church might well be the legacy of
original Congregationalism to the Baptists. Henry Jacob's catechism
of 1605 entitled *Principles & Foundations of Christian Religion*
at times sounds strikingly like Graves.

Henry Jacob, the "father of congregationalism," as Perry Miller referred to him, wrote in the same year he published his catechism, "I
affirme that No Synod under the Gospell hath power by God's ordinance
to prescribe & rule Ecclesiastically sundry whole Churches if they sever-
ally consent not."

The Jacob catechism thus explicitly presents the essentials of Congregational Puritanism. In summary, (1) the visible church is a particular
congregation, never a diocesan or national body; (2) the church is
formally gathered through mutual covenanting; (3) the church is composed of holy or regenerate believers; (4) the supreme head of the
church is Jesus Christ, from whom the church has immediate and full
power to order its entire life, without determination or control by any
overhead body.[9]

---

[8]*Ibid.,* p. 107.
[9]Smith, Handy, and Loetscher, *American Christianity,* p. 84.

However, for the first time, these elements were welded together into an effective, rigid, and logically tight system. It gathered momentum across the South to the extent that "Graves could boast in 1880 that only one Baptist weekly in the South (*The Religious Herald* of Virginia), out of a total of sixteen weeklies, editorially approved an 'alien immersion and pulpit affiliation.' "[10] Graves further declared that throughout the "whole South . . . 'Great West' and Northwest there was a 'heavy drift of sentiment . . . in favor of Baptist churches doing their own preaching, ordaining, baptizing, and communioning."[11]

At one time or another Graves and his disciples were in open conflict with the Convention over the policies of the Foreign Mission Board, the Bible Board, and the basis of representation in the Southern Baptist Convention. His challenges were finally successfully repulsed.

The force of the Landmark movement within the life of the Convention was greatly weakened by secessions sparked by the Gospel Mission movement of the 1880s, the Baptist Missionary Association organized in 1924, and the North American Baptist Association of 1950. These new organizations drew heavily upon Baptist churches in Arkansas and Texas. However, the influence of Landmarkism is far from a negligible force within the life and thinking of many Southern Baptists. This persistent influence explains, in part, the strong denominational consciousness and lack of interest in ecumenical ventures by Southern Baptists. There have been many other factors which have predisposed Southern Baptists to follow strictly a denominational line of action.

The numerical success of Southern Baptists has made them far less conscious of the need for developing strong interdenominational ties than some other much smaller bodies. The vigorous evangelism that characterized the Separate Baptists in the mid-eighteenth century has become the special legacy of Southern Baptists. And up to the present, the predominantly rural character of the South has rendered "old-fashioned revival" efforts fruitful.

The Modernist-Fundamentalist controversy, which occupied the energies and time of many other denominations, was for the most

---

[10]Cited by Hugh Wamble, "Landmarkism: Doctrinaire Ecclesiology Among Baptists," in *Church History*, XXXIII (December, 1964), 443.
[11]*Ibid.*

part safely bypassed by Southern Baptists. Although the Convention lost some churches to Landmark and Fundamentalist factions, it managed to avoid the fragmentation of its membership by adhering rather closely to a conservative theology. Until recently there have been no large segments of new citizens to engulf the cities of the South. As a result of this combination of factors, the ecumenical movement has never had the appeal for Southern Baptists that it has held for some other Baptists.

Yet, Southern Baptists have not been unaware of the ecumenical movement. Before J. R. Graves was dead, the Convention proposed a conference on faith and order. "We respectfully propose to the general bodies of our brethren of other denominations to select representative scholars, who shall seek to determine just what is the teaching of the Bible on the leading points of differences of doctrine and polity between the denominations."

They also suggested that their conclusions "be widely published in all denominational papers, so that the Christian public may be thoroughly informed concerning Christian union."[12]

The proposal by Southern Baptists precipitated correspondence with the Disciples of Christ on the basis of Christian union which was not terminated until 1894.[13] A paper on Christian Union was presented to the Southern Baptist Convention in 1900 by I. T. Tichenor. The attention of the Convention was called once again to a consideration of interdenominational relations by the Home Mission Board in 1909.

The Board had been invited to join the recently organized Home Missions Council, but instead of accepting the invitation outright, the Board referred the matter to the Convention for advice. Upon this occasion, the Convention told the Home Mission Board that while it was desirous that the Board maintain fraternal relations with other home mission bodies, it could not approve of "any relations with other Boards which can possibly circumscribe our independence or liberty as to the fields which we are to occupy, or the methods we are to adopt . . . Our churches . . . are independent of each other. . . and therefore cannot be lined up in any sort of federation that can subject them to any external authority, or commit them to any special line of policy."

¹²Barnes, p. 271.
¹³*Ibid.*, pp. 271-72.

Summing up its position, the Convention told the Board: "We deem it inadvisable to form any relations with the Home Missions Council which can in any way abridge its freedom, warp its policy or embarrass its action in the future."[14]

The Board chose not to join.

The Foreign Mission Board of the Southern Baptist Convention was confronted with a similar problem in regard to its relationship with the Foreign Missions Conference of North America. From 1893 to 1919, the Board was represented at the annual meetings of the Conference by its secretaries, who judiciously abided by the policies enunciated by the Convention relative to the Home Missions Council in 1909.

In 1916, the Foreign Mission Board, in order to alleviate any possibility of misunderstanding concerning its relations with the Foreign Missions Conference, issued its own policy statement under the title of "A Statement of the Foreign Mission Board of 1916." In this statement the Board proceeded to assure the Convention that it would not "enter into nor be committed to any compact by which arbitrary territorial boundaries or divisions are fixed for its missionary operations."

The Board said: "We cannot subscribe to any agreement providing for an interchange of church letters contrary to the recognized custom among the Baptist churches of the South."

The Board also promised the Convention that it would not "engage in any form of cooperation, hospital, publication, educational or other missionary activity, which is not fully reported to the Convention, and which does not meet the approval of the Convention, under the auspices of which it operates, and to the instructions of which it is subject."[15]

From 1919 to 1938 the Board was not represented at the annual meetings of the Foreign Missions Conference. It joined the Conference in 1938 and participated actively in its affairs until the Conference expressed its desire to merge with the proposed National Council of Churches. The Board, in order not to hinder the Conference or violate its own principles, unanimously voted to withdraw in March, 1950.

During the period in which the Foreign Mission Board of the

---

[14]*Annual of the Southern Baptist Convention,* 1909 (Nashville), pp 27-28.
[15]*Ibid.,* 1916, pp. 120-22.

Southern Baptist Convention was defining its own policies relative to the ecumenical movement, the Convention was struggling with the same problem. Shortly after the International Missionary Conference in Edinburgh in 1910, Bishop Charles Henry Brent and his fellow Anglicans initiated procedures looking toward a World Conference on Faith and Order. After unanimous approval of the idea by the House of Bishops and the General Convention of the Protestant Episcopal Church of the United States of America, a commission was set up to issue invitations and to make plans for the proposed gathering. The Convention, upon a motion by J. M. Frost, referred its invitation to a committee of seven, headed by the president of the Convention, with instructions to make "a fraternal response, and, if it is found possible, to attend the proposed Conference as fraternal messengers."

This action by the Convention initiated a number of pronouncements on interdenominational relations and Christian union by various committees appointed by the Convention over the next quarter of a century. The first of these was that of the committee appointed to draft a reply to the Commission of the Protestant Episcopal Church on Faith and Order.

The committee reported to the Convention that a plan had been outlined for the work of the conference which was "stated in general terms and does not involve any compromise of principles on the part of those who participate." "It merely looks," they assured the Convention, "to a fraternal and general conference on doctrine and polity with a view to a better understanding and closer union among all Christians."[16]

To the Commission, the committee expressed its general agreement with the purpose and plan of the proposed conference and their satisfaction at the signs of "increasing spiritual unity among all the true followers of the Lord." They also expressed their skepticism in regard to the prospects of organic union.

They were frank to say "that many of the tenets which are regarded as divisive between ourselves and our brethren of other communions are and ever must be cherished and defended by us as the clear teachings of God's Word, and on these matters we can never evade or compromise."[17]

---

[16]*Ibid.*, 1912, p. 12
[17]*Ibid.*, pp. 13-14.

The most definitive of all pronouncements of the Southern Baptist Convention concerning the ecumenical movement was that adopted by the Convention in 1914, known as "The Pronouncement on Christian Union and Denominational Efficiency." It has three main divisions: the introduction, with some basic assumptions; the body, which approximates a confession of faith; and a conclusion, entitled "Denominational Efficiency."

In the body of the pronouncement the historic Baptist position is carefully articulated with reference to the following points: (1) the relation of the individual to God; (2) the nature of the change which takes place in the individual when right relations are established with God; (3) the initial ordinance whose observance is enjoined by Christ at the outset of the renewed life; (4) the nature of the spiritual fellowship and life of the church into which the renewed man enters; (5) the relation of the church to the state and to the world at large.

In the conclusion, the committee expressed its conviction that denominational efficiency could best be promoted "by preserving a complete autonomy at home and abroad, unembarrassed by entangling alliances with other bodies holding to different standards of doctrine and different views of church order."

The Convention, while saying no to the ecumenical movement, did not intend to close the door to other avenues of interdenominational cooperation, as indicated by the following statement: "We hereby avow in the most emphatic manner our desire and willingness to cooperate in all practicable ways in every cause of righteousness. We join hands with Christians of all names in seeking these common ends."[18]

From this point on, Southern Baptists consistently, with few exceptions, turned their energies toward advancing the cause of Christ through purely denominational channels.

At the close of World War I, an ill-fated ecumenical experiment appeared to confirm Southern Baptists in the rightness of their position. The Interchurch World Movement, with its grandiose plans for world evangelism, attempted to capitalize on what its leadership felt was an opportune time to unite the forces of Christendom.

Southern Baptists, who were becoming increasingly suspicious of

---

[18]*Ibid.*, 1914, pp. 73-78.

the rash of ecumenical organizations, rejected this latest bid for their support. They were still smarting under what many Baptists considered the unfair treatment of evangelicals by the Army. They accused the chaplaincy program of attempting to erase denominational lines among Protestants and of showing favoritism toward the Roman Catholics.

A committee headed by J. B. Gambrell was charged with the responsibility of drafting a reply to the overtures of the Interchurch World Movement. Several statements are characteristic of the spirit of the Convention at this time. The first of these is concerned with ecumenical organizations in general.

The numerous and various schemes of federation, cooperation, or other forms of common action by Christian denominations which have been proposed, cannot be ignored without discourtesy. Such of these schemes as involve a leadership which we cannot appoint or dismiss, but to which we must in some degree surrender our autonomy, are impossible for Baptists.

The Convention also told the leaders of the Interchurch World Movement that a Baptist sense of destiny prohibited the Convention from impairing its witness in any way.

Baptists have, as we profoundly believe, a distinct witness to bear and our message must in no way be mutilated or enfeebled. It is our inescapable duty to bear this message unabated to the uttermost part of the world. To syndicate our denomination with other denominations would impair, if it did not destroy, this message.

The committee speaking for the Convention expressed its opinion that a question of methodology also prohibited union.

The practical and important question emerges, even if fundamental difficulties are removed, whether we cannot better promote the Kingdom of Christ by pressing on along lines that are familiar to us, using methods that are approved among us and have been favored of God, than by venturing on vague schemes of general cooperation with other Christian organizations. We think we can.

The Convention rejected the idea that denominational divisions are sinful per se.

We prefer to think of the denominational spirit, not as hateful and intolerant, though it may sometimes degenerate into hate and intolerance, but rather, as we have known it as growing out of clear individual convictions, out of loyalty to Jesus Christ and His Word. Such a spirit is neither to be contemned nor condemned. The loss of it would be a calamity to the world and to the Kingdom of Jesus.[19]

The collapse of the Interchurch World Movement took place in the same year in which Southern Baptists launched their most ambitious financial drive, the Seventy-Five Million Campaign. This campaign, projected over a five-year period, attempted to raise seventy-five million dollars for missionary expansion and other denominational needs. Actually the campaign had the effect of increasing immeasurably the denominational consciousness of Southern Baptists. Southern Baptists became so engrossed in their revitalized program that the first round of ecumenical conferences, at Stockholm, Lausanne, and Jerusalem, came and went virtually unnoticed.

In 1932, the Executive Committee of the Southern Baptist Convention received an invitation to send representatives to another proposed World Conference on Faith and Order. The Executive Committee referred the matter to the Convention. Thereupon the Convention approved a motion by A. J. Barton that it decline to appoint delegates to the World Conference of Faith and Order and that the Executive Committee be authorized and instructed to say in reply to the invitation that "the Southern Baptist Convention has no authority in such matters, being only a Convention organized for missionary, educational and benevolent purposes with no ecclesiastical functions."[20]

In 1937, the invitation was again extended. Upon this occasion the Executive Committee referred the correspondents to the 1932 action of the Convention.

When the Convention met for its annual session, a motion was made by W. O. Carver "that this Convention request Dr. George W. Truett, who has an itinerary in Europe for this summer as President of the Baptist World Alliance, if at all practicable, to arrange to attend the Conference on Church, State, and Community at Oxford, July 12-26, 1937, as spokesman of this Convention."[21] Truett sent word to the Executive Committee that due to prior engagements, he could not attend the Life and Work Conference

---

[19]*Ibid.*, 1919, pp. 111-13.
[20]*Ibid.*, 1932, p. 71.
[21]*Ibid.*, 1937, p. 70.

at Oxford. The Executive Committee then proceeded to elect President John R. Sampey, of Southern Baptist Theological Seminary, the "official representative and spokesman of the Southern Baptist Convention" to attend the Oxford Conference, as well as the Edinburgh Conference on Faith and Order, whose invitation the Committee had turned down a few months before on the basis of the 1932 Convention action. Dr. and Mrs. J. D. Franks were also elected as representatives.[22]

Sampey and his party found the atmosphere of the ecumenical conferences quite uncongenial. He was invited to address the Faith and Order Conference at a Plenary Session on the last day. The Baptist stalwart brought his brief talk to a close with this statement:

I have the distinct impression that in the findings of the Conference, though we affirm more than once our belief in the Saviourhood of the Lord Jesus and his sole mediatorship, yet time and time again the church and the sacraments are thrust between the individual soul and the Saviour, as in some sense essential to his salvation.[23]

The Convention, in adopting the report of a committee appointed the previous year to study interdenominational relations, reiterated the position as defined in the 1914 pronouncement.[24]

In 1940, the Southern Baptist Convention declined an invitation to join the World Council of Churches. The grounds of its action was stated by the committee of which Truett was the chairman.

Directly replying to your invitation, permit us to advise that the Southern Baptist Convention is a voluntary association of Baptists for the purpose of eliciting, combining and directing the energies of our denomination in missionary activity at home and abroad, and in education and benevolent work throughout the world. Our Convention has no ecclesiological authority. It is in no sense the Southern Baptist Church.[25]

The position as enunciated by the committee upon this occasion was essentially the position assumed by the Convention in 1932. However, in this instance, the action of the Convention was not taken without open opposition. Nineteen messengers out of the several thou-

---

[22]Barnes, p. 285.
[23]In *Ibid.*, p. 286.
[24]*Annual of the Southern Baptist Convention, 1939*, p. 25.
[25]*Ibid.*, 1940, p. 99.

sand present stood to register opposition to the report of the committee. In asking for the rising vote, the dissenters created an opportunity to express their convictions on the matter.

While we are fundamentally opposed to any step toward organic church union, we are convinced that the basic spiritual unity of all believers should have a channel through which to give united expression to the mind and message of Christ in a world in which all Christian ideals are challenged.[26]

There are indications within the Southern Baptist Convention that this sentiment is growing but it still apparently represents a minority opinion.

While the Convention has declined membership in the National and World Council of Churches, it has also steadfastly refused to force individuals and churches to conform with the stated position of the Convention. In 1949, E. P. Alldredge offered an amendment to Article VI of the Constitution of the Southern Baptist Convention which would have changed this policy. The proposed amendment read:

No one who belongs to or is affiliated with any state or local council of churches which is connected with or sponsored by the Intercouncil Field Department of the Federal Council or any one or more of its six affiliated councils shall be eligible to serve on any board, agency, or institution of this Convention—either as an official, employee, or board member.[27]

If passed, this amendment would have penalized individuals and churches which were cooperating with various organizational expressions of the ecumenical movement. It would also have been in violation of Baptist ecclesiological principles. This action the Convention refused to take. The issue was brought before the Convention again in 1963 at Kansas City, Missouri, by W. L. Snyder of Texas. Once again the Convention refused to reject messengers from churches that were affiliated in some way with the National Council.

During the same meeting of the Convention a new statement of faith was adopted. Attempts were made by both liberal and Land-

---

[26]*Ibid.*, p. 100.
[27]*Ibid.*, 1945, p. 43.

mark elements to change some parts of the confession but without success. The confession was based upon a previous statement of faith which had been adopted by the Convention at Memphis thirty-eight years before. Like the New Hampshire Confession, on which it was based, the 1925 declaration only discussed the local church in the article on the church.

The revised confession departed from this precedent by touching on the church in its universal dimension. Two paragraphs are given to a definition of the local church and its functions. The third paragraph reads, "The New Testament speaks also of the Church as the body of Christ which includes all of the redeemed of all the ages."[28]

Wendell Rone of Kentucky moved to amend the article by striking out the last paragraph. His motion failed.

It is possible that these two actions are indicative of a change in climate, which in time may move the Southern Baptist Convention to affiliate with national and international ecumenical organizations.

To date, apparently most Southern Baptists feel that there is still a need for a vigorous Baptist witness in the present age. They are extremely dubious about the possibility of maintaining the integrity of that witness within contemporary ecumenical structures. For theological, ecclesiological, and pragmatic reasons, Southern Baptists have held aloof from ecumenical Christianity, refusing to believe that the answer to humanity's woes lies in an organizational realignment of Christendom.

Others Without

The American Baptist Association with 719,100 members, the Progressive National Baptist Convention numbering some 505,000, and the Conservative Baptist Association with a constituency of 300,000 head a list of Baptist bodies in the United States, whose total numbers exceed three million, which have no direct relationship with either the National or the World councils.

A number of factors combine to produce this antiecumenical stance on the part of these Baptists. Landmarkism, conservatism, a love of independence, and a general feeling of self-sufficiency are the most prominent discernible elements. Often a combination of these elements forms the distinguishing characteristics of the group in question,

---

[28]*Ibid.*, 1963, p. 275.

with one or more predominating in the specific pattern of dissent.

The Landmark emphasis and the fundamentalist posture are inseparable in molding an esprit de corps within a group like the American Baptist Association, whereas, theological and ecclesiological, but not Landmark, concepts have been equally influential in forming the distinctive witness of the Conservative Baptist Association.

This much is quite clear from what Shelley has written in the first history of the Conservative Baptist Association:

In 1959 a bold but careful study presented striking evidence of the quiet revolution that had taken place in the American Baptist Convention. The results of Paul M. Harrison's social case study of the Convention gave ample documentation of the bureaucratic character of the organization and showed convincingly why the Fundamentalists were unable to implement their program. Delegates, Harrison asserts, have "little influence over the affairs of the Convention except in an indirect manner." The positions involving policy-making have shifted into the willing hands of salaried personnel, who, in order to accomplish the goals of the Convention, have gained increasing power, "in some cases considerably more than necessary for the performance of their task." Conservative Baptists, who became one of the organized protests against such centralization in policy, had learned all this by hard experience. They were convinced, even without Harrison's documentation, that the rights of the local churches had been sacrificed on the altar of efficiency and organization.[29]

Shelley categorizes the theological principles that undergird the Conservative Baptists under three headings: (1) Conservative Baptists are fundamentalists; (2) Conservative Baptists are Baptistic; and (3) Conservative Baptists are not inclusivists.

By the first category the Conservative Baptists are identified with fundamentalism in its historical development. However, since much of fundamentalism had fallen into disrepute, the Conservative Baptists were careful not to choose this term as a part of their name. Shelley quotes E. Myers Harrison, the first president of the Conservative Baptist Foreign Mission Society, who relates this development:

To many sincere though misinformed persons and churches, the term "Fundamentalism" carries a schismatic and otherwise derogatory con-

---

[29]*Conservative Baptists,* p. 15.

notation. Shall we seek to enlist them by not using what to them is an objectionable nomenclature?

Apparently enough of the founders of the CBFMS agreed with Harrison that the odium surrounding the term "fundamentalist" would best be avoided by using another term. "Conservative" was selected, and the name to this day testifies to the fact that these men had no desire to represent extremism, negativism, or obscurantism. But at the same time they were genuinely concerned to stand for conservative, orthodox Christianity. In order to do this, they thought it necessary to adopt a confession of faith.[30]

Under Baptistic, Shelley includes the Conservative Baptist emphasis upon the principle of voluntarism, or liberty of the individual under God, and the ideal of a regenerate church and the accompanying principle of autonomy, defined as "that divinely given ability of each local church to make responsible decisions of its own apart from ecclesiastical pressure of any sort, legislated, financial, or personal."[31]

The claim is made that Conservative Baptists "are not inclusivists." By this rather awkward terminology Shelley attempts to describe the concept of separatism.

Any confession will separate. Even the simple confession "Jesus is Lord" separates one, in some sense, from the world of unbelief. The confession of immersion as the proper mode of baptism separates Baptists, in some sense, from non-Baptists. That Conservatives are separatists in the sense of using confessions is, therefore, obvious.

The adoption of their confessions committed the Conservative agencies to a distinctively biblical position, a position which emphasized the doctrines of historic orthodoxy. By their action in this regard, Conservatives in effect said that this agency, whether school, mission society, or association, is not inclusivist. It will not endorse or sponsor teaching in the school, planting of churches by the association, or the sending of missionaries by the society which do not propagate the New Testament faith. Conservative Baptists, therefore, require those who teach, administer, or go as missionaries to subscribe to the agency's doctrinal statement.[32]

However, it is admitted by Shelley that strict separation is an impossibility. Here again Shelley indicates that in his opinion the Con-

---

[30]*Ibid.*, p. 96.
[31]*Ibid.*, pp. 98-99.
[32]*Ibid.*, pp. 99-100.

servative Baptists, in separating from the American Baptists, were on solid Baptist ground.

Sensing the impossibility of such separation, the CBA of A organizers left matters of other affiliations to the local church. The societies, the schools and the association have no power to dictate to churches concerning cooperative ventures. Individuals are free to protest, but any legislation in such matters would threaten both the nature of the local church and the Baptistic character of the Annual Meetings.[33]

The Conservative Baptists, while holding to a traditional Baptist concept of the church as composed of all the redeemed, confine their "ecumenical" outreach to those of the same basic theological stance. Their interest is in a "vital spiritual unity" rather than corporate union with the mixed multitude.[34]

In spite of this expressed desire for unity, the Conservative Baptists have not as yet affiliated with the Baptist World Alliance. Most Baptist bodies in the world do belong. However, some, as many as four million, do not. Among those that do there is no commonly agreed upon position relative to the ecumenical movement. At times the ecumenical movement has become a troublesome problem within the Baptist fellowship which cannot be ignored.

The Baptist World Alliance

Even though the majority of Baptists share Southern Baptists' feelings relative to the ecumenical movement, Southern Baptists have sometimes stood pretty much alone in stemming the ecumenical tide. Consequently, the cords that bind Baptists together in the Alliance have been strained almost beyond repair. In order to preserve their own unity, Baptists have had to learn to live together in an air of mutual respect, while differing on such an explosive issue as ecumenicity.

The Alliance first took note of the ecumenical movement at Philadelphia in 1911. Dr. John Clifford of England, president of the Alliance, voiced the feelings of most of those present when, after expressing interest in and concern for a deeper understanding and closer cooperation among all Christians, he said, "But with equal frankness we say that a visible, formal, and mechanical unity has no

---

[33]*Ibid.*, p. 102.
[34]*Ibid.*, p. 103.

charm for us whatever. It is not the unity Jesus prayed for. . . . Unity of life, of love, and of governing ideas and ideals, let us have by all means, but unity of 'order,' of machinery' or of 'creed,' is not in keeping with the 'unity in diversity' either of Nature or of Grace."[35]

At the Third Congress of the Baptist World Alliance in Stockholm, 1923, the Alliance addressed "A Message of the Baptist World Alliance to the Baptist Brotherhood, to other Christian Brethren, and to the World." The Message stressed the vital spiritual unity which Baptists feel with all "who have communion with God in our Lord Jesus Christ." The Message also enumerated basic Baptist insights relative to the individual, the church, the ministry, the lordship of Christ, and the authority of the New Testament. The implications of this document are clear. At that time, Baptists expressed little interest in the ecumenical movement and none at all in corporeal union.[36]

By 1939, the climate within the Alliance had changed considerably. The Sixth Congess of the Alliance, meeting in Atlanta, Georgia, heard reports of two commissions which had been appointed prior to the Congress. One commission was charged with a study of "The Baptist Contribution to Christian Unity," the other with a report on the Oxford and Edinburgh conferences of 1937. It is evident from both reports that there was much interest in ecumenicity on the part of Baptists. However, the majority still manifested hostility to the idea of both federation and organic union. All were agreed that there was still a need for a separate Baptist witness and that the unity of the Baptist world family was of prior importance.

The Seventh Congress, meeting in Copenhagen, 1947, was not as pacific as the Sixth had been. Henry Cook of England made an eloquent plea for Baptists to join hands with fellow Christians in the World Council of Churches. "And if we Baptist people," he concluded, "by joining this World Council of Churches, can stimulate it to evangelistic zeal, I say let us go forward to join it, believing that the hour demands our cooperation with all Christians and resolved, as God will help us, to prove ourselves worthy of the challenge the world is presenting to us."[37]

At the close of Cook's address, M. E. Dodd, a prominent Southern

[35]*The Baptist World Alliance, Second Congress*, 1911, pp. 62-63.
[36]*Third Baptist World Congress, Stockholm*, 1923, pp. 223 ff.
[37]*Seventh Baptist World Congress, Copenhagen*, 1947, pp. 58-59.

Baptist pastor from Louisiana, took issue with him, stating the generally accepted Southern Baptist position relative to the ecumenical movement. After he had completed his explanation of the Southern Baptist position, Ernest A. Payne of England pointed out that the constitution of the Alliance prohibited the Alliance from uniting with anyone. He further stated that the structure of the World Council made it impossible for an international body such as the Alliance to join. With this statement, the discussion ceased, but not the issue of the Baptist role in the emerging pattern of ecumenical Christianity.

The 1950 Congress of the Baptist World Alliance which convened in Cleveland, Ohio, lent itself to ecumenical propaganda as no previous Congress had. Only two years had transpired since the First Assembly of the World Council in Amsterdam, and the enthusiasm generated by this gathering had not yet subsided. English and American Baptists could not refrain from taking advantage of the opportunity to advance the fortunes of ecumenical Christianity among the noncooperating brethren, which included the Southern Baptist Convention and, at that time, the National Baptist Convention of the U. S. A., Inc., as well as the Baptists of Africa, Latin America, most of Asia, and most of Europe.

The tone of the Congress was indicated in the welcoming address delivered by Wade Hampton McKinney, pastor of the Antioch Baptist Church in Cleveland when, rhetorically, he asked, "What about the ecumenical movement? We are troubled about it also. Jesus Christ prayed that his followers might be one. But we are divided."[38]

Most of the featured speakers developed this theme. Johannes Norgaard, Edwin McNeill Poteat, Edwin T. Dahlberg, and M. F. McCutcheon all set forth eloquent arguments for Baptist participation in the World Council of Churches.

C. Oscar Johnson, who reflected a greater knowledge of the thinking of Southern Baptists on this question than any other speaker, attempted to pour oil on the troubled waters. In his presidential address, he asked, "What of our continuing fellowship?" Then he proceeded to plead for understanding, forbearance, and mutual respect:

This question emerges naturally out of our present-day world. Some bodies in our fellowship have established connections with other groups of Christians not of our Baptist family. These efforts at wider cooperation have in some unions and conventions been desirable for com-

---

[38]*Eighth Baptist World Congress, Cleveland,* 1950, p. 22.

mon interests and ends. Others in our family have not so united for good and sufficient reasons to them. These convictions must be respected and safeguarded for all times. This has been the genius of our Baptist heritage from the beginning. We must not allow these positions of our constituent bodies to mar or in any way to disrupt our fellowship in this great Alliance of fellow Baptists.[39]

The Report of the Commission on Contemporary Religious Movements was presented by its chairman, W. O. Carver. The Report was adopted by the Congress and became the official statement of the Alliance pertaining to the ecumenical movement. Two paragraphs are of such nature as to have perennial interest for all Baptists.

In all matters pertaining to ecumenicity, unity and union we would urge the importance of accurate information, clear thinking, and action in harmony with the essential nature and genius of Christianity, looking to its mission and destiny as the determinative fact and factor in human history. We should always pursue our passion for truth and learn the exact facts concerning all organizations making a bid for support of any Baptist group. . . . We must be loyal to the truth as it is in Christ Jesus: we must hold with unbreakable tenacity to the freedom wherewith Christ hath made us free: we must retain our own ecclesiastical integrity and autonomy as essential to the present and the future of the Christian religion and to its nature and goal.[40]

In subsequent congresses of the Alliance the ecumenical movement has not enjoyed such paramount consideration as it received in 1947 and again in 1950. In 1955, the Golden Jubilee Congress was held in London. Upon this occasion, F. Townley Lord, president of the Alliance, spoke very frankly to the issue.

On the question of participation in the World Council of Churches our Baptist people are divided. In this country for a long time now we have been predisposed to the warmest possible co-operation with the other Christian communions in concerted attacks on the problems which affect us all. . . But if I understand my own denomination aright, we decline to equate brotherly co-operation with the sacrifice of essential principles. We will pray with anybody and work with anybody for the extension of Christ's Kingdom. But we do not share the views of the ones who talk about the organizational divisions of Christendom as "sin." Nor do we think that the words of our Lord in His prayer in John 17, "that they all may be one," can, by any species of exegesis, be brought to mean a vast organization based either on papacy or episcopacy. There is a danger, I think, of taking the idea of unity in abstraction, as

---

[39]*Ibid.*, p. 67.
[40]*Ibid.*, pp. 243-44.

if it were the one shining and resplendent idea which spells salvation in our modern perplexities. The New Testament does not regard unity in such abstraction. At least two other ideas are found in conjunction with it—liberty and loyalty. And I know that our Baptist people, whether they are within the World Council or remain outside it, would agree on that.[41]

Quite clearly Dr. Lord, in presenting the English Baptist position, was careful not to injure the sensibilities of Baptists within the Alliance who were not so ecumenically minded. There is also apparent in this address the usual Baptist posture toward an interdenominational organization which would in any way call for a compromise of commonly held Baptist distinctives, or question the right of Baptists on ethical grounds to exist as a separate denomination of Christians.

The next Congress of the Baptist World Alliance met in Rio de Janeiro in 1960. The environment was quite different from that of London. For the first time in its history, the Alliance was meeting in a predominantly Roman Catholic country. Here the ecumenical movement has never had a great appeal. Ecumenists generally regard Protestant missionary efforts in Latin America as unwarranted proselytism and, therefore, an unethical operation. The evangelical movement has, therefore, been the result of the missionary efforts of bodies, for the most part, not related to the ecumenical movement.

Naturally, the ecumenical movement has made little headway in Latin America. Too, the delegates and the leadership of the Tenth World Congress of the Alliance seemed far more conscious of their responsibility to use the meetings of the Congress to bear witness to the redemptive power of Jesus Christ than to use them as a platform to advance the cause of ecumenicity.

The evening sessions of the Congress were open to the public. Some thirty thousand attended. On the closing Sunday an estimated two hundred thousand filled the Maracaná Stadium to hear an evangelistic message by Billy Graham. In addition to the other factors, the evangelistic thrust of the Alliance precluded, it appears, any discussion of the ecumenical movement.

The Eleventh Congress of the Baptist World Alliance convened on June 24, 1965, at Miami Beach, Florida. The ecumenical movement failed once again to make a comeback in the consideration of the delegates. Perhaps the unhappy experience of the Baptists of Ontario

---

[41]Cited in Roberts-Thomson, pp. 95-96.

and Quebec with the United Church of Canada, which led to a termination of cooperative efforts, was one of the contributing factors. Too, the election of Dr. João Soren of Brazil to the Alliance presidency marked the end of an era in which the influence of the English Baptists predominated. Subsequently, the Alliance has become less English and more cosmopolitan in its complexion. Doubtless, this trend will increase rather than diminish.

The General Secretary of the Alliance, Josef Nordenhaug of Norway, did touch upon the Christian unity in a most forceful address. He had little to say about ecumenicity but much to say about the ingredients of a universal Baptist credo:

In most of the nations of the world there are Baptists who have stood up to profess the faith they have in the Lord Jesus Christ. They have professed this through baptism upon their profession of faith. They believe in the sovereignty of God, in the lordship of Jesus Christ, in the guidance of the Holy Spirit, in the personal nature of faith, in believer's baptism, in the regenerate church membership, in the memorial nature of the Lord's Supper, in the priesthood of all believers, and in obligation upon all to bear witness to the Lord Jesus Christ. The objectives of the Alliance has [sic] been stated by the panel in showing the essential oneness of the Baptist people in the Lord Jesus Christ. But our impatience to get things done must not lead us to break with the genius of Baptist cooperation. Precisely because of its voluntary nature the Alliance needs the enthusiastic support of all Baptist groups. Baptists are right in opposing centralized ecclesiastical organization and should, therefore, give wholehearted support to the organization which seeks to develop a worldwide fellowship based upon mutual respect and voluntary participation.

The last sixty years has also seen an upsurge in a concern for Christian unity. The issues that during the Reformation days and in the wars that follow [which] divided Christendom still lingers [sic]. The Reformers all agreed in persecuting the Anabaptists of the early sixteenth century. Because they opposed the state as the custodian of the church they were practically annihilated by both Roman Catholics and by other Protestants. Yet, their witness is living on. Through the succeeding centuries the churches retained, on the whole, this posture of hostility. But in the face of present-day secularization, state-sponsored atheism, and the intensified missionary activity on the part of non-Christian world religions, the various church groups had to consider seriously the meaning of being together in their witness for Christ.[42]

---

[42]Tape of Josef Nordenhaug, "Summary and Highlights," Eleventh Congress of the Baptist World Alliance, June 25, 1965. Recorded by the Radio and Television Commission of the Southern Baptist Convention, Fort Worth, Texas.

The general secretary of the Alliance then called upon Baptists to give themselves with renewed dedication to the task of presenting the changeless gospel to a changing world. The implementation of this God-given task, Dr. Nordenhaug emphasized, calls for faith and love. "This, my dear Baptist friends, is the time for a kind of faith that overcomes the world. Above all, this faith must be linked with Christlike love, and this for all of us is the most difficult Christian achievement."[43]

There is in the Nordenhaug address an implied contrast between the Baptist World Alliance, which is based upon a rather well-defined theological stance, and the heterogenous complexion of the ecumenical organizations with their rather elusive credo. Perhaps the contrast is overdrawn. It may not even be implied. However, there is no mistaking the emphasis. Nor can there be a misunderstanding of the prior necessity of Christian love as the one absolute essential for an effective witness to the one Lord by all of his disciples.

It now appears that the Baptist World Alliance has not become an agency for the promotion of ecumenicity as some Baptists had so ardently desired and others had just as fearfully anticipated. On the other hand, it seems increasingly evident that it is becoming an effective international fellowship for the strengthening of the Baptist witness around the world.

---

[43] *Ibid.*

9

The Issues That Divide

Long before the modern ecumenical movement arose, Baptists possessed a basically ecumenical orientation. For them salvation was dependent upon a right relationship to God and not to a particular body of Christians. In Baptist ecclesiology, the church, which is the body of Christ, is made up of all the redeemed. In this concept of the church they share the insights of Wycliff, Luther, Calvin, and Schwenckfeld. However, this church, even though universal, in Baptist eyes must never be identified exlusively with any visible, historical entity.

While Baptists disagree with the vast majority of Christendom regarding the nature of the local church, its purpose and function, as well as the function of the ministry and of baptism in the church, they refuse to force their own convictions upon others either directly or indirectly.

The preaching of the gospel for Baptists, when they have been true to their highest insights, has always been predicated upon an uncoerced response. It is a Baptist conviction that faith must be a conscious commitment to Christ, freely given. There can be no discipleship without it. Such a postulate demands for its freest expression an atmosphere of complete religious liberty. This freedom Baptists have sought to achieve for all others as well as for themselves. It is possible that a genuine Christian faith may exist in spite of persecution, but faith is never the fruit of the inquisitor's methods.

These principles, which Baptists believe are derived from the nature of the gospel, the nature of the Christian commitment, and the teachings of Christ, have caused them to oppose the coercive measures of state churches wherever they persist. Theirs and other forms of the Christian faith have been more healthy and vigorous where

168

religious freedom has prevailed. It should not be at all surprising
that a people with such love of freedom would view the increasingly
elaborate ecumenical structures with mixed emotions.

However, Baptists are far more invovled in the ecumenical movement than their limited affiliation with the various national councils
and the World Council might indicate. The nature of this involvement
is more informal than formal, but the resultant dialogue, in which
Baptists are engaged with the remainder of Christendom, may be just
as meaningful, or even more so, than an unequivocal support of
ecumenical organizations would provide.

In almost any Baptist seminary, students have the opportunity to
hear and enter into discussion with professors and ministers from half
a dozen or more non-Baptist communions in a given year. The class-
room becomes a forum in which books by foremost scholars of the
world are read and discussed. The professors who teach in Baptist
seminaries study in institutions of varying affiliation and theological
complexion.

Baptist churches, even of the Southern Baptist Convention, are
sometimes affiliated with the local council of churches. Their ministers are members of the local ministerial alliances.

At times various denominational leaders are brought into consultation with those of the National Council as American Protestants and
Orthodox attempt to arrive at a consensus regarding an issue
of such magnitude as to demand nothing less than mutual understanding and concerted action by all interested religious bodies. Such a
meeting on religious liberty took place in 1964 under the leadership
of Dean Kelley. Dr. E. S. James, editor of the *Baptist Standard,* and
other prominent Southern Baptist leaders attended this conference.

The Faith and Order Committee of the World Council has from
time to time utilized the talents of Baptist theologians whose constituencies are unaffiliated with the World Council. Such involvement
by local churches and individual Baptists in a working relationship
with ecumenical organizations has, to date, constituted no major
problem in Southern Baptist life. Perhaps the same would not be
true of other unaffiliated Baptist bodies.

Whether Baptists are inside or outside the ecumenical organizations does not seem to change the basic problems which Baptists see
in a deeper involvement in the ecumenical movement. There are
issues which are deemed of sufficient importance as to constitute a
barrier which keeps most Baptists aloof from a direct relationship with

contemporary ecumenical structures. Even those who have joined are often uneasy in their new relationship for the same reasons. The issues that divide may be placed into four categories: theological, ecclesiological, methodological, and teleological.

The Theological Issue

Baptists are one in their agreement with the Trinitarian import of historic creeds. Very few Baptists would be inclined to reject the substance of the Apostles' Creed, or those creeds which antedate it from the Rule of Faith in Irenaeus to that of the Chalcedonian formula. However, no Baptist, acting in the Baptist tradition, is prepared to adopt a creed.

In the historical legacy of Baptists, all creeds are man-made. They believe them to be only approximations of divine truth. To them one can never compel assent. All too easily the creeds usurp the place of Christ. Confessions which do not attempt to absolutize for all time the Christian faith are both legitimate and necessary. From generation to generation these change, however, as Baptists attempt to interpret their faith in understandable terms for a world in transition. In these confessions, which speak of some divinely given truths that to Baptists are eternally valid, are recognizable theological barriers that continue to separate Baptists from others.

The first of these is the lordship of Jesus Christ. Perhaps no one has stated it better than did John Smyth in his confession of 1612. Article 84 of that confession reads:

> That the magistrate is not by virtue of his office to meddle with religion, or matters of conscience, to force or compel men to this or that form of religion, or doctrine: but to leave Christian religion free, to every man's conscience, and to handle only civil transgressions (Rom. XIII), injuries and wrongs of man against man, in murder, adultery, theft, etc., for Christ only is the king, and lawgiver of the church and conscience (James IV. 12).[1]

To this basic concept Baptists today give an unqualified allegiance. The New Hampshire Confession of Faith of 1833, which perhaps is the most popular Baptist confession of all time, has an article almost identical with that just quoted.

Article XVI, "Of Civil Government," reads: "That civil government is of divine appointment, for the interests and good order of

---

[1]Lumpkin, *Baptist Confessions of Faith,* p. 140.

human society; and that magistrates are to be prayed for, conscientiously honored, and obeyed, except [only] in things opposed to the will of our Lord Jesus Christ, who is the only Lord of the conscience, and the Prince of the kings of the earth." [2] It is this fidelity to the Lord Jesus Christ which makes Baptists at times seem obstinate, narrow, and exclusive. But in Baptist eyes, if Christ commands, the true disciple does not ask why, he obeys.

If the Baptist interpretation of the lordship of Christ seems deliberately perverse or counter to the will of the majority of Christendom, Baptists can only answer that the same God who made Christ Lord makes the believer a priest. This priesthood of believers implies that the individual Christian is competent to know, through the Holy Spirit, the will of his Lord.

The competence of the redeemed, the lordship of Christ, and the priesthood of believers comprise for Baptists an inseparable triad of divine truth. It is, of course, the concept that Christ is Lord and that of the corporate nature of all discipleship that keeps the concept of the priesthood of believers from degenerating into rank individualism.

The source of these concepts is the Bible. While Baptists may disagree about the exact nature of the biblical revelation, there is no question in the Baptist world fellowship, with some notable exceptions, of the authority of the Bible for the faith and practice in the Christian life, and that of the church. The church, in Baptist thought, is always under the judgment of the Scriptures, never the reverse.

Creeds and tradition must all be measured by the yardstick of Holy Writ. This does not mean for Baptists that the Bible is an object of worship. The Bible can never replace Christ. To the contrary, it is the one authentic witness to Christ. Here Baptists stand with the Reformers of the sixteenth century. *They take the historical nature of revelation seriously.*

Since the revelation of God in Christ was a historical phenomenon, it is subject to record. The New Testament alone contains this written record. It is the witness of the apostles of the first century to what they saw and felt. There is no other. When this witness is accepted as reliable, men come to know the God who "was in Christ, reconciling the world unto himself" (2 Cor. 5:19). Not that the witness in

---

[2]*Ibid.,* p. 366.

itself brings us to God, for the New Testament does not bear witness
to itself but to Christ. Thus, the authenticity of the witness finds
validity in the fact that men came to know God in Christ.

It is the Holy Spirit who makes the historical and apostolic witness effective to the salvation of the believer. Consequently, the norm
for the church in every generation is that apostolic witness of the first
Christian generation. Baptists are always disturbed when some other
authority is substituted for that of the New Testament.

The ecumenical movement has not always given the Scriptures
that priority which Baptists desire. When it comes to the Bible, Baptists, for the most part, have assumed a very conservative position.
They believe themselves to be utterly dependent upon biblical
authority for their theology. Consequently, they are quite uncomfor-
table around those who hold a rather low view of the Bible.

The priority of the New Testament norm has been determinative
in the Baptist doctrine of the church. While most Baptists hold that
the concept of the church in the New Testament has a particular and
a general usage, the emphasis is placed upon the local congregation.
In fact, some Baptists admit no other definition. For all Baptists, a
particular church must be made up of the regenerate, who upon
their own volition profess faith in Christ and follow him in baptism.

To Baptists, there is something terribly wrong about counting infants of a given communion and the whole population of a given
country among the redeemed. This seems to be the surest way to
perpetuate a nominal Christianity, violate the consciences of the
newly born, and guarantee a decadent Christianity. Baptists do not
believe that the grace of God follows racial, geographical, or even
confessional lines. They reject the idea that the grace of God is conveyed automatically with the use of the Trinitarian formula. Nor
are the sacraments, which most Baptists prefer to call ordinances,
expressions of divine magic in which the grace of God is *ex opere
operato*. Christ does not need to be mediated through the sacraments.
He is available by faith alone in response to the proclamation of the
gospel.

Baptism has already been alluded to. It is here perhaps that Baptists who are also ecumenists face their most difficult dilemma. This
is also the focal point of change in Baptist thought precipitated by
ecumenical pressure. Traditionally, Baptists have taught that, according to the New Testament, the sacraments are symbolic. They do
not convey grace.

Baptism is the initiatory rite and the Lord's Supper the continuing expression of faith and fellowship between the crucified and risen Lord and his own. When properly administered both portray in unfailing imagery the kerygma.

Baptism by immersion is reserved only for those who have reached the age of moral responsibility and upon their own initiative commit their lives to Jesus Christ. Baptism, so conceived, is a voluntary act of obedience to the command of Christ. It identifies one with Christ before the world and admits him to the fellowship of his brethren in the church. He comes under the watchcare and discipline of the church. It is therefore, both an individual act of discipleship and a corporate act of church membership.

Historically, Baptists have been quite consistent in rejecting a sacramental concept of baptism. This was one of the issues which separated Alexander Campbell and his followers from the Baptists.

Within the past decade, English, and some continental, Baptists have begun to attach to the teaching of baptism in the New Testament a quasi-sacramental significance. Beasley-Murray,[3] principal of Spurgeon's College, London, is the most effective contemporary spokesman of this group. Few Baptists, however, are willing to accept the view that baptism is a sacrament in which the participant receives grace, in some sense, as a part of the saving process.

There is also an apparent willingness on the part of some Baptists to accept into Baptist churches members of other churches who have never received believer's baptism. Of course, this act removes a major obstacle which continues to divide Baptists from their pedobaptist brethren.[4]

At New Delhi, the report of the section on unity devoted much of its space to a discussion of the problems related to baptism. The report incorporated the fruits of Faith and Order conferences at Toronto (1950) and St. Andrews (1960). After a rather thorough statement on the nature of Christian unity and the necessity of its manifestation, the report proceeds to discuss "Baptism and Unity."

Among other things, the report said: "Our failure to share in the one Table of the Lord, to live and act as one visible and united body, is an obvious contradiction to the baptismal gift that we all claim

---

[3]*Baptism in the New Testament.*
[4]Torbet, "Baptists and Protestantism in America," *Southwestern Journal of Theology,* Vol. VI, No. 2 (April, 1964), 108.

to possess." [5] The Report urged mutual recognition of baptism but suggested that this is not quite enough. It further exhorted and enjoined the conferees:

> It is important that disagreement as to the meanings and modes of baptism does not now entail outright denial or nonrecognition of non-approved baptism. Even more important is the wide agreement that the initiative in baptism is from God by his Holy Spirit and that the baptized person's appropriate response must be expressed in the entirety of the life of faith. Such an understanding of baptism would suggest to those churches which practice infant baptism that this entails a more serious enterprise of Christian nurture than is often the case—and, to those churches that practise "believers baptism," that they should reconsider the place of infants and children in the household of faith. Baptism recognizes God's claim on us as his children. It marks out a person's "Place" in the family so that even if that person does not "take his place" it is there for him, awaiting his response to be [a] faithful soldier of Christ in the Church militant.[6]

Most Baptists would doubtless conclude that the metaphors are not the only concepts that are mixed in this section of the "Report." It is difficult to refrain from asking, Where are the biblical norms in this apologetic for infant baptism? It is quite apparent that there is a vast gulf between Baptist teaching on baptism and the New Delhi position. Consequently, Baptists outside the World Council remain somewhat wary over their ability to maintain their doctrinal integrity within such an organization.

Communion is also singled out as a persistent problem, even among member churches of the World Council. Here, it appears, despite all protestations to the contrary, that the section which prepared the report on unity, is insisting on uniformity of acceptance at the Lord's table regardless of profound differences in the theology of the Eucharist. But Baptists, who possess an unusual degree of theological agreement among themselves on the meaning of the Lord's Supper, cannot observe it together. Their differing views regarding those who can partake of communion together and those who cannot do not follow organizational lines.

In every large Baptist body, historically, there have been the closed communionists who argue that only the baptized are eligible to sit

---

[5]*Ibid.*, 127.
[6]*Ibid.*, 128.

at the Lord's table, and since only those who possess believer's baptism by immersion are considered actually baptized, the communion table is open only to those of "like faith and order."

The logic used by these Baptists also underlies the New Delhi Report. However, the premise is different. The New Delhi report on unity assumes that all baptism, regardless of the meaning attached, whether of an infant or a believer, whether immersion, affusion, sprinkling, or salt and saliva, is baptism, and, therefore, an initiatory rite which permits one to partake of holy communion.

With Baptists the problem lies in the definition of baptism. It is really closed baptism which predetermines the position of some Baptists regarding the Lord's Supper.

Still there are other Baptists who insist that since the Lord's Supper is a church ordinance, it can only be observed by a particular congregation alone. Visiting Baptists who may be close relatives of some of the members of the church observing the Lord's Supper are not even invited to partake. This view of local church communion is more often than not a result of the Landmark legacy. There are others, however, who have no sympathy with Landmarkism and prefer to limit the observance of the Lord's Supper to the members of the local church, since these are the only members over which that particular church exercises discipline. The Lord's Supper, in their thinking, is to be observed only by those in unbroken fellowship within a given congregation.

Then there are those Baptists who view the Lord's Supper as a general Christian ordinance of which the churches are the custodians. All Christians, baptized, or like the Quakers and members of the Society of True Inspiration, unbaptized, are invited to the Lord's table. These Baptists simply enjoin those who are present, "Let a man examine himself, and so let him eat of that bread, and drink of that cup" (1 Cor. 11:28).

While it may not be surprising to the non-Baptist to learn of this variation among Baptists in general regarding the Lord's Supper, it may come somewhat as a shock to learn that each of these positions is held by sizable groups within the Southern Baptist Convention itself. This fact raises a number of questions about the nature of the Convention and its ability to commit its constituency to a movement which apparently is striving not only for unity but for a certain degree of uniformity which the Southern Convention does not even possess.

Of course, the Convention is not a church.[7] It ordains no one, baptizes no one, and celebrates no communion. It only performs functions which the churches have assigned to it.

This state of affairs raises a number of questions regarding Baptist ecclesiology that call for clarification.

The Ecclesiological Issue

The ecclesiological issue is raised, as far as most Baptists are concerned, every time communion is observed during the assemblies of the World Council. For Baptists, with some exceptions, it would be a hypocritical act to participate in the prayer preceding the separate communion services of a World Council gathering, asking divine forgiveness for the sin of schism. Most Baptists refuse to believe that denominational divisions are sinful per se. Therefore they reject a blanket condemnation of all acts of separation. There are times when the sin lies at the door of those who refuse to separate.

In short, Baptists do not subscribe to an uncritical ecumenical philosophy of union at any cost. They are not at all convinced that the New Testament makes the concept of corporate union the pearl of great price. To the contrary, they ask: Is Luther to be condemned for refusing to keep silent at Worms? Were the Anabaptists wrong when they refused to bring their infants for baptism upon the orders of the Great Council of the city of Zurich? Is it possible that Smyth, Helwys, Williams, Clarke, Backus, Ireland, and Leland were impelled by demonic forces as they followed the separatist pattern of dissent?

To condemn Baptists for being Baptists because they refuse to conform to a more "ecumenical pattern" is, in Baptist thought, presumptuous. It smacks entirely too much of an established church. To go against conscience for the sake of a superficial union is for Baptists, as it was for Luther, an utter impossibility. Besides, ecclesiological principles of Baptists call for no such sacrifice. Historically, the local church has assumed a rather prominent place in Baptist life. Organizational life beyond the local church was extremely slow in developing. Associations, from their beginning, were rather severely limited in the functions assigned them by the churches. In fact, the early popularity of the society method in carrying on the missionary

---

[7] The Convention, when it was first organized, did observe the Lord's Supper together, but this was upon the invitation of the First Baptist Church of Augusta, Georgia. This practice has never been repeated.

task among Baptists in England and America lay in the complete freedom which the churches felt from any possible domination by the societies. The societies offered no threat to the autonomy of the local church. That the associational type of connectionalism survived at all is remarkable.

Recently, some Baptists have attempted to change Baptist ecclesiological concepts to conform to what they conceive to be a more ecumenical pattern. But the autonomy of the local church, even in England, where some Baptists have no hesitancy in referring to the Baptist Union as "the Baptist Church," is a prized possession of the Baptist people. Henry Cook, writing as late as 1947, explains the outworking of this principle in its practical application among English Baptists.

This, therefore, means that no outside body, however influential or numerous, can impose on a Baptist church, even the smallest or humblest, a decision that it does not choose to accept. There is a Baptist Union, but the church enters the Union of its own free will, and, by its own free will, it can come out again. The Union works through Associations and both have Councils and Assemblies which pass a great many resolutions and do a great deal of business. These Councils and Assemblies are made up of delegates who act as they think best in the interests of the cause as a whole, but their legislative power is subject always to the consent of the constituent churches. Baptists are not subject to the control of Bishops, Presbyteries, or Synods. Officers of the Union or Association may advise or recommend, but they cannot compel. The church, in the long run, is the final arbiter in all matters that affect its well-being and destiny.[8]

The supreme judicature among Baptists has always been the local church. Torbet sees this as a later development of the nineteenth century.

This was true because those who believed that there was no church larger than a local congregation refused to recognize that gatherings of delegates from the local churches could constitute in any sense the church. By this strictly local view of the church, associations and conventions were stripped of ecclesiastical standing and reduced to human societies which in no sense were parts of the Body of Christ.[9]

The obvious reference here is to the Landmark movement. While

---

[8]*What Baptists Stand For,* p. 62.
[9]"Baptists and Protestantism in America," 105.

it is true that Landmarkism greatly heightened Baptist appreciation for the local church, its influence was not as great as some have imagined. Is it not possible that Professor Torbet is reading into Baptist history something that is not there? Of course, J. R. Graves was willing to identify the aggregate of Baptist churches as the kingdom of God, but not even the Landmarkers have followed him here. It is a Baptist axiom, as Barnes was fond of stressing with his students, that "Baptists are a people with churches, not a church with people." Baptists have rather consistently refused to give, with few exceptions, to extra-church organizations; i.e., associations, societies, and conventions, the authority or functions of a church. But this is an undeniable trend among some contemporary American and English Baptists. However, this fact hardly justifies one in attempting to rewrite Baptist history along these lines. To do so not only does violence to Baptist history, but it also makes more difficult the task of understanding Baptist ecclesiological concepts.

Long before Graves, the dominant ecclesiology among Baptists was almost exclusively that of the local church. The confessions, which have had marked acceptance among Baptists, tend to confirm this opinion. The Second London Confession of 1677, which became, with two additional articles, the Philadelphia Confession of Faith of 1742, sets forth in the twenty-third article the relationship between the invisible church and visible churches:

1. The Catholick or universal Church, which (with respect to internal work of the Spirit, and truth of grace) may be called invisible, consists of the whole number of the Elect, that have been, are, or shall be gathered into one, under Christ the head thereof; and is the spouse, the body, the fulness of him that filleth all in all.
2. All persons throughout the world, professing the faith of the Gospel, and obedience unto God by Christ, according unto it; not destroying their own profession by any Errors everting the foundation, or unholyness of conversation, are and may be called visible Saints; and of such ought all particular Congregations to be constituted.[10]

The sixth, seventh, and eighth paragraphs proceed to delineate the characteristics of a particular church.

6. The Members of these Churches are Saints by calling, visibly manifesting and evidencing (in and by their profession and walking) their

---

[10]Lumpkin, p. 285.

obedience unto that call of Christ; and do willingly consent to walk together according to the appointment of Christ, giving up themselves, to the Lord & one to another by the will of God, in professed subjection to the Ordinances of the Gospel.

7. To each of these Churches thus gathered, according to his mind, declared in his word, he hath given all that power and authority, which is any way needfull, for their carrying on that order in worship, and discipline, which he hath instituted for them to observe; with commands, and rules for the due and right exerting, and executing of that power.

8. A particular Church gathered, and compleatly Organized, according to the mind of Christ, consists of Officers, and Members; And the Officers appointed by Christ to be chosen and set apart by the Church (so called and gathered) for the peculiar Administration of Ordinances, and Execution of Power, or Duty, which he intrusts them with, or calls them to, to be continued to the end of the World, are Bishops or Elders and Deacons.[11]

It is significant that The New Hampshire Confession, drawn up almost a century after the adoption of the Philadelphia Confession, and which had nothing to say about the universal church, soon supplanted the older confession in all sections of the country. And the Landmark movement had not as yet materialized. Hiscox's *New Directory of Baptist Churches,* which from 1894 to 1946 had gone through twenty-two printings, sets forth a more restricted view of the church than the New Hampshire Confession.

They hold that a Church is a company of disciples, baptized on a profession of their faith in Christ, united in covenant to maintain the ordinances of the Gospel, and the public worship of God; to live godly lives, and to spread abroad the knowledge of Christ as the Saviour of men.

Consequently an ecclesiastical system consisting of many organic units, a confederation of religious societies under one general government or head, is not a Christian Church, though sometimes bearing that designation.[12]

It is quite evident that Baptists have not been particularly concerned with the Church Universal. Their energies have been directed toward the planting of churches in all parts of the world in order to win men to Christ. It is the church in the concrete, not the ab-

[11]*Ibid.,* pp. 286-87.

[12]Edward T. Hiscox, *The New Directory for Baptist Churches* (Philadelphia: The Judson Press, 1946), p. 15.

stract, which has compelled their interest. The results validate the wisdom of this emphasis, for here is where the work is done, the gospel preached, youth enlisted, lives strengthened, and men transformed. This is the church that permeates the world with "salt, leaven, and light." The man in the jungle, in the village lane, or on Fifth Avenue will be brought to a face-to-face encounter with the living Christ because a local church was there witnessing in the power of the Holy Spirit of God.

Southern Baptists have been particularly devoted to church-centered evangelism. Their mammoth organization has never conceived of itself as a church. It exists to serve the churches. This concept of its nature has entered into the ecumenical conversation from time to time. Wayne Dehoney, president of the Southern Baptist Convention, 1964-66, reiterates the position of Southern Baptists relative to the National and World councils:

The Southern Baptist Convention is a federation of independent democracies, local churches that recognize no ecclesiastical authority superior to themselves. This structure creates a mechanical problem with regard to the NCC and the WCC. These ecumenical councils are composed of denominations and do not accept affiliation by local churches. But no centralized body can deliver the 33,000 local Southern Baptist Churches as a unit into any such ecumenical affiliation or corporate unity.[13]

The question immediately arises then, if this be true, how can the Southern Baptist Convention be a part of the Baptist World Alliance and its recently created North American Committee? Perhaps the answer to this question lies in the nature of the organizations involved. At the 1964 meeting of the Southern Baptist Convention in Atlantic City the proposal to become a part of the North American Committee of the Baptist World Alliance was turned down. During the following year the Convention's leadership took special care to inform Southern Baptists concerning the safeguards inherent in the Alliance structure.

Whereas, the Bylaws of the Baptist World Alliance specifically limit this subcommittee as follows:
(a) It shall have no authority over any Baptist church or over any

---

[13]"Southern Baptists and Ecumenical Concerns," *Christianity Today,* IX (January 29, 1965), 15.

Baptist body or undertake any work for which the member bodies are responsible, and

(b) The work of this subcommittee shall be financed within the framework of the Baptist World Alliance budget by funds contributed by the North American member bodies, organizations and individuals.[14]

Even here there are problems for some Baptists who refused to have anything to do with the Alliance or the North American Committee of the Alliance.

Obviously there is a wide gulf between the commonly accepted Baptist ecclesiology and the implied ecclesiology of the World Council.

The Methodological Issue

If there were no theological and ecclesiological barriers which prohibit Baptists from giving the World Council their unqualified support, there would still remain the practical problems. These problems often have theological overtones. They cannot be completely divorced from the foregoing discussion and are only separated here for the sake of clarification.

The ostensible purpose which gave birth to the modern ecumenical movement was world evangelism. Ecumenically minded missionaries reasoned that the Christian witness to a pagan society would be greatly strengthened if it were one witness. Conscience-stricken over the sin of perpetuating homegrown divisions in virgin mission territory, they sought to unite the denominations in an ever accelerating round of cooperative efforts.

Have the results justified the expenditure of life or met the expectations of these "sturdy dreamers"? Some observers would answer with an unqualified "yes." However, the Baptist dissenters are compelled to disagree. And the research of Lindsell appears to support the Baptists:

On this continent the most famous of all church union movements is the United Church of Canada. Completed in 1925, this merger of Methodist, Presbyterian, and Congregational churches united people of unrelated denominational backgrounds. . . . Its ecumenical passion remains.

But since union has been justified in terms of furthering the witness of the Church, the question must be asked: How well has the United Church of Canada met this standard?

---

[14]Cited in Report of Committee on North American Baptist Fellowship, *Baptist Standard*, Vol. 77, No. 7 (February 17, 1965), 9.

The reply leaves much to be desired. At its annual session in 1961 the United Church of Canada was addressed by its retiring moderator. As weaknesses of this group he mentioned the need for renewed missionary zeal and for a quickening of spiritual life. Following the 1925 merger there had been a surplus of ministers. Now the moderator says a shortage exists which has reached emergency proportions; moreover, he says that membership growth for the United Church of Canada is lagging far behind the nation's population increase. The last annual report showed a drop in new members by profession of faith in every conference. In finances, 80 per cent of all monies gathered from the congregations remained in the congregational coffers.

What is more, the very reason usually given for union, namely, the fulfillment of mission, gets little confirmation. Year by year the United Church's foreign missionary force has decreased. From 452 missionaries in 1936, the number had declined to 245 by 1950. By contrast, the whole North American foreign missionary force of 11,289 in 1936 increased to 27,219 by 1960. While this total force increased almost 250 per cent, that of the United Church of Canada shrank to almost one half.[15]

Lindsell has also shown that this decline in missionary interest and effort on the part of the United Church of Canada is characteristic of the ecumenical movement as a whole. While sending bodies directly related to the National Council of the United States have experienced a steady decline during the past ten years, the nonrelated sending bodies have experienced a remarkable increase. Today as far as North America is concerned, twice as many missionaries are sent by those groups outside the National Council as by those within it. While these statistics in themselves do not necessarily indicate that the ecumenical movement threatens the missionary outreach of the church, they strongly suggest that it doesn't help.

Baptists are not at all convinced that the non-Christian world would be greatly impressed by the spectre of one world church organization. Is not such a concept foreign to the nature of genuine evangelism?

Are men won to Christ by spectacular displays, parades, councils, or pronouncements? Hardly. They are won one by one as the Holy Spirit brings conviction for sin, which is only the work of the Spirit, and always related to Christ. This Christ-bearing witness may appear in a variety of ways, but most often its most effective form is the transformed life of a neighbor or friend whose concern has found graphic expression in word and deed.

---

[15]*Op. cit.,* p. 5.

The indispensable ingredients of an effective witness are the Spirit and the Word. The vehicles of this witness are the disciple and the church. Baptists would feel much happier about the World Council if it frankly admitted, as at least one leading European theologian has, that state-church Christianity of Europe is little more than "baptized paganism." Perhaps this is asking too much.

In some respects the ecumenical movement displays the tendencies of an establishment. It finds it difficult to resist the temptation to speak for its constituency in political and economic matters. But the World Council has never taken a stand for the separation of church and state. There is no attempt here to depreciate what it has said on behalf of religious liberty. It simply has not gone far enough as far as most Baptists are concerned. One suspects that to much of the Council's constituency the lure of an established church with its status and prestige are yet too great to resist.

What the established churches have done in "gerrymandering" the Old World, the National Council's program of comity agreements has attempted to do in the New. However, it has not met with an overwhelming success. Scotford indicates some of the reasons for this situation.

Present comity arrangements are subject to a number of limitations. Their observance is restricted largely to the "standard brand" denominations: Methodist, Presbyterian, Congregational Christian, Baptist, Disciples, and some smaller groups. The Episcopalians sometimes listen to reason but often do as they please. The same is true of the United Lutheran Church; but the Missouri Synod Lutherans, the Southern Baptists, and the Fundamentalist and Pentecostal groups will move in next door to anybody's church if they feel the call to do so.[16]

Baptists object to comity agreements on at least two grounds: first, it consigns huge segments of the population to a particular denomination, making a choice of church a practical impossibility; and second, it deprives many communities of adequate spiritual ministry. In such areas the semi-Christian groups like Jehovah's Witnesses, Christian Science, and Theosophists move in. Since some denominations (the Episcopalians, for instance) who are a party to the agreement, ignore the provisions when they are displeasing to them, they are practically worthless.

---

[16]*Church Union. Why Not?*, p. 43.

The choice of denominations to serve in a given community is often arbitrary. For example, certain Council authorities pronounced a community in Ohio overchurched. The Baptists made a survey and discovered that in the community of thirty thousand people there were approximately ten thousand church members, including numerous infants and children. By whose standards was this community overchurched?

The same kind of thought processes would have kept Protestants out of Latin America. From its beginning, the modern ecumenical movement frowned upon mission endeavors in Latin American countries. Mission bodies operating in Latin America were not invited to Edinburgh, 1910. Subsequently Latin America has become one of the most fertile mission areas in the world. Numerous "faith missions," independent and interdenominational mission societies, as well as denominations not related to the ecumenical organizations have entered these countries. Consequently, they have made possible the eternal and abundant life which Christ promised those who commit themselves to him.

Not the least of the benefits of Protestant mission endeavors in Latin America is a more evangelical and revitalized Roman Catholicism. Still, ecumenically related denominations have only token, and for the most part only educational, work in Latin America. The Episcopalians, who have refused to work among Roman Catholics in Latin America because they belong to a sister communion, have had a field day proselytizing among Baptists and others, especially if they possess wealth and/or social status. The Episcopalians have followed this procedure very successfully in the United States as well.

Ordinarily Baptists, particularly Southern Baptists, have been insistent that Baptists pursue the task of world evangelism through methods which they know best. Their energies are, therefore, channeled into efforts of direct evangelism in bringing men face to face with the claims of the risen Christ on their lives. For Baptists no one becomes a Christian except by his own volition. This is why it is so important that the gospel be preached in the power of the Holy Spirit. Baptists themselves may not always accomplish the purpose which they feel is a divine mandate, but they feel, rightly or wrongly, that they can come much nearer the objective than they possibly could in uniting with those who apparently do not know what it is.

A state church mentality seems to characterize the World Council of Churches. This presents a number of problems for Baptists. How can Baptists accept with good grace the reprimands for proselytism by those who still resort to the tactics of the inquisition?

No nation belongs to any one denomination simply because it claims exclusive franchise and enjoys the traditional status of an established church within a given country. Therefore, to base its representation in the World Council upon a census of the population, or even its baptismal statistics, is quite unrealistic if not dishonest. When as high as 85 percent of the baptized of a national church ignores that church and minimal Christian norms throughout their lives and then expect Baptists to recognize them as Christians and their baptism as a "gift from God," is this not asking too much?

The Teleological Issue

J. B. Gambrell, a Baptist stalwart of the past generation, is quoted as having said in reference to Southern Baptists' refusal to join the interchurch world movement, "Baptists refuse to ride a horse without a bridle." Even though in this generation the horses have given way to automobiles, the Baptist attitude as reflected in Gambrell's homely metaphor still remains. Baptists persist in asking where the movement is headed. What is its goal, its ultimate purpose? The answer to this question by ecumenists is by no means clear.

Visser 't Hooft made it abundantly plain at Evanston, and also in his numerous works, that the World Council of Churches is not a superchurch and does not seek to become one. However, as has been demonstrated in previous chapters, not all ecumenical leaders are quite so willing to write off the ecclesiastical aspirations of the World Council so quickly. Even fewer are willing to freeze the movement at its present stage of development.

That corporate union is the goal is the clear implication of Younger's editorial in *Foundations* (April, 1961). "Are we afraid of unity, or have we come to the place where we can serve our Lord by discussing questions of cooperation, of mutual recognition and intercommunion, and even of corporate unity with other members of the Body of Christ?"

Buchanan and Brown are also under the impression that the goal of the movement is a monolithic ecclesiastical structure. In a widely publicized article which first appeared in the *Saturday Evening Post* and was reprinted in *Christianity Today,* they write:

Suppose that the ecumenical movement should succeed. Suppose that all the churches unite into one, and that this one church becomes the sole repository of religious doctrine, the sole arbiter of man's spiritual destiny. Where will the dissenter, the nonconformist, the individualist go? Where will a man go if he finds himself at variance with a doctrine, or worse still, the governing authority of that one church? The ultimate theological implications of the one-church concept are obvious.[17]

Glenn Hinson, in a reply, plays down the ultimate goal of the ecumenical movement but he does not deny it. "All of this indicates that the fears expressed by Buchanan and Brown are premature and greatly exaggerated. At best, organic union of Christendom is as far ahead of us as the Reformation is behind." [18]

Robert T. Handy, a Baptist historian who has long lived and worked in ecumenical circles, expresses the fear that in the drive for organizational uniformity, church membership will become a meaningless experience. "The drive for total organizational unity inevitably forces anew the question of who is a heretic. In the effort to escape the harsher aspects of that question, while pressing for total organizational unity, standards of membership would be lowered and the nature of the church would, in effect, be presented in minimal terms." [19]

Surely there is within the ecumenical movement that which causes each of these interpreters of the movement to assume that its goal is corporate union, however remote. Is this an unwarranted assumption? The solution to the problem is suggested by Roberts-Thomson, who carefully distinguishes between the World Council and the ultimate purpose of the ecumenical movement:

We should get clearly in our minds that the World Council can never become other than a Council of Churches. Its own Constitution forbids this. But at the same time we should recognise what has been said earlier, that the World Council, particularly through its Faith and Order branch, is the present means whereby ecumenism can be directed towards challenging the churches with the sin of division, until eventually, with conscience stabbed wide awake, they face those divisions, and seek to effect reconciliation of them. Thus the World Council of Churches, whilst being in no way the *Una Sancta*, is a means towards its ultimate realisa-

---

[17]Henry A. Buchanan and Bob W. Brown, "The Ecumenical Movement Threatens Protestantism," *Christianity Today*, Vol. IX, No. 4 (November 20, 1964), 22.

[18]"Ecumenism: Threat or Hope?" *The Christian Century*, Vol. LXXXI, No. 52 (December 23, 1964), 1593-94.

[19]"The Ecumenical Task Today," *Foundations*, Vol. IV, No. 2 (April, 1961), 105-6.

tion. If Baptists understood this they would face the issues of ecumenism more realistically.[20]

Roberts-Thomson is undoubtedly correct in his delineation of the ultimate purpose of the ecumenical movement. His conclusions can easily be substantiated from the writings of Visser 't Hooft alone. Therefore Baptists, who may not have always had their terminology correct or the ecumenical structures properly related to the goal of the movement, have not entertained an altogether mistaken apprehension as to its ultimate goal. Baptists are practically unanimous in their lack of interest in corporate union. They might help build the "scaffolding," but never the permanent structure. Baptists do not believe that the *una sancta* of ecumenical dreams is the will of God or the answer to Christ's prayer as recorded in John 17. They see no basis for such a concept of the church in the Scriptures. If they repudiate it for themselves, how could they be expected to embrace it with others?

Baptists, who hold aloof from the ecumenical movement, were not born yesterday. They are not completely naïve as their pietistic characteristics might lead the outsider to believe. Buchanan and Brown reflect a typical Baptist awareness of the issues when they write:

> We are afraid of a superchurch, just as we are afraid of a superstate, and not because of a lack of faith in God. What we recognize is the fact that man cannot be trusted without checks and balances upon his power and authority—not even in the church. The various branches of Christendom now act as checks and balances, one upon the other, and they have a purifying effect on each other. Remove this tension, and we could be back to the pre-Reformation struggle between church and state with the individual man caught in the middle.[21]

Despite all disclaimers to the contrary, the World Council of Churches is beginning to reveal characteristics associated with ecclesiastical hierarchical structures throughout the centuries.

Liston Pope, an ardent ecumenist, expresses the fear that the World Council is becoming so much like a church that it may become the end of ecumenical aspirations rather than a means to that end. In a revealing chapter, "The World Council of Churches: Uncertain

[20]*Op. cit.*, p. 39.
[21]Buchanan and Brown, *op. cit.*, 23.

Samaritan," in an ecumenical symposium entitled *Unity in Mid-Career,* Pope relates the existence of a self-perpetuating establishment within the Central Committee controlled by the secretariat which is referred to as "the steel hand in a velvet glove." This "in-group," he charges, "controls the Council and ultimately determines its policies." [22]

He declares the Central Committee is not truly representative of the World Council. "In practice, the Central Committee is handpicked by the General Secretary with the advice and approval of the officers and the Executive Committee. The Assembly, as New Delhi showed, has very limited possibilities for either veto or initiative in regard to the Central Committee membership." [23] The power structure headed by the Geneva secretariat is not rationally organized nor is it constitutionally recognized, according to Pope. Therefore, it is difficult to curb and impossible to control.

Whether the World Council is the scaffolding or the superstructure is really beside the point. A superchurch of ecumenical aspirations could not have less bureaucracy or fewer interhierarchical struggles. Baptists have enough such problems within their own severely limited denominational structures without helping to build a modern Tower of Babel with finite hands in the name of the Lord.

---

[22]Cited in Bridston and Wagoner, *Unity in Mid-Career,* p. 36.
[23]*Ibid.*

10

Guidelines for Christian Unity

The heart of the New Delhi report on unity is found in paragraph two under the subtitle "The Church's Unity."

We believe that the unity which is both God's will and his gift to his Church is being made visible as all in each place who are baptized into Jesus Christ and confess him as Lord and Saviour are brought by the Holy Spirit into one fully committed fellowship, holding the one apostolic faith, preaching the one Gospel, breaking the one bread, joining in common prayer, and having a corporate life reaching out in witness and service to all and who at the same time are united with the whole Christian fellowship in all places and all ages in such wise that ministry and members are accepted by all, and that all can act and speak together as occasion requires for the tasks to which God calls his people.[1]

This is undoubtedly one of the finest and most balanced statements on Christian unity which has come out of the ecumenical movement. There is much within it that carries the ring of truth. However, it appears that the theological presuppositions which have dictated its final formulation make it unacceptable for most Baptists.

In spite of an emphasis on unity as a gift of God, unity is apparently conceived of more as an outward expression than as an inward reality. To subscribe to such a document implies the acceptance of all kinds of "baptism" and intercommunion. The commentary on the report further points up the necessity of the recognition of infant baptism on the part of Baptists if they are to become a constructive part of the movement. "The mutual recognition

---

[1]Visser 't Hooft, p. 116.

of baptism, in one sense or another, has been a foundation stone in the ecumenical discussions of the present century."[2] The commentary continues to point out the wide discrepancy in the understanding and practice of baptism among participants of the World Council. In paragraph 35, those who practice believer's baptism are urged to conform to the thinking of the authors of the report.

It is important that disagreement as to the meanings and modes of baptism does not now entail outright denial or non-recognition of non-approved baptism. Even more important is the wide agreement that the initiative in baptism is from God by his Holy Spirit and that the baptized person's appropriate response must be expressed in the entirety of the life of faith. Such an understanding of baptism would suggest to those churches which practise infant baptism that this entails a more serious enterprise of Christian nurture than is often the case—and, to those churches that practise "believers' baptism", that they should reconsider the place of infants and children in the household of faith.[3]

Are the framers of this Report asking Baptists to cease to be Baptists? It would appear so. G. W. Bromiley is far more blunt about the matter.

A short word might be included at this point on the specific issues of re-baptism and inter-communion. As regards the first, Baptists have to learn two lessons if they are to make the contribution which they might to practical unification in orientation on the one baptism (Eph. 4:5). They have to learn that baptism is basically the sacrament of Christ and His work, not of me and mine; so that baptism itself stands even though my own response may yet be lacking, or if I am an adult, insincere. And they also have to learn that in their baptismal teaching and practice they are called to genuine evangelism and edification, not to contention and propaganda. On the other side, the more traditional churches have been slow to recognize that what Baptists do is real baptism even though its theology may be one-sided, but willingly to concede to them this particular form and humbly to accept the genuine lesson which it carries.[4]

If Baptists find the New Delhi report on unity impossible to accept in toto, then what alternative guidelines for Christian unity do they have to offer? Perhaps no one Baptist could draw up a document that would be completely acceptable to all Baptists. But Baptists have written enough on the subject and have lived long enough

---

²*Ibid.*, pp. 118-19.
³*Ibid.*, pp. 127-28.
⁴*Op. cit.*, p. 88.

with the issues for a careful student of Baptist history to comprise some guidelines to Christian unity based on a Baptist consensus. This is admittedly a dangerous procedure and, therefore, the author makes no pretensions of infallibility.

1. The unity for which Christ prayed is not achieved by man, regardless of how sincere or well-meaning his efforts may be. *It is a gift of God through the Holy Spirit.* To profess this unity in reality means to be born of God; to become a recipient of his saving grace through faith in Jesus Christ; to be so hid in Christ that God's will in redemptive purpose may be achieved through the redeemed, as it was in Christ. This is the oneness which the Holy Spirit uses to convince the world that "God was in Christ reconciling the world unto himself." Unless this vital union with God through Christ is a personal possession, all talk of manifesting our unity in Christ is nonsense.

2. *The indispensable center of Christian unity is Christ.* The centrality of Christ in the quest for Christian unity is a growing conviction on the part of Baptists and non-Baptists alike. Barth states it clearly.

> The quest for the unity of the Church must in fact be identical with the quest for Jesus Christ and the concrete Head and Lord of the Church. I repeat: Jesus Christ as the one Mediator between God and man is the oneness of the Church, is that unity within which there may be a multiplicity of communities, of gifts, of persons within one Church, which through it a multiplicity of Churches are excluded.[5]

The New Delhi Report contains an almost identical statement: "It is in Jesus Christ, God's Son and our only Mediator, that we have union with God. It is he who has given this gift to us through his coming into our world. Unity is not of our making, but as we receive the grace of Jesus Christ we are one in him."[6]

Rather than a goal toward which the Christian world feverishly strives, Baptists view unity as a reality which belongs to the new man in Christ, only to be recognized in order to be realized. This is the import of Handy's words as he pens his own commentary on the St. Andrews (1960) statement of the Faith and Order Commission on unity, which was incorporated in *The New Delhi Report.*

---

[5]*The Church and the Churches.*
[6]Visser 't Hooft, *New Delhi Report,* pp. 117-18.

The final goal of Christian unity is sometimes thought of in static terms, but it seems to me that Christian unity must always be considered as a dynamic and living thing. In this sense, it is not even quite correct to think of unity as a "goal" to be won, but as a reality always in danger of being lost and always needing to be rewon in the ongoing life of the church.[7]

3. *The church universal is not an institution.* It can never be identified with one particular denomination exclusively. Baptists do not claim this distinction. In this sense the church is composed of those who are in Christ, the redeemed of every race, denomination, and nation. It cannot be destroyed, divided, or defeated. It is one and a present reality wherever redeemed men walk.

4. The New Testament emphasis is upon *visible churches* to which are committed the tasks of *preaching, teaching,* and *discipling,* and *the observance of the ordinances commanded by Christ.* These churches find the *source* of their life in Christ, the *strength* of their witness in the Holy Spirit, and the *substance* of their faith and practice in the Bible. They do confess "one Lord, one faith, and one baptism," but they permit no organization or person to usurp the place which Christ has reserved for himself. He alone is Lord in the church. And the church is a self-governing entity which knows no higher judicature in Christendom than itself.

5. Baptists under the lordship of Christ *cannot forfeit* the *convictions which they believe are of God* for any amount of organizational solidarity in Christendom, regardless of how high and noble and advantageous such an arrangement may appear. *They abhor cheap unity.* No less of a theologian than Barth agrees with this position:

Modestly though the claim should be made, a genuine Church separation will always possess a preponderant rightness over against any nonchurchly motives for union, and only through its faith can and must a living Church know itself to be called to abandon its separateness.

(3) Such a surrender must not imply the abandonment in one iota, of anything which a Church believes it necessary to assert in a certain way and not otherwise. The step away from a particular to a common confession must have no taint of compromise or of an assent to forms and formulae of union which would camouflage division without transcending

[7]Handy, *op. cit.,* p. 107.

it. A Church taking such a step must be known to act with perfect truthfulness and loyalty.[8]

Even though Baptists believe many other Christian communions are seriously in error in matters of faith and practice, they respect the right of others to practice their faith according to their own theological presuppositions. Even though they may believe them to be wrong, sometimes tragically so, yet Baptists do not on this basis withdraw their hand of Christian fellowship. *Fellowship with those in Christ and respect for the diversity which characterizes human discipleship are to Baptists inseparable qualities.*

6. *The manifestation of Christian unity is seen primarily in expressions of genuine Christian fellowship.* Bradbury expresses the relationship between Baptist convictions and the broader Christian fellowship in typical Baptist terms:

> In insisting, therefore, upon our Baptist witness, as New Testament Christians, we in no sense whatever isolate ourselves from believers in other ecclesiastical organizations; we hail them in Christian fellowship. But there is no need for them to ask us to compromise our own tenets for the sheer pleasure of organizing that fellowship which is freely offered to them by us as Baptists.[9]

This fellowship of which Bradbury speaks has been a living reality in Baptist life through the centuries. It has not often found organized expressions, and sometimes in moments of fierce controversy with other groups or under the lash of persecution or the sting of unjust laws of discrimination it has been a neglected aspect of Baptist life. Nevertheless, the kinship which Baptists feel with all those who know Christ as Lord and Saviour has survived. It is, indeed, an inextinguishable flame that lights up a darkened world filled with hate and misunderstanding.

It finds its overt expression in a thousand and one indescribable but tangible ways among missionaries far from home, in ministerial alliances or union evangelistic meetings, or in cooperative ventures in projects of mutual concern as individuals and local churches where convictions are not compromised or the lordship of Christ abrogated.

---

[8] *Op. cit.,* p. 51.
[9] *Watchman Examiner* (Feb. 19, 1948), p. 177.

7. *Baptists may from time to time continue to be related to ecumenical structures in various ways.* The exact nature of this relationship, at this time, is difficult to predict. As the pressure for organizational unity grows, some Baptists will likely become more wary of even the scaffolding (the World Council), to say nothing of the "coming great church."

It is admittedly much easier to work with the mechanics of an organization, to subscribe to some grandiose proclamation on Christian unity, to condemn a brother because he isn't quite as "ecumenical," or in the same way as yourself, than it is to do the work of an evangelist. But which is Christ's way?

What Joseph Martin Dawson has written of Southern Baptists might express the attitude of some other Baptists as well:

Prophets of doom are predicting that Southern Baptists will eventually crack up on the rock of ecumenicity. The notion is based on the failure of Southerners to join up with the National Council of Churches, the World Council, and kindred organizations. One who has endeavored to live fraternally with all men, especially with those of evangelical tenets as I have done, can well understand how I could wish that my people, with proper understanding, might co-operate with these lofty dreamers. Yet I am emboldened to say, I do not concede that Southern Baptists will perish by staying outside these folds.

It might be, as James Madison contended, that religious liberty for all is dependent upon diversity of religious creed and organization. It could be, too, that separation of church and state, the great bulwark of religious liberty, would be imperiled in a world organization composed of so many members that enjoy the privilege of being state churches. Above all, I am compelled to acknowledge the difficulty of formulating sincere statements of faith with so many who hold to sacramental views of eternal salvation. It is altogether possible that Southern Baptists, in affirming that they will not fight ecumenical organizations but prefer to work in their own, are not so perverse after all. It also might be that in declining to give up three Sundays in the month to exploiting the glittering generalities of ecumenicity while reserving a lone Sunday to present the claims of their own body, these Southern Baptists have chosen a practical way of promoting the Christian cause. It is probable, too, that in proposing to work for spiritual unity, which they genuinely seek and cherish, and agreeably practice it with their neighbors, rather than uniting in a formal way, an act which they distrust because of what has happened for a thousand years, they are traveling on a road that will lead to the answer of Jesus' prayer that all his may be one.[10]

---

[10]"What Future for Southern Baptists?" *Christianity Today,* Vol. II, No. 8 (January 20, 1958), p. 13.

Bibliography

ABBOTT, WALTER M. and GALLAGHER, JOSEPH (eds.). *The Documents of Vatican II*. New York: Association Guild; American Press, 1966.

ARMINJON, PIERRE (ed.). *Le Mouvement Oecumenique*. Paris: P. Lethielleux, 1955.

BAINTON, ROLAND. *Studies on the Reformation*. Boston: Beacon Press, 1963.

————. *The Travail of Religious Liberty*. New York: Harper & Bros., 1951.

BAKER, ROBERT ANDREW. *Relations Between Northern and Southern Baptists*. Fort Worth: Seminary Hill Press, 1948.

————. *A Summary of Christian History*. Nashville: Broadman Press, 1959.

BARNES, WILLIAM WRIGHT. *The Southern Baptist Convention, 1845-1953*. Nashville: Broadman Press, 1954.

BARTH, KARL. *The Church and the Churches*. London: James Clarke & Co., Ltd., n.d.

BASS, ARCHER B. *Protestantism in the United States*. New York: Thomas Y. Crowell Co., 1929.

BATTEN, SAMUEL ZANE. *The Social Task of Christianity*. New York: Fleming H. Revell Co., 1911.

BEASLEY-MURRAY, G. R. *Baptism in the New Testament*. London: The Macmillan Co., 1962.

BELL, G. K. A. *Documents on Christian Unity*. London: Oxford University Press, 1948.

BERKOUWER, G. C. *The Second Vatican Council and the New Catholicism*. Translated by Louis B. Smedes, Grand Rapids, Michigan: William B. Eerdmans Publishing Co., 1965.

BRIDSTON, KEITH R., and WAGONER, WALTER P. *Unity in Mid-Career*. New York: The Macmillan Co., 1963.

BROMILEY, G. W. *The Unity and Disunity of the Church*. Grand Rapids: William B. Eerdmans Publishing Co., 1958.

195

BROWN, ROBERT MCAFEE. *Observer in Rome.* Garden City, N. Y.:
Doubleday & Co., Inc., 1964.
BROWN, WILLIAM ADAMS. *Toward a United Church.* New York: Charles
Scribner's Sons, 1946.
CANNON, WILLIAM RAGSDALE. *History of Christianity in the Middle
Ages.* Nashville: Abingdon Press, 1960.
CAVERT, SAMUEL MCCREA. *Twenty Years of Church Federation.* New
York: Federal Council of Churches of Christ in America, 1929.
CHAVAZ, EDMOND. *Catholicisme Romain Et Protestantisme.* Paris:
Casterman & Tournai, 1958.
COLE, STEWART G. *The History of Fundamentalism.* New York:
Richard R. Smith, Inc., 1931.
CONGAR, M. J. *Divided Christendom.* Translated by M. A. BOWSFIELD.
London: The Centenary Press, 1939.
CONNOLLY, JAMES M. *The Voices of France.* New York: The Macmillan
Co., 1960.
COOK, HENRY. *What Baptists Stand For.* London: The Kingsgate Press,
1947.
ELLIOTT-BINNS, L. E. *The Beginnings of Western Christendom.* London:
Lutterworth Press, 1948.
ESTEP, WILLIAM R. *John XXIII and the Papacy.* Fort Worth: Deering
Publications, 1958.
————. *The Anabaptist Story.* Nashville: Broadman Press, 1963.
EUSEBIUS. *The Ecclesiastical History.* Translated by J. E. L. OULTON.
London: William Heinemann Ltd., 1958.
FAIRWEATHER, E. R., and HETTLINGER, R. F. *Episcopacy and Reunion.*
London: A. R. Mowbray & Co., 1952.
FISHER, GEORGE PARK. *History of Christian Doctrine.* New York:
Charles Scribner's Sons, 1904.
FREMANTLE, ANNE. *The Papal Encyclicals.* New York: The New
American Library of World Literature, Inc., 1956.
GAIRDNER, W. H. T. *Echoes from Edinburgh.* New York: Fleming H.
Revell Co., 1910.
GRANT, FREDERICK C. *Rome and Reunion.* New York: Oxford University Press, 1965.
GREENSLADE, S. L. *Early Latin Theology.* Philadelphia: The Westminster Press, 1956.
GULOVICH, STEPHEN C. *Windows Westward.* New York: The Macmillan Co., 1947.
HANAHOE, EDWARD FRANCIS. *Catholic Ecumenism.* Washington: The
Catholic University of America Press, 1953.
HAKER, RICARDO STRUVE, PBRO. *Inquisicion, Tolerancia E Idea Ecumenica.* Bogota: Centro Mariano Nacional de Colombia, 1959.
HASELMAYER, LOUIS A. *Lambeth and Unity.* New York: Morehouse-
Gorham Co., 1948.
HEICK, O. W., and NEVE, J. L. *A History of Christian Thought.* Philadelphia: The Muhlenberg Press, 1946.

HISCOX, EDWARD T. *The New Directory for Baptist Churches.* Philadelphia: The Judson Press, 1946.

HOGG, WILLIAM RICHEY. *Ecumenical Foundation.* New York: Harper & Bros., 1952.

HOPKINS, CHARLES HOWARD. *The Rise of the Social Gospel in American Protestantism 1865-1915.* New Haven: The Yale University Press, 1950.

JEFFRIES, CHARLES. *Towards the Centre.* London, S.P.C.K., 1958.

KENNEDY, JAMES W. *Ventures of Faith.* New York: Morehouse-Gorham Co., 1948.

KIK, J. MARCELLUS. *Ecumenism and the Evangelical.* Grand Rapids: Baker Book Co., 1957.

KÜNG, HANS. *The Council, Reform and Reunion.* Translated by CECILY HASTINGS, New York: Sheed & Ward, 1961.

LATOURETTE, KENNETH SCOTT. *The Emergence of a World Christian Community.* New Haven: Yale University Press, 1949.

LIGHTFOOT, J. B. *The Apostolic Fathers.* Grand Rapids: Baker Book House, 1956.

LUMPKIN, WILLIAM L. *Baptist Confessions of Faith.* Chicago: The Judson Press, 1959.

MACFARLAND, CHARLES S. *The Progress of Church Federation.* New York: Fleming H. Revell Co., 1917.

MACHEN, J. GRESHAM. *Christianity and Liberalism.* Grand Rapids: William B. Eerdmans Publishing Co., 1946.

MACKINNON, JAMES. *From Christ to Constantine.* London: Longmans, Green & Co., 1936.

MARTY, MARTIN E. *Church Unity and Church Mission.* Grand Rapids: William B. Eerdmans Publishing Co., 1964.

MASTER HISTORIANS. *The Great Republic.* New York: The R. S. Belcher Co., 1902.

MCINTIRE, CARL. *Twentieth-Century Reformation.* Collingswood, N. J.: Christian Beacon Press, 1945.

MCNEILL, JOHN T. *Unitive Protestantism.* Richmond: John Knox Press, 1964.

MIEGGE, GIOVANNI. *The Virgin Mary.* Translated by WALDO SMITH. Philadelphia: The Westminster Press, 1955.

MINEAR, PAUL S. *The Nature of the Unity We Seek.* St. Louis: The Bethany Press, 1958.

MOONEYHAM, W. STANLEY. *The Dynamics of Christian Unity.* Grand Rapids: Zondervan Publishing House, 1963.

MORRISON, CHARLES CLAYTON. *The Unfinished Reformation.* New York: Harper & Bros.

MORROW, E. LLOYD. *Church Union in Canada.* Toronto: Thomas Allen, 1915.

MUELLER, WILLIAM A. *Church and State in Luther and Calvin.* Nashville: Broadman Press, 1954.

MURCH, JAMES DEFOREST. *Cooperation Without Compromise.* Grand Rapids: William B. Eerdmans Publishing Co., 1956.

NEILL, STEPHEN. *Men of Unity.* London: SCM Press Ltd., 1960.

PAYNE, ERNEST A. *The Baptist Union.* London: The Carey Kingsgate Press Limited, 1959.

_____. *The Fellowship of Believers.* London: The Kingsgate Press, 1944.

_____. *The Free Church Tradition in the Life of England.* London: Hodder & Stoughton, 1965.

RAUSCHENBUSCH, WALTER. *A Theology for the Social Gospel.* New York: The Macmillan Co., 1917.

ROBERTS, DONALDSON, and CROMBIE, F. (eds.). *The Writings of the Apostolic Fathers.* Edinburgh: T. & T. Clark, 1868.

ROBERTS, ALEXANDER, and RAMBAUT, W. H. *The Writings of Irenaeus.* Edinburgh: T. & T. Clark, 1868.

ROBERTS-THOMSON, E. *With Hands Outstretched.* London: Marshall, Morgan & Scott, 1962.

ROY, RALPH LORD. *Apostles of Discord.* Boston: The Beacon Press, 1953.

ROUSE, RUTH, and NEILL, STEPHEN CHARLES (eds.). *A History of the Ecumenical Movement, 1517-1948.* London: S.P.C.K., 1954.

RYNNE, XAVIER. *Letters from Vatican City.* New York: Farrar, Straus & Co., 1963.

SANDERSON, ROSS W. *Church Cooperation in the United States.* Hartford: Association of Council Secretaries, 1960.

SCHULTZ, SELINA GERHARD. *Caspar Schwenckfeld Von Ossig.* Norristown, Pa.: Board of Publication of the Schwenckfelder Church, 1947.

SCOTFORD, JOHN R. *Church Union. Why Not?* Boston: The Pilgrim Press, 1948.

SHARPE, DORES ROBINSON. *Walter Rauschenbusch.* New York: The Macmillan Co., 1923.

SHELLEY, BRUCE L. *Conservative Baptists.* Denver: Conservative Baptist Theological Seminary, 1960.

SLOSSER, GAIUS JACKSON. *Christian Unity.* New York: E. P. Dutton & Co., 1929.

SMITH, H. SHELTON, HANDY, ROBERT T., and LOETSCHER, LEFFERTS A. *American Christianity.* New York: Charles Scribner's Sons, 1960.

SPENCER, DAVID. *The Early Baptists of Philadelphia.* Philadelphia: William Sychelmoore, 1877.

STRONG, JOSIAH. *The Next Great Awakening.* New York: The Baker & Taylor Co., 1902.

SUBILIA, VITTORIO. *The Problem of Catholicism.* Translated by REGINALD KISSACK. Philadelphia: The Westminster Press, 1964.

TAVARD, GEORGE H. *Two Centuries of Ecumenism: The Search For Unity.* New York: The New American Library of World Literature, Inc., 1960.

TORBET, ROBERT G. *A History of the Baptists.* Philadelphia: The Judson Press, 1950.

TULGA, CHESTER E. *The Case Against the Federal Council of Churches.* Chicago: Conservative Baptist Fellowship, 1948.

————. *The Case Against the World Council of Churches.* Chicago: Conservative Baptist Fellowship, 1949.

UNDERWOOD, A. C. *A History of the English Baptists.* London: The Carey Kingsgate Press, Ltd., 1947.

VERDUIN, LEONARD. *The Reformers and Their Stepchildren.* Grand Rapids: William B. Eerdmans Publishing Co., 1964.

VISSER 'T HOOFT, W. A. (ed.). *The New Delhi Report.* New York: Association Press, 1962.

————. *The Evanston Report.* New York: Harper & Bros., 1954.

————. *The First Assembly of the World Council of Churches, Official Report,* Amsterdam Assembly Series, Vol. V. London: SCM Press, Ltd., 1949.

————, and OLDHAM, J. H. *The Church and Its Function in Society,* London: George Allen & Unwin, 1937.

Index